THE FOREIGN SERVICE
OF THE UNITED STATES

Westview Library of Federal Departments, Agencies, and Systems
Ernest S. Griffith, General Editor

†*The Library of Congress,* Second Edition, Charles A. Goodrum and Helen W. Dalrymple

†*The National Park Service,* William C. Everhart

The Forest Service, Second Edition, Michael Frome

†*The Smithsonian Institution,* Second Edition, Paul H. Oehser; Louise Heskett, Research Associate

The Bureau of Indian Affairs, Theodore W. Taylor

The United States Fish and Wildlife Service, Nathaniel P. Reed and Dennis Drabelle

The Foreign Service of the United States: First Line of Defense, Andrew L. Steigman

†Available in hardcover and paperback.

About the Book and Author

The Foreign Service of the United States
Andrew L. Steigman

Heir to a tradition that predates the founding of the Republic, the Foreign Service of the United States has been representing U.S. interests abroad for more than two centuries. During that time, it has undergone organizational changes and acquired new functions in a process of adaptation to changing circumstances. Today, Foreign Service personnel in five different foreign affairs agencies work together and join with other elements of the federal government to help shape and execute the foreign policy of the United States.

After tracing the Service from its origins to the structure established by the Foreign Service Act of 1980, Andrew Steigman describes the composition of the modern Foreign Service and offers a succinct account of the work done by its members at home and abroad. He concludes with an assessment of the problems posed for the Service by societal change and by the spread of terrorism and offers some cogent thoughts about the Service's future.

Andrew L. Steigman has been a Foreign Service officer since 1958. His career includes assignments as ambassador to Gabon, ambassador to São Tomé and Principe, and deputy assistant secretary of state for personnel. He is currently a research professor of diplomacy at the Institute for the Study of Diplomacy, Georgetown University.

THE FOREIGN SERVICE
OF THE UNITED STATES
First Line of Defense

Andrew L. Steigman

Foreword by Carol C. Laise

Westview Press / Boulder and London

Westview Library of Federal Departments, Agencies, and Systems

All photographs in this book have been provided by the Department of State. The photographs in Chapter 2 are from the diplomatic reception rooms; pictures of training at the Foreign Service Institute are from FSI files and were taken by Tom Bash; the photograph of the Operations Center is by Bob Kaiser; and the remaining photographs are from the files of *State* magazine. Many from this group were taken by Donna Gigliotti of the magazine's staff, who also assisted in their selection.

Copyright © 1985 by Westview Press, Inc.

Published in 1985 in the United States of America by Westview Press, Inc., Frederick A. Praeger, Publisher, 5500 Central Avenue, Boulder, Colorado 80301

Library of Congress Cataloging in Publication Data
Steigman, Andrew L.
    The Foreign Service of the United States.
    (Westview library of federal departments, agencies,
and systems)
    Bibliography: p.
    Includes index.
    1. United States. Foreign Service.   2. United
States—Diplomatic and consular service.   I. Title.
II. Series.
JX1706.Z5S74   1985   353.0089′09   85-5078
ISBN 0-8133-0167-X

Printed and bound in the United States of America

10   9   8   7   6   5   4   3   2   1

To Meryl
Who has shared it all

CONTENTS

ILLUSTRATIONS

FOREWORD

Although the position of the United States today as a global power with worldwide interests calls for an active and effective diplomatic role, there is remarkably limited public understanding of the diplomatic process and the organizational underpinnings essential to the conduct of that diplomacy. This situation is not helped by the fact that frustration over foreign policy problems and our seeming inability to tame them leads to public blame and critical analyses being aimed at those who execute the policy—the members of the Foreign Service. It is the old syndrome of shooting (or, at a minimum, reforming) the messenger if you don't like the message. In such an environment, it is small wonder that so many misconceptions about the Foreign Service continue to prevail. When I traveled around the country as assistant secretary for public affairs, it was not unusual to find people equating the Foreign Service with the Foreign Legion and something alien rather than an arm of the U.S. government.

The purpose of the present volume is to deal with this problem and to dispel some of the illusions, without at the same time diminishing the significance and challenge that characterize the more complex mission of the Foreign Service today. The author, himself a career officer, has served at home and abroad in senior positions and thus is well qualified to undertake this task.

The book lives up to the promise in the preface to provide a guidebook to what "the Foreign Service really is, how it got to be that way, and what its members do to justify their existence."

The special contribution of this book is to give a candid account (warts and all, at times) of what a career in the Foreign Service is currently like and the organizational environment within which the Service functions.

The author writes from an overview of the Foreign Service gained from having managed an embassy abroad and policy decisions at home, as well as from having managed the whole Foreign Service personnel system. To give his account color as well as greater realism, he develops cases and examples drawn from his own operating experience. The result is a lucid explanation of the sometimes complex Foreign Service system, its organization, and its functions. For this reason, the book is to be welcomed as filling a gap in current literature, and it should be especially useful to those who are contemplating a career in diplomacy. I salute my fellow laborer in the vineyard for being one of the few who has been able to synthesize the Foreign Service experience and share it with others in a succinct and intelligible manner.

Whether this candid look at the Foreign Service will serve to enlarge its constituency is another question, since there is always the risk that familiarity may breed contempt. After all, the prevailing mystique and all the public confusion and illusion about the role of the Foreign Service have not stood in the way of the profession's being widely regarded as prestigious. Nevertheless, the risk must be taken. Only by peeling off the glamour and the various misleading labels that have stuck to the Foreign Service like barnacles over the years can we get a true measure of what is needed to pursue the interests of the United States in its relations with other nations—a task that is, in fact, being performed with distinction by the relatively small but dedicated group that composes the Foreign Service of the United States. One hopes that a better understanding of the realities will lead to greater support for maintaining the kind of Foreign Service that will continue to give the United States the excellence and competence it both deserves and needs to advance its interests abroad.

Carol C. Laise
Former Assistant Secretary of State, Ambassador,
and Director General of the Foreign Service

PREFACE

The Foreign Service of the United States has been the subject of innumerable studies, histories, and descriptive volumes. Only a handful, however, have been intended to serve the purpose for which this book has been written. Just as a good guidebook leads a traveler gently through the country being visited, so this volume is designed to tell the reader just what this thing called the Foreign Service really is, how it got to be that way, and what its members do to justify their existence. The most recent book of this kind appeared in 1969. Much of what its author wrote then about the Foreign Service is still true today, but the intervening years have brought such changes to the Service and its world that a retelling of the story seems very much in order.

As is the case with any writer, a great deal of this book inevitably draws on personal experience, in this case over twenty-five years as a career Foreign Service officer, as an ambassador, and most recently as the number two in the State Department's personnel operation. The book also depends, however, on information and insights generously provided by the foreign affairs agencies and by many friends and colleagues in and out of the Foreign Service. Among this group, I am particularly grateful to Barry Fulton at the United States Information Agency, to Mary Frances Costantino of the Foreign Commercial Service, to Bill Sigler and Frank Kenefick at the Agency for International Development, to Tim Blackburn of the Animal and Plant Health Inspection Service, and to Larry Thomasson and Dick Welton of the Foreign Agricultural Service for filling in the gaps in my knowledge about their agencies and for reviewing portions of the draft, and to Bill Bacchus and Art Tienken at the State Department for their willingness to read the entire manuscript and for the invaluable suggestions which resulted from their labors. Since I did not always take their advice, it is only fair to add that any errors of fact or interpretation are my sole responsibility.

I also owe much to the generosity of the State Department for a one-year Foreign Affairs Fellowship, which made it possible for me to devote full time to the writing of the book, and to that of Georgetown University and its School of Foreign Service for their hospitality and support during this period. Dean Peter Krogh and Ambassador David Newsom, associate dean of the school and director of the Institute for the Study of Diplomacy, made me feel at home at Georgetown while Charlie Dolgas of the school's staff proved an unfailingly cheerful source of good advice and logistic assistance. Ambassador Newsom also undertook the onerous chore of reading the full manuscript, and many suggestions based on his distinguished career are embodied in the final text. The Una Chapman Cox Foundation, through its Outreach Fund, provided a grant that greatly facilitated production of the final manuscript. The royalties from this book are being donated to the Scholarship Fund of the Association of American Foreign Service Women.

Thanks are also due to the editors who helped shape this book. In Washington, Dr. Ernest S. Griffith, consulting editor for the series of which this volume forms a part, reviewed the text at two different stages of its preparation and offered a number of constructive recommendations. Two thousand miles away in Boulder, Kellie Masterson showed great skill and patience in leading a novice author and his book through the editorial process; her encouragement, help, and sense of humor made the entire task far lighter than I would have believed possible. Once the draft had been completed, Libby Barstow and Megan Schoeck took on the task of putting it into fit condition for publication, and they too deserve much of the credit for its final form.

Finally, and most important, this book reflects the influence of my wife, Meryl, in a myriad of ways. It would not have been possible in its present form without her incalculable contribution, and it is only right that it should be dedicated to her. In addition to all we have shared at home and abroad, Chapter 8 of this book owes more to her wisdom and sensitivity than to any other source, and the entire manuscript has benefited greatly from her perceptive editing.

Andrew L. Steigman
Bethesda, Maryland

THE FOREIGN SERVICE
OF THE UNITED STATES

1

INTRODUCTION

The art of negotiating with sovereign Princes is of so great importance, that the fate of the greatest States often depends on the good or bad conduct, and on the capacity of the ministers who are employed therein.

—Francois de Callieres, 1716

The Foreign Service has never been easy to explain. For years, its members often encountered a blank look from friends and acquaintances when they mentioned their profession for the first time. The Foreign Service was little known to people in the United States, and its work was neither understood nor appreciated. Most U.S. citizens never met a member of the Foreign Service unless they had trouble while traveling abroad and thus needed help from the nearest embassy or consulate. If they thought about the Service at all, it tended to be in terms of stereotypes—the "striped-pants diplomats" or "cookie-pushers" image of a bygone age. And as to what the Foreign Service did (aside from bailing out stranded tourists), they had even less idea, beyond the general impression that its members dealt, as Elbridge Gerry of Massachusetts sourly put it two hundred years ago, "with those foreigners."

To a considerable extent, the Foreign Service suffered from a general lack of understanding of diplomacy and its purposes. "The American people," said one former ambassador, "have long looked on diplomacy as a mysterious activity on another plane."[1] Even sophisticated commentators used the term "diplomacy" indiscriminately to indicate both the making of foreign

1

policy and its subsequent execution, although the career Foreign Service personnel were responsible only for the latter. There was little appreciation of the view—expressed repeatedly over the centuries by statesmen, academicians, and diplomatic practitioners—that "the diplomatic establishment, not the military establishment, is the first line of defense."[2]

Then, beginning late in 1979, the Iranian hostage crisis suddenly and dramatically made the American people aware of the Foreign Service as they never had been before. By the time the 444 days of captivity were at an end, the United States had a new set of heroes—and the Foreign Service had a new image. The dangers and hardships faced by members of the Service had been vividly demonstrated in Teheran, and the courage of the hostages had earned new respect for the entire Foreign Service.

But who were these men and women who had shown such courage under pressure? And what was their job like under more normal circumstances? Did it consist entirely of the crisis and drama that prevailed in Teheran, or was there—as seemed more likely—a great deal of relatively routine work being done at posts around the world? The goal of this book is to attempt to answer these questions: to describe both the structure and composition of today's Foreign Service of the United States and the kind of work its members do.

One of the difficulties in defining the Foreign Service lies in the fact that it has undergone considerable change during its lifetime of just over two hundred years. It began as the overseas arm of the U.S. government, responsible for carrying out the full range of the nation's diplomatic and consular business beyond its borders. For nearly a hundred and fifty years after independence, the United States was represented abroad by a Consular Service and a Diplomatic Service, which were carefully kept separate and distinct. Until late in the nineteenth century, neither of these services had career employees in the modern sense, and all but a handful of their members tended to hold office only until the next change of administration. Through most of this period, U.S. representatives overseas were attached loosely to the State Department, and other government de-

A new image for the Foreign Service: Teheran hostages come home to heroes'
welcome, March 1981. (Top) White House ceremony; (bottom) crowds cheer
near West Point, New York.

partments needing help simply called on State's "man on the spot" to provide it.

As foreign policy grew in complexity during the twentieth century, the Foreign Service, as "the eyes and ears of the State Department," was supplemented by overseas representatives of other U.S. government agencies. The core functions continued to be performed by the State Department contingent abroad, which retained the responsibility for both consular services and the basic elements of traditional diplomacy. There were, however, new tasks to be performed, and these were largely undertaken by agencies other than the State Department. Even though some of the personnel of these agencies had career patterns that were not too different from those of State's representatives abroad, they were not formally part of the Foreign Service until after World War II, when several other agencies—most important, the United States Information Agency (USIA) and the International Cooperation Agency (later to become the Agency for International Development, or AID)—were authorized to appoint personnel under the Foreign Service system. In 1979, the Foreign Commercial Service (FCS) of the Department of Commerce came under the Foreign Service umbrella. The Foreign Service Act adopted the following year added the Foreign Agricultural Service (FAS) of the Department of Agriculture to the Foreign Service "family," and an executive order two years later extended the umbrella to include Agriculture's Animal and Plant Health Inspection Service (APHIS).

As this thumbnail history suggests, the Foreign Service is not itself an agency of the U.S. government. Indeed, its career personnel belong to the five different organizations just named— State, USIA, AID, Commerce, and Agriculture—collectively referred to as "the foreign affairs agencies."[3] There are, of course, other U.S. government agencies involved in foreign affairs, a number of which regularly assign employees abroad. The personnel of these other agencies, however, are not members of the Foreign Service; for them, overseas assignments in most instances are the exception in careers spent predominantly in the United States.

To the casual observer, the number of U.S. officials serving abroad might seem excessive. Several administrations, of both parties, have sought to cut their numbers, but ultimately have come to the reluctant conclusion that the needs of the U.S. government cannot be met in full if overseas staffs are significantly reduced. In light of the global responsibilities of the United States, its decision-makers must have up-to-date information from every corner of the world. The requirements of the country's complex executive bureaucracy and those established by Congress demand that personnel overseas monitor activities with an attention to detail unique among the western democracies. This need results in a substantial official presence abroad, one that accurately reflects the great power role of the United States.

Within each of the foreign affairs agencies, the Foreign Service component is only part of the total workforce. At the State Department, which has the largest Foreign Service population (over nine thousand), Foreign Service employees represent roughly two-thirds of all U.S. personnel. At the other end of the scale, FAS and APHIS combined have only about three hundred Foreign Service employees in a total Department of Agriculture workforce of a hundred and ten thousand, reflecting that department's primary focus on domestic agriculture programs. The other agencies fall between these extremes (see Appendix A for the distribution of Foreign Service personnel among the foreign affairs agencies).

The non–Foreign Service members of each agency consist primarily of career Civil Service employees, many of whom are as deeply involved in foreign affairs issues as their Foreign Service counterparts. Like the personnel of other government agencies interested in foreign affairs, the Civil Service employees in the foreign affairs agencies differ from their Foreign Service counterparts primarily in that they serve their careers almost entirely in the United States.

Since members of the Foreign Service belong to five different agencies, why write of *one* Foreign Service of the United States, as the title of this book implies? All Foreign Service personnel, regardless of their parent agency, share several important characteristics that give them a considerable degree of common identity. They share, for example, the responsibility (defined by the Service's own recruiting brochure) "of assisting the President and the Secretary of State in planning, conducting, and implementing our foreign policy at home and abroad."[4] The definition of that responsibility carefully excludes policy-*making*, which, subject only to those powers reserved to Congress, is the basic responsibility of the president. Nonetheless, the Foreign Service has considerable influence in the decision-making process, both through its reports from abroad, which furnish much of the information on which decisions are ultimately based, and through the judgments and recommendations its members offer to decision-makers.

Indeed, Foreign Service personnel are often more intimately involved in decision-making than their Civil Service counterparts working outside the field of foreign affairs. Particularly since the end of World War II, career Foreign Service officers have regularly been called upon to fill policy positions at a higher level than comparable career officers in other executive departments. When serving as an assistant secretary or under secretary, as is often the case, Foreign Service officers walk a narrow and delicate line, for in such positions, they are at the same time career personnel and officials of the current administration at a policy-making level, and thus they must have both an expert knowledge of the issues and sensitivity to the political concerns of the administration.

For the most part, however, the Foreign Service is not a policy-making body but, rather, the instrument that executes agreed-upon policies in the field of foreign affairs, both at home and abroad. Although the work of Foreign Service personnel on the domestic scene is shared with their Civil Service colleagues, in the foreign affairs agencies and elsewhere, the function they perform overseas is indeed unique. Members of the Foreign Service are, in the words of one former secretary of state, "soldiers in the front-line trenches of our foreign policy."[5] Their sense of the importance of the tasks they perform is one of the strongest bonds among them.

The statutory base of the Foreign Service is common to all five foreign affairs agencies—the Foreign Service Act of 1980. Prior to the 1980 Act, some of the agencies that had personnel spending the bulk of their careers abroad were in the Foreign Service system and some were not, and the system had become such a patchwork quilt after years of tinkering and accretions that it even accommodated some nominal Foreign Service employees who were not expected ever to serve abroad. Under the terms of the 1980 Act and its implementing regulations, members of the Foreign Service are now subject to a personnel system that is fairly uniform from agency to agency. Its most critical element, for all Foreign Service employees, is the commitment to spend the greater part of their careers at posts overseas—on average, about 60 percent.

Although this stipulation brings with it certain allowances and benefits unique to the Foreign Service, it also entails an obligation on the part of Foreign Service personnel to displace themselves and their families at intervals, usually ranging from two to four years, and to serve anywhere in the world. And, of course, some of the places where Foreign Service posts are located are far from being garden spots, often involving adverse climate, endemic diseases, severe isolation, and, to an increasing extent in recent years, real physical danger from terrorist activity. This common commitment to worldwide availability, with its corollary of shared hardship, contributes enormously to the Foreign Service employees' sense of belonging to a service that is special and unique.

Despite these elements that help to forge *one* Foreign Service, there are other factors that tend to keep the Foreign Service components of each of the five foreign affairs agencies separate and distinct. Most important, each of the agencies has its own mission, and for all but the Department of State, the mission is fairly clearly defined by the nature of the agency itself. The Agency for International Development, as its name implies, is responsible for devising and administering programs to assist the economic growth of the world's developing nations. The United States Information Agency manages the overseas information and cultural activities of the U.S. government, and the Foreign Commercial Service is charged with promoting U.S. trade with other nations by developing markets, assisting U.S. exporters, and seeking to reduce or eliminate barriers to U.S. trade. Like the Foreign Commercial Service, the Foreign Agricultural Service also seeks to expand U.S. exports but concentrates its efforts on agricultural products. The other foreign affairs service in the Department of Agriculture, the Animal and Plant Health Inspection Service, works with other governments to protect the United States against diseases and insect pests that are potentially harmful to U.S. agriculture. Finally, the State Department is responsible for consular services abroad; for administrative support to all agencies represented at Foreign Service posts; for reporting, negotiation, and representation in the broad political and economic fields; and for the overall coordination of foreign policy.

Given the highly specialized nature of many of these tasks, a totally integrated Foreign Service clearly would not be easy to achieve. Largely in recognition of the fact that each of the foreign affairs agencies needs particular qualifications and experience, the Foreign Service Act of 1980 called for "maximum compatibility" among the agencies "to the extent practicable" and instructed the secretary of state to "encourage . . . the development of uniform policies and procedures."[6] To underline the point that this statement was *not* a mandate to the secretary (and to reassure the smaller agencies, which feared they might be "swallowed up" by the State Department), the act added an extra caveat that "nothing in this chapter shall be construed as diminishing the authority of the head of any agency authorized by law to use the Foreign Service personnel system."[7] In effect, the authority of each agency head to run a separate Foreign Service was left essentially intact, and to a considerable extent, they have in fact exercised that authority.

As previously noted, there are many common elements in the Foreign Service personnel system, and its members share both responsibilities and commitments. By themselves, however, these common elements are not enough to forge all the personnel into a single Foreign Service so long as many of the critical decisions affecting their lives and careers are coming from five different agencies. In consequence, it is not surprising that members of the Foreign Service have a dual loyalty and see themselves as belonging both to their parent agencies and to the Foreign Service. Only overseas, when members of the Foreign Service are fused into a cohesive team under the leadership of an effective ambassador, are they likely to transcend agency lines and feel themselves part of a single body. On the whole, the Foreign Service thus falls short of total integration and remains elusive to define—but, as we shall see, its organizational anomalies do not keep its members from getting their jobs done.

To understand the modern Foreign Service, it is helpful to trace the process by which it evolved from the heady days of Benjamin Franklin and his colleagues. The next chapter will describe the steps in that process, and succeeding chapters will discuss the structure of the Service, its work at home and abroad, and the problems that it faces today.

Notes

1. Hugh S. Gibson, quoted in Elmer Plischke, ed., *Modern Diplomacy: The Art and the Artisans* (Washington, D.C.: American Enterprise Institute, 1979), p. xiii.

2. Thomas A. Bailey, "Advice for Diplomats," in ibid., p. 231.

3. The Peace Corps is also staffed by personnel on Foreign Service appointments, but since its governing statute limits the tenure of its employees to a maximum of five years, it has no *career* Foreign Service employees. Thus, its work will not be discussed in detail in this book, which focuses on the agencies utilizing the career Foreign Service personnel system.

4. U.S. Department of State, *Foreign Service Careers*, Department of State Publication 9202 (Washington, D.C.: U.S. Department of State, 1984), p. 2.

5. John Foster Dulles, quoted in Plischke, *Modern Diplomacy*, p. 223.

6. PL 96-465 (22 USC 3927), sec. 204.

7. Ibid., sec. 203(b).

THE FIRST
TWO HUNDRED YEARS

In the Old Days . . . diplomacy was a quiet and restful t
on in soothing inanity among a hundred shady legations a
all over the globe.

—Lawrence D

Although the Declaration of Independence marked
appearance of the United States on the world sce
there had already been official American representat
for a number of years.[1] The earliest such agent
London, where they dealt with British authorities
several of the individual colonies. The best known
dozen colonial agents in England in the decade
pendence was Benjamin Franklin, who held comm
Massachusetts and New Jersey in addition to his h
Pennsylvania. When the First Continental Congre
negotiations with the British in 1774 in the hope
peaceful solution to the problems between the
Britain, these agents served as the channel for the
petition—thus becoming the first to act abroad
the soon-to-be-born nation.

By 1775, Franklin was back home, and th
Congress had begun to explore the possibilities
and support in case its differences with Britain
resolved peacefully. For the purpose, it create
Committee of Correspondence (soon to be rena
mittee of Secret Correspondence) "for the so

11

corresponding with our friends in Great Britain, Ireland, and other parts of the world"[2] and named Franklin as the committee's chairman. The committee designated as its agents abroad Arthur Lee, then in London (where he had previously represented Massachusetts along with Franklin); Charles W. F. Dumas, a Swiss residing in The Hague who was dedicated to the American cause; and Silas Deane, who was sent to Paris. Deane's early diplomatic activity was limited largely to sounding out the French foreign minister as to French reaction if the colonies should be "forced to form themselves into an independent state,"[3] but he made a major contribution in getting munitions and supplies rolling soon after his arrival in France in the middle of 1776.

Recognizing the potential importance of French support for the revolutionary effort, Congress named a three-man commission later in 1776 to represent the new nation in Paris. Deane, already in the French capital, was joined by Franklin and Arthur Lee. During the course of the conflict with Britain, this distinguished trio assured a constant flow of French support, which proved a critical element in the eventual American victory. Their counterparts elsewhere in Europe, notably John Jay in Spain and John Adams in the Netherlands, found the going more difficult, but they also secured important backing for the revolutionary cause. After the decisive battle at Yorktown, Franklin, Jay, and Adams teamed up (later joined by Henry Laurens, who had sat out the war in the Tower of London after being captured by the British while en route to represent the new nation in the Netherlands) to negotiate the final—and highly favorable—peace treaty that established the United States as a nation. (The desk on which this historic treaty was signed has found an appropriate home in the diplomatic reception rooms on the eighth floor of the State Department.)

The new nation's early representatives abroad necessarily operated on the basis of fairly general instructions and with a great deal of leeway in their interpretation. Not only were communications slow and hazardous, with Britannia pretty much in control of the Atlantic, but there was also considerable disorganization at home in the management of foreign affairs. In 1777, Congress changed the Committee of Secret Corre-

The desk on which the Treaty of Paris was signed on September 3, 1783.

spondence to the Committee for Foreign Affairs and provided it with a secretary (revolutionary pamphleteer Tom Paine), but the fluctuating membership of the committee made for a lack of continuity in policy and for a diversity of instructions to agents abroad. Not until 1781 was this situation partially re-

medied by the creation of a Department of Foreign Affairs. The
first secretary, Robert R. Livingston of New York, set up shop
in a small house in Philadelphia in October of that year with
an initial staff of two under secretaries, a translator of French,
and a clerk. Although Congress never gave him a very free
hand, he managed to play a fairly substantial role in policy-
making. Perhaps most important, he provided a single locus
for correspondence between the U.S. government and its representatives abroad, who, for the first time, were provided
information and guidance on a regular basis and were enjoined
to report regularly and in detail on events in the countries in
which they served.

Livingston was succeeded in 1784 by John Jay, who previously
had served successively as the country's representative in Madrid
and as a member of the team negotiating the peace treaty with
Great Britain. The seat of government was then in New York,
and Jay established his office first in Fraunces Tavern, at Pearl
and Broad Streets, and later on lower Broadway. Following the
adoption of the Constitution, the Department of Foreign Affairs
was reorganized and expanded to become the Department of
State. Its principal officer was designated secretary of state, and
Thomas Jefferson—then concluding four years of service as
minister to France—was chosen by President Washington as
the first incumbent of the new office, and he began his duties
early in 1790.

The Constitution (Article 2, Section 2) also gave the president
the power to appoint, subject to the advice and consent of the
Senate, "Ambassadors, other public Ministers and Consuls," a
task previously performed directly by the Congress. Subsequent
appointments have all been made under this broad constitutional
umbrella, but U.S. overseas representation already had a solid
foundation on which to build. Benjamin Franklin, whose diplomatic career long predated the Constitution, is generally considered the father of the U.S. Foreign Service. As already noted,
he served as colony agent in England for some fifteen years
prior to 1775, acted as agent of the First Continental Congress
in London in 1774, and was included in the original trio of
full-fledged U.S. diplomatic representatives to France in 1776.
When he presented his letters of credence to Louis XVI on

The statue of Benjamin Franklin, America's first professional diplomat, in the garden of the U.S. Embassy in Paris.

March 23, 1779, he became the new country's first minister plenipotentiary.

Franklin, however, was but primus inter pares in a distinguished galaxy. In the early years, when the United States was striving to establish and consolidate its independence, the business of foreign affairs required the nation's best talent—and the best men were ready and willing to serve. Every president between George Washington and Andrew Jackson had prior diplomatic experience: Thomas Jefferson, James Monroe, John Adams, and John Quincy Adams all served in diplomatic posts abroad, and all but the older Adams served as secretary of state. James Madison did not represent his country abroad, but he was secretary of state for eight years and was thoroughly briefed on foreign affairs. Washington himself was keenly sensitive to the importance of foreign relations, and on taking office, he read through and made notes on the entire diplomatic correspondence (then only a few volumes). Many leading citizens known for other attainments in the early years of the Republic also spent part of their careers serving the nation overseas— among them Albert Gallatin, Gouverneur Morris, and Robert Livingston.

The Nineteenth-Century Service

For most of the nineteenth century, the dominant issues in the United States were domestic rather than foreign. Only during times of crisis such as the Mexican War, the dispute with Britain over Oregon, and the Civil War (when preventing aid to the Confederacy became crucial) were U.S. diplomats called upon to play a prominent role. In the absence of external threat, the prevailing attitude toward the outside world was one of indifference, and diplomacy as a profession had relatively little appeal for the country's ablest talents.

Meanwhile, the spoils system initiated by President Jackson took a firm hold on the distribution of federal offices, and it was not long before diplomatic and consular appointments came to be governed almost exclusively by domestic and partisan political considerations. By the late 1850s, consul Nathaniel Hawthorne (himself a beneficiary of the system) was led to write, "It is not too much to say, (of course, allowing for a brilliant exception here and there,) that an American never is thoroughly qualified for a foreign post, nor has time to make himself so, before the revolution of the political wheel discards him from his office."[4] (Hawthorne, incidentally, was not the only distinguished literary figure to serve overseas during the nineteenth century. Washington Irving and James Russell Lowell were respectively ministers to Spain and to Britain, while Bret Harte and William Dean Howells, like Hawthorne, held consular posts.)

Despite this relegation of foreign affairs to a metaphorical back burner, U.S. diplomatic and consular representation abroad grew dramatically during the three decades preceding the Civil War. The number of diplomatic posts more than doubled, from fifteen in 1830 to thirty-three in 1860. Most of these posts still consisted only of the U.S. minister or chargé d'affaires and a local clerk; fewer than half of the diplomatic establishments included a U.S. secretary of legation to assist the principal representative. During the same period, the Consular Service— reflecting the foreign trade boom of the times—nearly doubled its number of posts from 141 to 279, though, here again, the consul was normally the only U.S. official at the post.

The Consular and Diplomatic Services were separate entities throughout the nineteenth century, the former staffed largely by businessmen in search of commercial advantage who kept their consular fees in lieu of salary, and the latter by individuals who required private means to supplement the meager compensation paid them by the government. Under the spoils system, neither service offered much in the way of career prospects, and rare indeed were the individuals who spent more than a few years in the nation's service overseas.

Under these circumstances, consular representatives of integrity and ability were the exception rather than the rule. Rapaciousness and fraudulent practice on the part of consular officials were all too common, and there was no effective mechanism to police consular activities. In the diplomatic field, some able and distinguished men rendered outstanding service— notably in the key posts of London and Paris—but it became a fact of spoils-system life that many U.S. political appointees to diplomatic posts did not compare in knowledge and competence, and certainly not in experience, with the professional diplomats of the European powers.

By the 1830s, the subject of reform began to run like a perennial thread through the history of what was to become the Foreign Service. In 1833, Secretary of State Edward Livingston prepared the first comprehensive recommendations aimed at putting the separate Diplomatic and Consular Services on a sounder footing, primarily by providing appropriate salaries for overseas personnel. Despite the further impetus of a congressional investigation in 1846, it took over two decades to get action on Livingston's reform proposals. In an act of 1856, To Remodel the Diplomatic and Consular Systems of the United States, Congress fixed salaries for ambassadors, ministers, and chargés d'affaires, and generally cleaned up the consular system by placing compensation on a salary basis, making it illegal for consuls to earn more than fifteen hundred dollars a year from engaging in private business, establishing a uniform tariff of consular fees, and rendering consuls accountable to the State Department for what they collected. The 1856 Act also made a start toward the merit principle by providing for a corps of "consular pupils" to be appointed on the basis of qualifications and fitness for office.

The 1856 Act was potentially a basic charter for a career foreign service, but it could only serve that purpose through follow-up legislation, executive order, and active administration within the Department of State—none of which was forthcoming. First there was the Civil War, then postwar reconstruction and industrial development—and, with it, renewed U.S. absorption in domestic affairs. The spoils system continued to hold sway. Because of loopholes in the consular fee schedule, fiscal irregularity did not noticeably abate, and the actual number of consular pupils with any kind of permanent tenure never rose above thirteen.

Nonetheless, the movement for reform of the domestic spoils system was gaining strength throughout the country. In 1883, its proponents pushed through the Civil Service (Pendleton) Act, which established the principle of selection by competitive examination. This act did not apply to appointments in the Diplomatic Service or the Consular Service, however, since they were made by the president with consent of the Senate. Toward the end of the century, U.S. businessmen sparked fresh efforts to reform the Consular Service in order to make it more effective in promoting U.S. exports. Encouraged by the business community, President Cleveland tried to push consular reform through Congress, but he finally acted by executive order when he was unable to move the legislative branch to take the action he sought. His 1895 order made a start by requiring oral and written examinations for appointment to the Consular Service, but the order lost much of its potential effectiveness when the McKinley administration lowered the appointment standards.

Early Twentieth-Century Reforms

When Theodore Roosevelt became president, he renewed the attack on the spoils system, reiterating in successive annual messages his conviction that foreign service appointments should be based on merit rather than on partisan considerations. In 1906, Congress finally fell in line, voting on April 5 for a thorough reorganization of the Consular Service. Posts were classified and graded, positions paying a thousand dollars or more per year had to be filled by U.S. citizens who were not permitted to engage in private business, inspection was mandated, and a clear-cut system of fee accountability was introduced.

The 1906 Act did not itself prescribe a merit system, but it made the application of such a system possible. In June of the same year, Roosevelt issued an executive order that, in effect, established a consular merit system by bringing appointments and promotions in the Consular Service under the Civil Service Act of 1883. This consular reform paved the way for parallel action affecting the Diplomatic Service, and a 1909 executive order from President Taft extended the merit principles of the Civil Service Act to all diplomatic positions below the rank of minister. Taft's executive order also directed the secretary of state to report to the president the names of those diplomatic secretaries who had demonstrated special capacity for becoming chiefs of mission. A board of examiners was established to evaluate candidates for the Diplomatic Service, along with qualifying examinations for appointment, and a system of efficiency reports was introduced as a means of judging the performance of members of the Service. More than one hundred years after the founding of the Republic, a foreign service based on merit began to appear possible.

There was still no statutory recognition of the merit principle for U.S. overseas representatives, however, and the existing regulations were considered overly inflexible because both grade and compensation were determined by post of assignment rather than by ability and performance. These shortcomings were rectified by Congress in 1915 in a law that gave statutory confirmation to the merit principle, established a new personnel classification system for both services, and introduced greater flexibility in manpower deployment by providing for the commissioning of officers to grades rather than to posts.

World War I and its aftermath imposed new demands on the Diplomatic and Consular Services, from repatriating U.S. citizens in the path of hostilities to providing new kinds of support for U.S. business in a postwar situation of greatly expanded government intervention in the economies of the principal trading nations. The resultant pressure on the services spotlighted the defects that remained even after the progress achieved under Roosevelt and Taft and through the 1915 Act. In particular, the absence of any provision for shifting personnel between the Diplomatic Service and the Consular Service—a lacuna that was reinforced by sharp disparities in the salary levels of the two services so that the former was reserved almost exclusively to individuals who had private incomes—caused serious problems in attempting to ensure appropriate staffing of the State Department and overseas posts.

Reform found a new champion in Representative John Jacob Rogers of Massachusetts, who had gained first-hand knowledge of the problems confronting the Diplomatic and Consular Services during a visit to Europe in 1919. He became convinced that effective U.S. representation abroad required unification of the still-separate services. This view was enthusiastically shared by members of the Consular Service, who believed that unification would bring an end to their perceived status as second-class citizens. The idea was even coming to be accepted by the Diplomatic Service, which faced serious recruitment problems stemming in large measure from low diplomatic salaries. Equally important, the search for a more effective structure received strong support from Secretary of State Charles Evans Hughes, for whom the foreign services had become even more important as mechanisms for international communication in the wake of the United States' repudiation of the League of Nations.

Over the next several years, Rogers worked closely with the State Department to develop legislation that would firmly establish a single career foreign service. Their collective efforts finally bore fruit on May 24, 1924, the effective date of a new statute known ever since by the name of its principal congressional patron.

The Rogers Act combined the Diplomatic and Consular Services into the unified Foreign Service of the United States; all subsequent changes in the Service have built on this foundation. The act designated permanent officers below the rank of minister as Foreign Service officers (FSOs) and made them subject to diplomatic or consular assignments interchangeably. It provided for appointment by open, competitive examination with promotion strictly on a merit basis, established new salary and retirement scales, and gave authority for a system of representation (entertainment) and housing allowances, thus putting the Service for the first time on a secure professional basis.

The Rogers Act brought about a great improvement in the quality and morale of U.S. overseas representation, but no single piece of legislation could magically cure all the problems of the Foreign Service. Old habits and old attitudes persisted, and the "diplomatic branch"—whose members had traditionally looked down on their consular colleagues—manipulated the administrative mechanisms of the State Department to their own advantage. In particular, it soon became apparent that the ex-diplomats were exerting inordinate influence on the personnel board, so that the promotion rate for former members of the Diplomatic Service was twice as rapid as that for ex-consuls. This practice was sharply criticized in a 1928 report by the Senate Foreign Relations Committee, and a series of proposals to rectify personnel and other inequities culminated three years later in the Moses-Linthicum Act of 1931. The most important provision of the new act was one that assured an impartial promotion process, but the act also provided for improvements in both salaries and allowances.

Most of these material benefits were deferred, however, when government expenditures underwent severe curtailment as a result of the Great Depression. The Foreign Service was particularly hard hit, suffering not only the salary cuts that affected all departments but also reductions in allowances, a suspension of new recruitment, and a loss of purchasing power abroad when the dollar was depreciated and revalued in 1933 and 1934. Not until midway through the 1930s were the cuts restored and the gains promised by the 1931 legislation fully realized.

Other Agencies Enter the Scene

Prior to 1924, the Diplomatic and Consular Services were the only organizations with personnel whose careers were devoted exclusively or predominantly to service overseas. Under the Rogers Act, the newly unified Foreign Service (still part of the State Department) continued to represent the interests abroad of all federal departments and agencies. Then, in 1927, Secretary of Commerce Herbert Hoover persuaded Congress to authorize a separate Foreign Commerce Service—a corps of commercial attachés and trade commissioners operating under the general supervision of Foreign Service posts and devoting their efforts to the promotion of U.S. exports. Next, in 1930, the Department of Agriculture succeeded in gaining congressional authorization for its own foreign service, albeit on a more modest scale, in the form of a small group of agricultural specialists attached to posts abroad. Finally, the Bureau of Mines of the Department of the Interior was authorized in 1935 to place its own representatives in foreign countries, and it assigned a few minerals specialists abroad.

Both Commerce and Agriculture had in fact been sending their own personnel abroad for a number of years before their services received this separate career status, as had such other agencies as the Treasury Department. The presence at overseas posts of representatives from several government departments, each reporting directly to his home office, made for duplication of effort, waste of public funds, and frequent jurisdictional disputes, the most serious of which involved overlapping economic and commercial responsibilities between officers of the State and Commerce Departments. To remedy this situation, President Franklin Roosevelt gained congressional approval in 1939 to fold the overseas activities of the Commerce and Agriculture Departments into the Foreign Service (the few Bureau of Mines specialists were added in 1943). The reorganization brought 105 commercial attachés and 9 agricultural attachés into the Foreign Service, which acquired, in the process, sole responsibility for commercial and agricultural reporting and for trade promotion. Thus, the United States entered World War II with the Rogers Act principle of a unified Foreign Service firmly reestablished.

World War II and Its Aftermath

Although the country may have had a unified Foreign Service, it did not have one that was adequate to the demands imposed on it either by the war or by the radically changed situation of the postwar world. Hampered by the suspension of recruitment for several years during the early 1930s, the Foreign Service in 1941 lacked both the numbers and the specialized know-how it needed to handle a new and vastly altered situation. In addition, even though the Foreign Service had kept Washington well informed of critical developments in the decade leading up to war, it was held in generally low esteem by President Roosevelt, who regarded it (with some justification) as a bastion of conservatism and traditionalism and thus unsympathetic to the goals of his administration.

In consequence, when the expansion of U.S. foreign activities at the onset of the war outstripped the capacity of the Service to keep pace, Roosevelt opted to meet the need by creating new agencies rather than by expanding the Foreign Service. The Service did acquire some extra help during the war in order to perform its regular functions, though in the form of a temporary Foreign Service Auxiliary since regular recruitment was suspended for the duration of the conflict. But nearly all the problems and demands generated by the war were addressed by organizations that were essentially independent of the Foreign Service and the Department of State. Principal among the separate wartime entities given such status were the Economic Defense Board (later Board of Economic Warfare), the Lend-Lease Administration, the Coordinator of Inter-American Affairs, the Office of War Information, and the Office of Strategic Services. Under these circumstances, it was not surprising that an estimated 90 percent of the additional civilian officer personnel assigned to foreign duty between 1939 and 1944 worked for agencies outside the Foreign Service—or that this multiplicity of agencies inevitably gave rise to serious problems of jurisdiction and policy coordination.

The Foreign Service returned to a more central role in the foreign policy process during the immediate postwar years as temporary wartime agencies were disbanded and their functions either dropped entirely or transferred to long-established government departments. State, for example, picked up many of the responsibilities of the Office of War Information and became the operating agency for the overseas information and cultural programs of the U.S. government. It might have wound up with even more operational responsibilities had it been prepared to seek them, but the Foreign Service was loath to accept the dilution of either its numbers or its traditional activities that would have come with such an expanded mandate.

Both the Foreign Service and the State Department leaders recognized that the Service had to adapt to the demands of the postwar world, but their proposals for change differed. Working closely with the Bureau of the Budget, Dean Acheson (then under secretary of state) sought to broaden the Foreign Service by folding in a number of domestic State Department personnel as well as new additions from the former wartime agencies. However, most members of the Service opposed such a course of action and found allies in Congress to help thwart Acheson's plan. In the end, the views of the career officers largely prevailed and were embodied in the Foreign Service Act of 1946.

That act revised and codified all previous legislation and introduced a number of changes with respect to working conditions and the recruitment, classification, training, and utilization of personnel. Salaries, allowances, and retirement conditions were substantially improved; an additional personnel category (Foreign Service reserve officer) was introduced to facilitate the hiring of specialized personnel for limited periods; new offices and institutions were created to strengthen the administration of the Service; and a modified version of the U.S. Navy's promotion-up-or-selection-out system was introduced to encourage a more rapid advancement of the ablest officers and the separation of those whose performance was judged less strong.

Although these changes, combined with the resumption of recruitment, gave the Foreign Service a much more solid base, critics charged that it still was not capable of dealing effectively with the complexities of the postwar scene. In 1947, the Commission on Organization of the Executive Branch of the Government—called the Hoover Commission after the former president who chaired it—was the first of several such groups to reopen the whole question of overseas representation. A principal recommendation of the commission's report, submitted to Congress in 1949, was that personnel of the State Department and the Foreign Service above certain levels should be amalgamated into a single foreign affairs service, to serve both overseas and at home. The report noted that Foreign Service officers, because of long duty abroad, lost touch with their own country (a complaint previously voiced by Thomas Jefferson on the basis of his own experience), while departmental officers had too little contact with or understanding of other nations and the problems of those officials who worked directly with them. This recommendation proved unpopular with both of the groups potentially affected by it: Foreign Service officers once again resisted losing their exclusive status, and many Civil Service officers had no wish to go overseas for protracted periods or be subjected to the more exacting Foreign Service promotion system. Largely because of this hostile reception, the recommendation was quietly shelved.

Although its time had not yet come, the idea of incorporating a significant part of the State Department staff into an expanded Foreign Service was far from dead. It took two more study

groups and five more years before it became reality, with the
final push coming from a Public Committee on Personnel
appointed in 1954 by Secretary of State John Foster Dulles and
headed by Brown University President Henry M. Wriston. The
chief recommendation of the Wriston report, echoing the Hoover
Commission findings, was to integrate the personnel of the
Department of State and the Foreign Service when their official
functions converged—and to do so within a two-year period.
Secretary Dulles accepted the recommendation, including the
draconian insistence that it be done in short order, and the
integration process that came to be known as "Wristonization"
was under way. As a result of both mandatory integration and
stepped-up recruitment, the Foreign Service officer (FSO) corps
tripled between 1954 and 1957, growing from around twelve
hundred to a new total of nearly thirty-five hundred members.

Throughout this period, the principal focus was on Foreign
Service officers—but they were only part of the total Foreign
Service. Even within State Department ranks, the FSOs were
complemented by employees in the other two principal personnel
categories established by the 1946 Act: Foreign Service reserve
officers (FSRs) and Foreign Service staff (FSS) employees. The
former consisted primarily of specialists in such fields as labor
or economics, still underrepresented among FSOs, while the
latter comprised secretaries, communicators, and similar support
personnel. Together, they outnumbered the FSOs roughly two
to one. Although the FSRs have since disappeared as a personnel
category, today's successors of the former FSS employees remain
an indispensable element of the Foreign Service.

New Agencies Take the Field

Equally important to the future shape of the Foreign Service
was its extension to the new agencies that were emerging on
the foreign affairs scene. The substantial U.S. commitment to
postwar reconstruction had quickly been transformed into a
longer-term program of economic assistance to other nations.
Although responsibility for these programs was initially given
to the State Department and the Foreign Service, the magnitude

of the effort was clearly beyond their immediate resources. In consequence, foreign assistance became the province of a series of agencies created specifically for that purpose. The Economic Cooperation Administration, responsible primarily for the rebuilding of Europe, was succeeded in 1951 by the Foreign Operations Administration, in 1955 by the International Cooperation Administration, and in 1961 by the Agency for International Development (AID). Their employees serving abroad received either Foreign Service reserve or Foreign Service staff appointments. Despite the nominally "temporary" nature of each of these agencies, many able individuals remained with them for extended periods. These were career employees in all but name, but they were to be kept waiting until 1979 to have that status given formal recognition.

The overseas information programs of the U.S. government followed a similar course. Initially assigned to the State Department when the Office of War Information was disbanded in 1945, these programs were stripped away in 1953 and consigned to the newly created United States Information Agency (USIA). This action was in keeping with a recommendation made four years earlier by the Hoover Commission that State generally should not be given responsibility for the operation of specific programs, but should instead concentrate on policy formulation and coordination. The move also reflected the steady growth of the information effort and the strain it was placing on State Department resources; by 1952, its last full year under the State umbrella, the information and cultural program represented roughly half the total State Department budget. A substantial part of the information effort, particularly its overseas arm (which operated then, as it does today, under the name of United States Information Service, or USIS), was staffed from the beginning by personnel with Foreign Service appointments. As in the case of AID and its predecessors, the initial appointments were made in either the FSR or FSS categories. With USIA, however, there was earlier recognition that its functions were likely to endure, and in 1968 Congress granted career status to that agency's Foreign Service personnel by authorizing a new corps of Foreign Service information officers under the same terms and conditions governing the FSO corps in the State Department.

The 1950s also saw the reemergence of a separate Foreign Agricultural Service (FAS), set up by Congress in 1954 largely in response to growing problems associated with the marketing of surplus agricultural products. The FAS, like the much larger AID and USIS, used Foreign Service appointments for its agricultural attachés and support personnel abroad. During the decade of the 1960s, the Foreign Service system was also applied to the newly created Peace Corps, but no problem of career appointments arose because personnel of that agency are limited by statute to a maximum service of five years. The establishment of the Arms Control and Disarmament Agency (ACDA) meant yet another candidate for the Foreign Service appointment system, but ACDA chose to have its personnel appointed and then detailed by the State Department rather than to develop a distinct body of ACDA Foreign Service employees.

The final entrant on the scene during the lifetime of the 1946 Act was the Foreign Commercial Service (FCS), set up by Congress in 1979 as the overseas arm of the Department of Commerce and assigned the export promotion and related functions formerly carried out by the State Department. The legislation creating the FCS put its overseas employees under the Foreign Service umbrella, and provided for career appointments on terms identical with those applicable to the other agencies already in the system.

As the number of agencies utilizing the Foreign Service system continued to grow, the concept of a single Foreign Service of the United States envisaged by the framers of the 1946 Act was fading fast. An effort was made in 1965 to create a new structure capable of absorbing all U.S. government personnel engaged in foreign affairs, but the draft legislation to this effect never made it beyond committee consideration. During this same period, other shortcomings in the structure created by the Foreign Service Act of 1946 became apparent, and a series of amendments were adopted to respond to these more specific problems as they surfaced. The most important of these amendments changed the number of classes in the FSO corps, significantly improved the total package of allowances and benefits for members of the Service, liberalized provisions for integrating qualified personnel from other government agencies, and added a major policy statement in support of training in foreign languages and area studies.

By the mid-1970s, however, it was becoming clear that the Foreign Service required something more than the tinkering that had been done in three decades of amendments to the 1946 Act. The Foreign Service personnel system had been stretched like a rubber band to cover the often divergent needs of the several foreign affairs agencies, and had come to encompass employees in a profusion of personnel categories that often bore little logical relation to the duties they performed. The FSR category, for example, had been devised to meet temporary needs for particular specialized skills, but it had come to be used for career personnel not only in such "temporary" agencies as AID but even in the State Department. Still more anomalous, agencies had employees on Foreign Service appointments who were in fact never expected to serve abroad—a category that came to be known by the incongruous name of "domestic Foreign Service."

The search for new formulas began in the State Department in 1975 with an effort to restructure the system from within. Although the initial recommendations were not adopted, they laid the groundwork for a subsequent effort, which started three years later and culminated in passage of the Foreign Service Act of 1980. A critical step along the way was the Civil Service Reform Act of 1978, which provided a statutory base for the non–Foreign Service personnel of the foreign affairs agencies and a model for several of the provisions subsequently incorporated in the 1980 legislation. Congressional action on the Civil Service Reform Act also served to put the final seal on a debate that had been raging for years within the State Department: whether the goal should be a single personnel system, embracing both domestic and overseas personnel working in the foreign affairs area, or whether there should continue to be two separate systems, one for employees expected to serve abroad and another for those whose careers would be spent exclusively in Washington. In the wake of the strong congressional support given to the Civil Service Reform Act, State

Department officials concluded that the political realities required two systems, with domestic personnel remaining in the Civil Service. Their decision cleared the way for ultimate passage of the 1980 Act.

The basic purposes of the act were straightforward: to distinguish clearly between Foreign Service and Civil Service employment, and in the process to do away with the anomalous "domestic Foreign Service" category; to simplify and rationalize the various Foreign Service personnel categories; to put all Foreign Service employees on a single salary schedule and under the same terms and conditions of employment; to bring about greater compatibility among the foreign affairs agencies and with the Civil Service; to establish a Senior Foreign Service paralleling the Senior Executive Service created by the Civil Service Reform Act; and to consolidate in one place the provisions relating to the Foreign Service enacted both in amendments to the Foreign Service Act of 1946 and in various authorization and appropriation acts. Although the draft initially proposed by the foreign affairs agencies underwent some modifications in the course of congressional consideration, its essential elements emerged intact and provide the basic charter for today's Foreign Service.

Notes

1. The history of the Foreign Service through 1960 is based largely on William Barnes and John Heath Morgan, *The Foreign Service of the United States* (Washington, D.C.: Historical Office, Bureau of Public Affairs, U.S. Department of State, 1961); Warren Frederick Ilchman, *Professional Diplomacy in the United States, 1779–1939* (Chicago: University of Chicago Press, 1961); and on the retelling of this history in W. Wendell Blancke, *The Foreign Service of the United States* (New York: Frederick A. Praeger, 1969), pp. 3–30. Blancke is also the source for some of the developments during the decade of the 1960s.

2. Quoted in Barnes and Morgan, *Foreign Service*, p. 5.

3. Ibid., p. 13.

4. Ibid., pp. 105–106.

THE STRUCTURAL FRAMEWORK

*. . . a career foreign service, characterized by excellence and profes-
sionalism, is essential in the national interest to assist the President
and the Secretary of State in conducting the foreign affairs of the
United States.*

—Foreign Service Act of 1980

The 1980 Act greatly simplified the Foreign Service in several
respects—yet in other ways made it more difficult to explain.
In the wake of the new act, the broad concept of the Foreign
Service underwent a sea change. Although personnel in several
agencies had previously used Foreign Service appointments, it
was only the State Department employees under the Foreign
Service umbrella (and among them, only those personnel who
actually served abroad for the bulk of their careers) who really
identified themselves with the Service. Asked what they did
for a living, people in the other foreign affairs agencies usually
replied that they worked for AID or USIA, not that they were
in the Foreign Service.

One major cause of this situation was the pre-1980 difference
in nomenclature, and thus in status, between the Foreign Service
officers (FSOs) on State Department rolls and their counterparts
elsewhere in the foreign affairs community. For only the State
officers had the FSO designation, and thus the presumed heritage
of diplomats past; individuals with equivalent responsibility in
other agencies were clearly tagged as a breed apart by holding
Foreign Service reserve officer (FSR) appointments, even when
serving on a career basis. The one exception was in USIA,

which had a career officer corps, but as a matter of policy, that agency had obtained from Congress a separate designation of Foreign Service information officers (FSIOs) for its personnel.

In the wake of the 1980 Act, the multiple personnel categories that had made these invidious distinctions possible gave way to a much cleaner system—and to a congressional mandate that the new system should be so operated as to promote "maximum compatibility" both among the agencies using the authority provided by the Foreign Service Act and between the Foreign Service and the Civil Service systems, in which all the domestic personnel of the foreign affairs agencies are now lodged.[1] As we have seen, however, the act also qualified its hortatory injunction to promote compatibility by reaffirming the management rights of the head of each of the foreign affairs agencies. Nonetheless, the implementing regulations for the act were in fact prepared, to a considerable extent, jointly by all the affected agencies. In consequence, the rules of the game for administering the Foreign Service are substantially the same from agency to agency, even though the kinds of skills sought and the career prospects offered necessarily vary in keeping with the particular mission of each organization.

Compatibility between the Foreign Service and Civil Service systems raises an entirely different set of issues. In view of the congressional reaffirmation, in the 1980 Act, that a career Foreign Service "is essential in the national interest,"[2] it seems clear that there will be two separate systems for the foreseeable future. Given this circumstance, the fundamental differences between the two systems limit the extent to which they can be aligned. The Foreign Service system is designed to meet the special needs of a service committed to worldwide availability and characterized by frequent transfers among posts that on occasion offer conditions of severe hardship. Rank in the Foreign Service lies with the individual employee, as it does in the military, and does not change according to which job the person may hold at any given moment or the nominal rank of the position occupied (that is, a colonel is a colonel wherever he or she may be assigned, and the same is true of Foreign Service employees). The Civil Service, on the other hand, operates under rules that assume a career will be spent entirely or predominantly in the United States. The ranks of its members depend, with minor exceptions, on which positions they hold, so that advancement is dependent on the ability of a qualified individual to find an appropriate job graded at a higher level.

Although compatibility is clearly limited by these basic differences between the systems, there is—as so often in Washington—a political dimension to the issue. The Office of Personnel Management (OPM), which is responsible for directing the Civil Service personnel system, has over the years felt varying degrees of frustration at seeing the Foreign Service remain outside its managerial grasp. At times, OPM has been extremely supportive, most recently during the debates that led to the Foreign Service Act of 1980. At other times, it has sought to extend to the Foreign Service, insofar as possible, the rules and judgments that it imposes on the Civil Service. This sporadic "turf battle" has not impaired the ability of the foreign affairs agencies to manage the Foreign Service system, but it does add to the complexity of their task.

Foreign Service Appointments

One of the major contributions of the Foreign Service Act of 1980 was a greatly simplified structure of appointments, grades, and salaries for the entire Service. Where previously there had been ten personnel categories bearing a Foreign Service label—some utilized only in single agencies, some applying to individuals who never left Washington—there are now only three types of career Foreign Service appointments, and all who receive them share an obligation and a commitment to worldwide service. Equally important, the same appointment categories are used by all the foreign affairs agencies and are applied under a set of regulations applicable throughout the Foreign Service.

The total number of U.S. employees in the career Foreign Service is about thirteen thousand (see Appendix A). The three categories into which they fall are Senior Foreign Service (SFS), Foreign Service officers (FSOs), and Foreign Service specialist and support personnel (FPs). In addition, the Foreign Service also includes more than eighteen thousand Foreign Service national (FSN) employees, who support the U.S. staff at posts abroad.

Senior Foreign Service

Prior to the 1980 Act, the FSO corps consisted of ten classes, from a minimum entry level of class eight up to class one and then to the "supergrades" of career minister and career ambassador. These grades roughly paralleled those of the military services, with class three corresponding to colonel (or captain in the U.S. Navy) and the higher grades to general- or flag-officer rank. The Foreign Service grade structure also reflected that of the Civil Service in having a single grade ladder for professional personnel (in the Civil Service, from GS-7 through GS-18), with class three equating to GS-15 and classes two and one to the Civil Service "supergrades" of GS-16 and above.

In 1978, however, the Civil Service Reform Act introduced a new element into the Civil Service structure by creating the Senior Executive Service (SES), a government-wide corps of senior managerial personnel characterized both by reduced assurance of tenure and by access to an innovative program of performance incentives. Congressional initiatives to include senior members of the Foreign Service in the SES were deflected in part by promises that the framers of the Foreign Service Act would adopt the SES as a model and build a comparable SFS into the new legislation. In addition to honoring their commitment to Congress, they did so for two additional reasons: first, in the belief that senior officers in the Foreign Service should have an equal chance for the kinds of cash awards offered under the SES incentive system, and second, in hopes that a carefully structured SFS would solve the recurrent dilemma of overpopulation in the senior ranks of the Foreign Service. The latter problem arose periodically when, for a variety of reasons, the number of senior officers with certain types of skills exceeded the number of jobs for which they were qualified. When this situation occurred, skilled officers found themselves "walking the halls" (in fact, almost always employed but on temporary projects), not needed for regular positions in the foreseeable future but entitled to remain on the rolls until they had served as long as twenty-two years at senior levels.

The new SFS, intended by Congress to be (in the words of the 1980 Act) "the corps of leaders and experts for the management of the Service and the performance of its functions,"[3] embraces the four most senior grades in the old Foreign Service structure—those equivalent to the general- or flag-officer rank in the military services. The roughly twelve hundred SFS officers, all of whom are appointed by the president with the advice and consent of the Senate, hold ranks that are designated by name rather than by number. What had been class two became counselor, class one was transformed into minister-counselor, and career minister and career ambassador remained unchanged at the top of the ladder. Members of the SFS are paid on the same salary scale as their Civil Service counterparts in the SES. Again like SES members, they are eligible each year for performance pay both within their individual agencies and in a government-wide competition (in this case, within the entire SFS). Awards within the agencies range up to ten thousand dollars, and as much as one-third of the SFS may receive them in any single year; presidential awards for which the entire SFS competes are for either ten thousand or twenty thousand dollars, but they may not be given to more than 6 percent of the total SFS (and not more than 1 percent at the higher award level).

Along with this opportunity for greater monetary reward, however, SFS members have had to accept a considerable reduction in the security of tenure that previously characterized the senior ranks of the Foreign Service. Whereas officers holding the old ranks of FSO-2 or FSO-1 were assured (assuming satisfactory performance) that they could remain in either of these grades for twelve years, or for twenty-two years in the sequence of the two grades, today's SFS members have a far shorter allowance of "time-in-class." For counselors (the former FSO-2), the limit is seven years; for minister-counselors (previously FSO-1), the maximum is five years; and for career ministers, never before subject to any limit at all, there is now a four-year ceiling. Each of these officers, in the last year of time-in-class, competes for a limited career extension of three years, which is awarded by independent evaluation panels on the basis of written performance records. Since the number of limited career extensions to be granted in any given year is determined by the management of each agency, this clearly is a powerful tool for dealing with any future problem of surplus officers at the senior level.

Officers normally enter the Senior Foreign Service by promotion from the top grade of the FSO or FP structure. The Foreign Service Act also provides for direct appointment into the SFS of individuals from outside the Foreign Service, but this authority is subject to two limitations to guard against political abuse: the total number of such appointments may not exceed 5 percent of the total SFS; and any appointment of this kind must be a temporary one, with career status obtainable only after several years of satisfactory performance and a subsequent reevaluation of the individual's qualifications.

Foreign Service Officers

Within the modern Foreign Service, the FSOs are the lineal descendants of the secretaries of legation and consular pupils who were the first career members of the original Diplomatic and Consular Services. When the two services were merged in 1924, their professional-level members became FSOs, and the functions they performed then, while expanded, would appear reasonably familiar to many members of today's FSO corps in the State Department. What has changed is the extension of the FSO category throughout the foreign affairs agencies under the provisions of the 1980 Act.

The current total of over fifty-five hundred FSOs (and FSO career candidates) is spread across several agencies (see Appendix A). Regardless of the agency to which they belong, FSOs have the same grade and salary structure. What had been classes eight through three prior to the 1980 Act were renumbered following establishment of the SFS and became classes six through one—again, roughly equivalent to the commissioned military ranks of second lieutenant/ensign through colonel or navy captain.

Classes six and five are the normal entry grades for newcomers to the Foreign Service, though exceptionally qualified applicants are occasionally appointed at class four. Following a probationary period, officers move into the mid-career ranks of class three through class one, at which level they compete to cross the final threshold into the SFS. The time allowed to complete each step of this process is limited, as it is for officers within the SFS. FSOs may not remain more than fifteen years in any single mid-level class before being promoted, nor more than twenty-two years from the time they are awarded career status until they enter the SFS. Should either of these time-in-class limits be reached, the FSO concerned faces mandatory retirement from the Service.

Like their senior colleagues in the SFS, all FSOs are presidential appointees. When they complete their probationary period, usually between three and four years, new FSOs have their names submitted by the president for the advice and consent of the Senate. With Senate approval, each FSO is given a commission as a Foreign Service officer of the United States—and, along with it, career status in the Foreign Service.

As a result of the transition process that followed adoption of the Foreign Service Act of 1980, a number of today's FSOs came directly to their present status either from one of the personnel categories abolished by the 1980 Act or, in some cases (as in the Department of Agriculture), from Civil Service ranks. Most of these individuals formerly held appointments as Foreign Service reserve officers (FSRs), a catch-all category that included both career employees and those whose services were needed for only a short period of time. FSRs who were available for worldwide service, and whose skills could be utilized overseas, were incorporated into the new structure either as FSOs or as Foreign Service specialists (FPs), and those who were identified as domestic personnel were incorporated into the Civil Service. Now that this transition period has been completed, it is envisaged that most future FSO appointments will be made to the entering grades by examination.

Foreign Service Specialists

The final category of U.S. career Foreign Service personnel is in some ways the most critical of all. The Foreign Service specialist group is the largest in the Service, and its members perform the greatest variety of functions. Included within its ranks are the secretarial personnel who serve all the foreign affairs agencies abroad, as well as the communications specialists on the State Department rolls who assure the link between Washington and the overseas posts. The State Department's FP contingent runs the gamut from doctors and nurses to security officers, building engineers, and diplomatic couriers, and the range in the other agencies, while different, is equally impressive.

Foreign Service career employees in the FP category are paid on the same salary scale as their FSO colleagues, except the former have three additional lower classes—FP-7, -8, and -9. (To add confusion, salary grades for all Foreign Service personnel, whether FSOs or FPs, are designated FS—so that an employee who is, for example, either an FSO-3 or FP-3 is at the same time identified as an FS-3 for salary purposes.) The entering grade and career opportunities for FP personnel vary with the specialty in which they are employed, but several of the FP career fields offer openings up to class one and beyond into the SFS.

Where the FPs differ most visibly from their FSO colleagues is in the nature of their appointments, which are made by the heads of the foreign affairs agencies rather than by the president. In consequence, FP personnel do not receive a basic employment commission and are not normally accorded the additional commissions given to FSOs, which empower them to hold certain diplomatic and consular titles and to perform the functions associated with those titles. There is no bar to commissioning FP personnel in these capacities, however, and FP personnel do on occasion receive consular training and commissions to meet particular staffing needs at overseas posts.

Like the FSO corps, the FP ranks also received an infusion of former FSR employees during the post-1980 transition period. The largest single group of these was in AID, which had made the most extensive use of the FSR category since, for many years, AID lacked the authority to grant clear career status. Although AID initially converted all its Foreign Service personnel to FP status, in 1984 the agency commissioned nearly eight hundred of its personnel (all tenured members of the Service at grade FP-3 or above), thus putting them in a category more nearly akin to that of their counterparts in the other foreign affairs agencies.

Foreign Service Nationals

The final career category in the Foreign Service is that of Foreign Service nationals (FSNs), who are specifically recognized in the 1980 Act as "members of the Service." In the words of the act, these are employees "who provide clerical, administrative, technical, fiscal, and other support at Foreign Service posts abroad."[4] By definition, they are not U.S. citizens (though family members of U.S. employees do on occasion occupy FSN positions). They are usually nationals of the country in which they are employed, but in fact, they may be citizens of a third country. FSN employees are paid according to a wage scale "based upon prevailing wage rates and compensation practices,"[5] which is usually on a level that is competitive with the leading local and multinational companies. Thus, FSNs are generally well paid by host country criteria, and the Foreign Service has been able to retain many loyal employees on a career basis.

The value of capable FSNs to a post would be hard to exaggerate. The U.S. staff depends on its national employees not only to fill a host of relatively menial occupations such as janitor and driver, but also to provide essential continuity at a more professional level in support of their transient bosses. FSN ranks around the world include consular specialists, who cope with the daily crush of visa applicants; procurement experts, who handle the purchasing of a variety of supplies on the local market; economists competent to analyze a balance of payments or a nation's debt situation; engineers to supervise development projects; information specialists skilled at placing material in the local media; and a host of other able professionals. These FSNs contribute not only their basic talents and training but, equally important, a knowledge of the language, customs, conditions, and people of the host country that Americans find hard to equal during their relatively short tours.

It must be added that the lot of an FSN working for the U.S. government is not always an easy one. Although embassy or consulate employment may convey a certain social status in a number of countries, association with the United States can bring with it harassment, physical abuse, and even imprisonment and torture at the hands of an unfriendly government. Whereas U.S. personnel are protected by their diplomatic or consular status, FSNs have no such shield. More than one has paid a price—and some have given their lives—for loyal service to a U.S. Foreign Service post.

Limited Appointments

In addition to the career categories, the Foreign Service also includes, at any given time, a certain number of employees on time-limited appointments. These are made primarily to meet two needs: to obtain specialized skills that are not available within the Service but are required to fill a particular position abroad (in one recent case, a Turkish-speaking labor attaché to serve in Ankara) or to hire potential career employees, who are placed on limited appointments for a probationary period. By law, such appointments may not be for longer than five years and may not be extended or renewed.[6] These provisions are designed to ensure that limited appointments will not become a route to permanent tenure except through the demanding evaluation process required for career status. Unlike the FSR appointments, which were used in similar fashion prior to the 1980 Act, limited appointments may be used only for individuals who will serve overseas. Personnel to meet domestic vacancies must be hired in the Civil Service system.

Evaluation, Promotion, and Selection-Out

One of the major differences between the Foreign Service and Civil Service systems is between the "rank-in-person" concept of the former and the "rank-in-job" structure of the latter. Since promotions in the Foreign Service are not determined by the grade level of the particular job an individual holds, the Foreign Service Act of 1980 (like similar earlier legislation) provides for promotion decisions to be made by a series of impartial selection boards working solely from the written record of each employee's performance.

Although the implementing procedure varies slightly from agency to agency, the basic approach is the same throughout the Service. Each career Foreign Service employee is rated at least once a year by his or her supervisor (more often if the employee changes jobs or gets a new boss during the rating year). The annual evaluation covers actual performance over the past twelve months, the employee's strengths and weaknesses in a series of skill areas relevant to the work of the Foreign Service, and the supervisor's judgment of the employee's potential for the future. The supervisor next up the line (usually the boss of the individual who writes the initial rating) is required to add an independent evaluation of the employee, a double check that is particularly important in cases in which a report may be adversely influenced by an underlying personality clash between an employee and the first-line supervisor. Finally, the rated employee—who is shown the entire report before it is submitted—has an opportunity to add comments about his or her past year's work or future aspirations (the former is mandatory for State Department personnel), and this opportunity may be used to rebut criticism that the employee feels is unjustified.

If the supervisor has been doing his or her job properly, there will have been several meetings during the year at which the employee's performance has been frankly discussed. Under the regulations, employees should be informed of any perceived shortcomings early enough in the rating period so that an attempt can be made to overcome them. If this procedure has been followed, any critical observations that appear in the annual evaluation report should come as no surprise to the recipient.

The personnel office of each of the foreign affairs agencies is responsible for maintaining a performance file on each of the agency's employees, and it is to these dossiers that the new evaluation is added. Once a year, each of the agencies convenes a series of selection boards to recommend which employees are qualified for promotion to the next higher grade. The independence of the Foreign Service promotion process has long been one of the Service's most cherished features (as noted in Chapter 2, it owes its origin to the Senate's unhappiness in the 1920s with a process that was then dominated by an "old-boy" network). As reaffirmed in the 1980 Act, the key element of the promotion process is the requirement that the rank-ordering of candidates for promotion be done by independent selection boards composed of both career members of the Service and outsiders, including at least one public member—that is, an individual from outside government service—on each board. To guard against the possibility of unequal treatment, the act also calls for "a substantial number of women and members of minority groups" to be among the members of each selection board.[7] Finally, the 1980 Act makes it clear that the boards do indeed have the last word by requiring that the head of each foreign affairs agency make promotions "in accordance with the rankings of the selection boards."[8] (The wording of earlier statutes, which called for promotions "on the basis of" board rankings, led to efforts some years ago by one agency head to alter a list of board recommendations for essentially political reasons—and to the unequivocal language that appears in the current legislation.)

The selection board process is a demanding one. Each board is asked to read and rank-order the files of all the employees in one or more grades or specialties, a task that may involve the careful screening of as many as six hundred folders, each covering perhaps fifteen to twenty years of service. To ease their burden, the boards are instructed to concentrate on the most recent five years of ratings, or those ratings since the individual was last promoted, but the process still means that board members must spend an average of from four to eight weeks reading and ranking. The board always includes a public member, for whom the jargon is often bewildering at first, and often has at least one member from another government agency with some knowledge of the type of work being performed by the employees under consideration. This broad membership effectively rules out any possibility of promotion on the basis of favoritism or personal friendship, and has proved a solid guarantee of a fair and impartial selection process.

Although the mechanics of the board process work well, the weakness in the system lies in the total dependence of each selection board on the quality of the written evaluations that form the basis of their judgments. Because individual Foreign

Service jobs vary so widely in content even when they bear the same formal job title, boards sometimes feel they are being asked to compare apples and oranges within a supposedly homogeneous group. Added to this problem, in recent years there has been a serious tendency to inflate evaluations. In one year when percentile ratings were tried, over 80 percent of mid-level State Department FSOs were judged by their supervisors to be in the top 10 percent of their class, and proliferating adjectives have made it difficult to distinguish which employees are most deserving of promotion. Each of the foreign affairs agencies is constantly struggling to ensure that supervisors report candidly on the failings as well as on the accomplishments of their subordinates, but none has yet found the magic formula for success. (The Foreign Commercial Service has introduced an evaluation system that is more closely tied to quantifiable goals than the systems utilized elsewhere; to the extent that it can be adapted to the needs of the other agencies, it may offer a way out of the current dilemma.)

In addition to promotion decisions, the selection boards also bear the heavy responsibility of identifying which employees have performed below the acceptable standards for their grade and should therefore be considered for "selection-out" of the Foreign Service. This concept, borrowed from the U.S. Navy and first introduced in the 1946 Act, is designed to pare away the deadwood—those relatively rare individuals who are no longer capable of doing a satisfactory job, even at their current grade levels. The selection-out mechanism initially applied only to the commissioned FSO corps, but it was extended by the 1980 Act to cover all career members of the Foreign Service.

The files of employees judged by the selection boards to be performing unacceptably are referred to a separate Performance Standards Board, constituted in accordance with the same criteria that govern selection boards, and it is this latter body that makes the decision as to whether a particular individual should be separated from the Service. Any employee identified for selection-out through this process has the right of appeal, either to yet another review board or through a formal grievance process, and he or she may, of course, take the further step of challenging the decision in the courts. In recent years, an average of twenty to twenty-five State Department employees have been referred annually to the Performance Standards Board, and about half of those ultimately separated from the Service; the numbers in the other agencies have been proportionately lower.

As noted in the discussion about the Senior Foreign Service, a final responsibility of the selection boards rating SFS officers is to establish a rank-order list of SFS members in their last year of time-in-class who are competing for limited career extensions (LCEs). The process is closely akin to that used for promotion, with LCEs being granted in strict accordance with the rankings of the boards concerned.

The boards have authority only to recommend individuals for promotion, not to ensure that they are promoted. The actual number of promotions each year to each grade and in each specialist field is decided by management officials before the boards convene and is based on their determination as to how many more employees are needed in the next higher grade. This number is often smaller than the number of individuals recommended for promotion by a selection board (in some years, and in some grades, the number of promotions allowed may in fact be zero). At this point, management's only obligation is to ensure that the available promotions go in strict rank order according to the recommendations of the selection boards, not to promote all those who received a positive recommendation from the boards. Not surprisingly, employees recommended but not promoted find this a frustrating system, but with continued strong performance they can usually expect to move up in the rank-ordering in succeeding years.

Assignments

Like career military personnel, members of the Foreign Service accept an obligation to serve wherever they are needed, whether at home or abroad. The head of each of the foreign affairs agencies is authorized by the Foreign Service Act of 1980 to decide which of that agency's jobs shall be filled by Foreign Service employees and then to "assign a member of the Service to any position" with a Foreign Service label on it. More important, the agency head also "may assign a member from one such position to another such position as the needs of the Service may require"[9]—the basic statement of both worldwide availability and assignment in response to "Service need" that sets the Foreign Service apart from its domestic counterparts.

In addition to the designated positions within the foreign affairs agencies, members of the Foreign Service may be assigned to a wide variety of jobs elsewhere in the U.S. government or in the private sector. Both the 1980 Act and its predecessor provide for assignment of Foreign Service personnel to international organizations (for example, the United Nations and its specialized agencies, the North Atlantic Treaty Organization, or the Organization for Economic Cooperation and Development), a relatively straightforward extension of their normal work. Perhaps more surprisingly, both statutes also permit (and Congress has encouraged) assignments to state or local governments (ranging from the governor's office in Tallahassee, Florida, to the city manager's office in Billings, Montana), to congressional offices, to educational institutions, and to a range of other organizations including trade associations and even private corporations. As a result of this remarkable flexibility, members of the Foreign Service have had opportunities for direct exposure to aspects of the U.S. scene that make them more effective representatives of the United States when they return abroad; at the same time, they contribute their unique skills and perspective to their host organizations.

The assignment mechanism varies from agency to agency within the Foreign Service family, but in each case, it seeks to balance a number of elements in reaching assignment decisions. "Service need," in its most basic definition, means that each agency must be able to accomplish its assigned mission by putting qualified individuals where they are most needed to get the job done. Set against this need as each proposed assignment is being weighed are a number of other factors—for example, the preferences of the employee and his or her family (including the educational needs of children and, to an increasing extent, employment opportunities for spouses); the employee's career development requirements (whether formal training or a particular kind of work experience); and the special skills or background called for by a given position. There may be competition from several posts or areas for the services of an individual with a particularly strong record; there may be a conflict between the immediate requirement to get a particular job done and the desirability of preparing an employee carefully for future responsibilities; the employee's preferences and the agency's sense of urgent need may prove irreconcilable. Given the inherent conflicts, perhaps the real surprise is that nearly all Foreign Service assignments do manage to meet both the preferences of the employee and the needs of the Service; only rarely do members of the Service have to be ordered to posts against their wishes. In the end, however, it is the agency's decision that is final, and an employee who is unwilling to accept an assignment has only the option of resigning from the Service.

The duration of individual assignments also varies among the foreign affairs agencies, largely as a reflection of the differences in both their work and their workforces. Tours of duty for Foreign Service personnel in the State Department range from a minimum of eighteen months to a normal maximum of four years in any one country; the usual tour abroad tends to be three years at the more attractive posts and two years where hardship conditions prevail. It has long been recognized that such relatively short tours of duty make it difficult for employees to become fully effective at any given post, but this price has been accepted by the State Department in order to give its employees a wider range of both functional and area experiences to prepare them for more senior responsibilities.

The State Department preference for shorter tours also reflects a concern that personnel who stay too long in a single post may become afflicted with "localitis"—a condition that means that diplomats abroad have grown so close to their host governments that they have lost sight of the basic interests of their own country. It is not uncommon for members of the Foreign Service to exaggerate the importance of the country to which they have been sent; one ambassador called this tendency "the jungle clearing syndrome," in which the chief of mission who has stayed too long at a small post comes to believe firmly that "my jungle clearing is the most important jungle clearing." In its more dangerous form, localitis becomes "clientitis," and the diplomat becomes an advocate for his or her host country rather than for the government back home. When this condition occurs, it is time for a transfer.

In the other foreign affairs agencies, where the type of work done by an individual tends to be more uniform throughout a career than in the State Department, tours of duty tend to be considerably longer. (The one notable exception is in Agriculture, as the Animal and Plant Health Inspection Service has tours of eighteen months or two years and encourages personnel to extend for up to four years, but does not require the longer tour.) AID, for example, although most of its overseas positions are in the developing world where living conditions tend to be more difficult, sets a standard tour of four years in order to provide a greater continuity of personnel working on individual development programs or projects abroad. Similarly, the Foreign Commercial Service places heavy emphasis on the desirability of keeping employees at posts overseas long enough to become fully effective and to make use of their language and area skills. Taking advantage of the fact that most FCS positions abroad are at relatively attractive posts in developed countries, the agency assigns its personnel for standard tours of four or five years. Both USIA and the Foreign Agricultural Service, which like the State Department have posts more evenly divided between the developed and developing worlds, also tend toward longer tours of duty than those set by State.

For stateside assignments, the rules are more uniform among the foreign affairs agencies. The statutory provisions only require a tour at home at some point during each fifteen years of service (reflecting once again Jefferson's concern about personnel losing touch with their own country) and set a limit of eight years on any single period of domestic service. In practice, the foreign affairs agencies usually limit tours in Washington to four years, with a fifth year granted fairly routinely to accommodate training or personal considerations. In the words of the 1980 Act, "Career members of the Service shall be obligated to serve abroad and shall be expected to serve abroad for substantial portions of their careers";[10] the limits on Washington assignments are intended to help ensure that the intent of the act is fully honored.

Allowances and Benefits

It took a long time for Congress to recognize the special difficulties and hardships involved in service abroad. Nineteenth-century archives are replete with pleas from members of the Diplomatic and Consular Services for more adequate compensation, or at least for funds to cover necessary office expenses. In the early years of U.S. overseas representation, diplomatic officers received salaries and "outfits"—a lump-sum advance of funds to cover everything from transportation costs to office rental—from which they were expected to meet all their personal and official expenses. Most consular officers received no salaries at all, but instead were expected to cover all of their costs from the consular fees they collected for services rendered.

Gradually, in response to repeated supplications and congressional investigations, greater order was brought into funding overseas operations. The first step, taken midway through the nineteenth century, was to provide for official expenditures in addition to salary as an alternative to the unsatisfactory "outfit" system. A second step, achieved as part of the overall reform effort, was to establish more adequate salaries for both services, though only in the Consular Service was the level set high enough to make positions accessible to individuals without an independent income. And finally, beginning in the present century, special allowances and benefits began to appear to offset the unique costs and problems faced by U.S. representatives abroad.

The first of these steps, authorized only in 1906, was a provision for the government to pay the travel costs of a Consular or Diplomatic Service employee en route to or from his post. Not until 1919 was the authorization extended to cover the travel costs of family members and the expense of shipping a family's household effects. In the interim, World War I had caused severe hardship to personnel in the belligerent countries, where inflation was rampant, and Congress had responded by granting a compensatory cost-of-living allowance (ranging, in most cases, from two hundred to six hundred dollars per employee). World War I also forced a number of family separations as dependents were evacuated from belligerent countries, and the resultant hardships gave rise to a new separate maintenance allowance to compensate for the additional costs incurred in maintaining one household for the employee and another for the remaining members of the family.

These limited measures stood alone until 1924, when the Rogers Act took a systematic approach to the entire question of allowances and benefits in the course of establishing the Foreign Service as a unified organization. In addition to reaffirming the existing entitlements, the 1924 legislation introduced two significant new allowances and a major new benefit. For the first time, personnel abroad were granted a quarters allowance to cover their rent, light, and heat, as well as an allowance to reimburse them for the costs of official entertaining. The new benefit was home leave, which meant that each employee became eligible to return with family to the United States every three years with transport costs paid by the government.

This provision of allowances and benefits remained essentially unchanged for the next twenty years. Immediately after World War II came the fresh restructuring embodied in the Foreign Service Act of 1946, which echoed its predecessor in reaffirming existing allowances and benefits and providing a vehicle for additions to the list. In the 1946 Act, Congress for the first time granted an allowance to cover the extra cost of transferring from one climate zone to another; funds for the additional expense incurred in maintaining an official residence abroad of the size required for representational entertaining; and a pay supplement ranging from 10 percent to 25 percent of base salary for Foreign Service staff employees assigned to duty at hardship posts (those characterized by danger, isolation, endemic diseases, adverse climates, and the like). The act also reduced to two years (from three) the minimum period of service overseas required to qualify for home leave at government expense.

A series of 1955 amendments to the Foreign Service Act extended the hardship differential beyond the FSS category to all members of the Service and authorized allowances to cover the costs of educating Foreign Service children. Rest and recuperation (R&R) travel, an annual trip at government expense to a different climate zone, was instituted in the early 1960s for personnel serving at hardship posts, and provisions for government-paid travel in the case of family emergencies were added later in the decade.

The final elements of the existing allowance and benefit structure were put into place by the Foreign Service Act of 1980. New salary supplements were authorized for particularly dangerous posts and for posts that are especially difficult to staff; employees were authorized to draw part of their salary in advance of an overseas assignment to help defray the expenses of the move; the separate maintenance allowance, previously authorized only when the government determined that family members could not accompany an employee to post, was made available to families on request; and a new allowance was introduced to cover the travel of children whose parents are separated or divorced.

In the wake of passage of the 1980 Act, some concern has been expressed on Capitol Hill that the total package of allowances and benefits available to members of the Foreign Service may now be too generous. After nearly a century of evolutionary growth, that package provides personnel serving abroad with transportation for the employee and his or her family and, within prescribed limits, for the family's household goods; with housing (in the form either of a quarters allowance or, more often, of a government-furnished house or apartment); with an allowance for representational entertaining, if the employee's job requires it; with allowances to give the employee's children an education equivalent to that which would be available to them in the Washington area; and with an allowance to compensate for living costs that are higher than those prevailing in Washington. If the employee is serving at a hardship post, he or she will also receive a taxable supplement (hardship differential) of between 10 percent and 25 percent of base salary, depending on the degree of hardship encountered at the particular post, and possibly either danger pay or extra incentive pay as well. Hardship post service also brings with it entitlement to an R&R trip each year for the employee and his or her family, with travel paid all the way to the United States if the post is classified at the 20 or 25 percent level. And, of course, all employees may draw pay advances before each transfer to a post abroad, may request a separate maintenance allowance for spouse and children, and may request application of the other provisions designed to respond to special circumstances.

The package is indeed an impressive one, but is it really *too* rich? Many of the allowances, notably those relating to travel, apply to all U.S. government civilian employees abroad, not just to Foreign Service personnel. Each of the existing allowances and benefits was carefully developed to meet a demonstrated need and to respond to a situation in which members of the Service had experienced hardship because the necessary support was not available to them. Generous as the package may seem, the allowances and benefits still compensate only in part for the costs and dislocations of a Foreign Service career. Especially in light of the new problems facing the Service and its members (see Chapter 8), any attempt to reduce the hard-won allowances and benefits now available to Service personnel would seem inappropriate.

Retirement

Federal retirement programs have occasioned considerable debate in recent years, both in Congress and within the administration, and are once again being reshaped as this book is written. The retirement and disability system initially established for the Foreign Service in 1924 is broadly parallel to that for the Civil Service, but it has several unique features that were designed to meet the special circumstances of service abroad.

Like their domestic colleagues, members of the Foreign Service who joined the ranks of the Service prior to 1984 contribute a portion of their salaries to a retirement fund and then qualify for pensions based on both age and length of service. The contribution, 5 percent of annual base salary when the system was first set up, currently stands at 7 percent and is matched by a like contribution from the government. In return for their contributions, members of the Service are eligible for retirement at age fifty, so long as they have at least twenty years of service, and they must retire not later than age sixty-five. Their pensions are calculated by multiplying the number of years they have served the U.S. government (including military service and work for non–foreign affairs agencies) by 2 percent of their highest three-year average salary. The maximum allowable pension is 70 percent of the top salary received prior to retirement. As examples of the way this formula is applied, a Foreign Service employee who retires at age fifty with twenty years of service receives 40 percent of his or her "high-three" salary; the employee who completes thirty-five years of service can qualify for the maximum pension of 70 percent. Survivor annuities are provided for both spouses and dependent children, and there is an annuity for any member of the Service who is forced to retire because of disability after at least five years of service.

Three of the features just described set the Foreign Service retirement system apart from its otherwise similar Civil Service counterpart: mandatory retirement at age sixty-five (there is no age limit in the domestic service); the option of voluntary retirement at age fifty with twenty years of service (the comparable Civil Service provision requires age fifty-five and thirty years of service), and the pension cap of 70 percent of salary (the Civil Service maximum is 80 percent). The first two of these features specifically recognize both the particularly demanding nature of service around the world and the unique needs of a system that expects a certain number of its employees to be retired involuntarily, either through selection-out or through expiration of their allowable time-in-class. By the time Foreign Service personnel reach their fifties, about one-third of them face some limitation, for health reasons, on their ability to serve worldwide. Others, contemplating the strains and disruptions inherent in moving overseas again, may lose their zeal for the profession. In either circumstance, it has long been recognized to be in the interest of the Service as well as of the individual to give such employees the opportunity to seek another career— and the availability of an early pension encourages acceptance of that opportunity. An immediate annuity is also available to most employees who leave the Service involuntarily after having reached the level of FSO-1 or FP-1 with at least twenty years of service; those not meeting these minimum criteria may choose either a deferred annuity or a refund of their contributions.

A significant new feature introduced into the retirement system by the Foreign Service Act of 1980 provides protection for both spouses and former spouses of members of the Service. Under the terms of the act, the spouse of a Foreign Service retiree cannot be left without a survivor annuity (payable following the death of the former employee) unless the spouse agrees in writing to waive such payments; previously, the decision to deny a survivor annuity to a spouse could be made by the retiree alone. Even more innovative is a provision by which former spouses—those divorced from members of the Service—are assured a share of the retirement benefits. This section was added to the 1980 Act by Congress in recognition of the difficulties faced by a Foreign Service spouse in attempting to pursue a career while moving around the world and of the need of such a spouse for some source of retirement income in the event of a divorce. A former spouse who was married to a Foreign Service employee throughout the employee's service now receives half the annuity for which the employee qualifies; if married for only part of the period of service (but at least ten years), the spouse is entitled to half of that portion of the employee's annuity deriving from those years during which the marriage coincided with the service of the employee.[11]

Those individuals who joined the Foreign Service after January 1, 1984, may retire under a system that differs considerably from the one described above. As of that date, all new U.S. government employees contribute to Social Security and will ultimately receive Social Security benefits when they retire. At the time of writing (early 1985), Congress was beginning the difficult process of redesigning future federal retirement systems as supplements to Social Security for federal retirees in this post-1983 employment category, but the final shape of the benefits package was far from clear.

Labor-Management Relations

Another new element introduced by the 1980 Act was a statutory basis for labor-management relations in the Foreign

Service.[12] Although federal employees gained the right to organize as far back as 1912 (in the Lloyd-LaFollette Act), it was not until a series of executive orders in the early 1970s that their unions gained the further right to engage in adversarial bargaining with agency managements. When the first of these new orders became effective for federal workers, the State Department's initial reaction was to seek to exclude the Foreign Service from its provisions. What emerged instead was a separate executive order covering the Foreign Service (EO 11636, December 17, 1971), which paralleled the government-wide labor-management system in most respects (management and employee rights, election of an exclusive representative, unfair practices, and other aspects) but contained a few provisions that are unique to the Foreign Service. In particular, the order called for "consultation" rather than "negotiation" on proposed personnel policies, required a single agency-wide bargaining unit for all Foreign Service employees in each agency, and was more liberal in defining the categories of supervisors who are permitted to be members of bargaining units.

The American Foreign Service Association (AFSA), which had been a professional organization for members of the Service, won the first exclusive representation elections in 1973 in State, AID, and USIA (though it was subsequently displaced from USIA in 1976 by the American Federation of Government Employees, or AFGE). Over the ensuing years, AFSA and AFGE engaged the foreign affairs agencies in active bargaining on a wide range of employee issues, but they and their union counterparts elsewhere in the federal structure were uncomfortable about the absence of a statutory base for their role. The first step toward filling this gap was taken in 1978, when labor-management relations provisions were incorporated into the Civil Service Reform Act. These provisions, in turn, became a model for a comparable section in the Foreign Service Act of 1980, under which employees' rights to exclusive representation, adversarial bargaining, and referral of disputes and unfair labor practice charges to neutral outside bodies were all put on a firm foundation.

Today, the three agencies initially covered by the 1971 executive order retain the representatives they elected in 1976—

AFSA for the Foreign Service employees of the State Department and AID; AFGE for Foreign Service personnel at USIA. To date, Foreign Service employees of the Foreign Commercial Service and the Foreign Service components of the Department of Agriculture have not chosen an exclusive representative, though they retain the right to do so at any time under the terms of the 1980 Act.

In the three unionized agencies, management and the exclusive representative organizations consult and negotiate on a wide range of issues affecting Foreign Service personnel. Essentially, any regulations or management decisions regarding conditions of employment are negotiable. So too is the impact on employees of the implementation of management decisions in areas that are otherwise excluded from the bargaining process. The volume of negotiations has been particularly heavy over the past few years because of the need to rewrite a substantial number of regulations in the course of implementing the 1980 Act. In an effort to achieve the maximum compatibility mandated by the act, the five foreign affairs agencies have often participated jointly in negotiations with the two unions. This cumbersome process has achieved generally positive results in the form of agreed joint regulations for the entire Foreign Service, but it has also created a heavy workload for negotiators on both sides of the bargaining table.

One final responsibility of the unions is to represent individual members of the Foreign Service who seek redress under the statutory grievance system available to them under provisions of the 1980 Act and its predecessor. A grievance, for the purposes of this process, is defined by the act as "any act, omission, or condition subject to the control of the [head of the agency] which is alleged to deprive a member of the Service . . . of a right or benefit authorized by law or regulation or which is otherwise a source of concern or dissatisfaction to the member."[13] Although grievances can, and do, deal with such issues as separation and disciplinary action, the largest number represent unhappiness with allegedly inaccurate or prejudicial material in employee evaluation reports or with the denial of allowances to which an employee believes he or she is entitled. If an employee's supervisor is unable to resolve a grievance informally, it is investigated by a special staff within the individual foreign affairs agency, and a decision is rendered at that level. If the grievant is not satisfied with the agency's ruling, he or she may appeal to an independent Grievance Board, which conducts a second investigation and issues a final ruling. The union provides advice and counsel to the grievant, both at the agency level and before the Grievance Board, and has a right to be present (unless the case involves separation from the Service) even if the grievant has an outside attorney.

Notes

1. PL 96-465 (22 USC 3927), sections 101(b) and 203–205.
2. Ibid., sec. 101(a)(1).
3. Ibid., sec. 103(3).
4. Ibid., sec. 103(6).
5. Ibid., sec. 408(a)(1).
6. Ibid., sec. 309.
7. Ibid., sec. 602.
8. Ibid., sec. 605.
9. Ibid., sec. 502(a)(1).
10. Ibid., sec. 504(a).
11. Ibid., sections 806(b) and 814.
12. This section is based on ibid., chap. 10, and on William I. Bacchus, *Staffing for Foreign Affairs* (Princeton, N.J.: Princeton University Press, 1983), pp. 141–146.
13. PL 96-465, sec. 1101(a)(1).

4

THE SHAPE OF A CAREER

Our State Department emissaries accumulate none of the glory or glamour of military men. . . . These quiet heroes are entitled to more credit than they ever receive. It should not take death to inscribe their names on our national roll of honor.
—*New York Times* editorial, 1948

Given the widely varied missions of the several foreign affairs agencies, it should come as no surprise that the careers of Foreign Service personnel differ significantly from one agency to another. There are, of course, some similarities arising from the common features of the 1980 Foreign Service Act, but beyond this base, the career paths of members of the Service—the way they are hired, assigned and trained; the work they do; and the kinds of positions to which they can aspire—are so divergent that we will look at them on an agency-by-agency basis.

The Department of State

Recruitment and Hiring

As a general rule, candidates planning to make a career of the Foreign Service come in at the bottom, regardless of the agency or the employment category they enter. The best-known segment of the total Service is the FSO corps, whose new members normally come to careers in the State Department (and in USIA and the Foreign Commercial Service) by way of a written examination offered annually on the first or second

Saturday in December. The famous (or infamous) Foreign Service
exam once spread over three or four days. Writing about the
examination in 1939, the State Department described it as
comprising

> a wide variety of subjects, including . . . elements of international
> maritime and commercial law, arithmetic as used in common
> statistics, tariff calculations, exchange, and simple accounting;
> modern languages . . . ; elementary economics, including the
> natural, industrial and commercial resources of the United States;
> political and commercial geography; American history, government
> and institutions since 1776; and the history of Europe, Latin
> America and the Far East since 1776. Candidates will also be
> examined in political economy, and will be rated in English,
> composition, grammar, punctuation, spelling and penmanship as
> shown by their examination papers.[1]

Today's written examination, prepared and administered for the
Foreign Service by the Educational Testing Service, is not unlike
the Scholastic Aptitude Test (SAT) or the Graduate Record
Examination (GRE), which the same organization administers
to college applicants. The examination consists entirely of mul-
tiple-choice questions and requires only half a day to complete.

It has two sections, testing, respectively, general background
and English expression. The former seeks a broader understanding
of institutions and concepts than appears to have been the case
in 1939 and covers a wider range of subject matter than in the
days before World War II. Reflecting the enlarged mission of
the agencies composing the Foreign Service, the examination
measures knowledge of "the literary, artistic, and philosophical
heritage of the United States, current trends and developments
in the arts, and basic scientific and management principles"[2] in
addition to topics more traditionally associated with the field
of foreign affairs. Additional questions scattered throughout the
first section of the examination test the knowledge and skills
required for each of the functional areas of work into which
the candidates will be hired by the three agencies utilizing this
process—information and cultural affairs for USIA; commercial
work for the FCS; and the administrative, consular, economic,

and political fields for the State Department. The English expression portion of the examination measures skill in written English through questions testing a candidate's ability to express ideas clearly and accurately and to recognize errors in grammar and structure.

The written examination, offered throughout the United States and at diplomatic and consular posts abroad, has attracted over fifteen thousand candidates in each of the past few years. Yet it is only the first step in the selection process, and only the highest scorers will be invited to step two—the oral assessment. In an average year, about twenty-five hundred candidates are invited to this second stage, which for many years consisted only of a one- to two-hour oral examination not unlike that involved in defending a thesis before a professorial panel. Today's all-day assessment is given both in Washington and by panels of traveling examiners in major U.S. cities. It still includes an individual session with the examining panel (though reduced in length to forty-five minutes), but now it also encompasses a written summary exercise, a written essay, a group exercise, and a problem-solving "in-basket" exercise. Here again, the selection is severe, and only about one candidate in five can expect to emerge with a passing score.

Those who survive both the written examination and the oral assessment are nearly there, but their final eligibility still awaits completion of both a physical examination and a thorough background investigation to determine their suitability for employment. In light of the sensitive nature of much of the work in which they engage, all career members of the Foreign Service require security clearances at the top-secret level and therefore are vetted with particular care before being hired. These formalities being successfully completed, the candidate is certified as eligible for appointment, and his or her name is placed on one or more registers in strict rank order according to the composite score earned during the examination and screening process.

The multiple registers represent the six functional areas specifically tested by the written examination—the work done by USIA, by FCS, and in the four State Department FSO career fields. A candidate is placed on each register for which he or she scored high enough on the examination (and some of the top candidates have appeared on all six registers). Each candidate's name is carried for only eighteen months on the registers for which he or she has qualified. The clock begins to run for each candidate when his or her name is first placed on a register; if no appointment is offered or accepted within eighteen months, the name is removed from the register, and the candidate must begin the entire process from step one in order to become eligible once again. The uncertainty inevitably discourages some potential FSOs, who take up alternative careers rather than take their chances on an appointment that may never come.

When the State Department is ready to bring in a new class of junior officers, offers are made to candidates on the appropriate registers in order from the top until the number of acceptances matches the target size for the entering class. Since each entering FSO class usually includes individuals hired into each of State's four FSO fields, offers are apportioned among the four State registers. A candidate who receives an offer for one field but really wants to work in another functional area faces a difficult decision. He or she may decline the initial offer, but takes a gamble in doing so as there is no assurance of being reached later on the register of choice. Accepting the offer, on the other hand, can mean spending a number of years doing work of no real interest, since it is difficult to change agencies or even functional fields within the State Department.

The procedures for hiring Foreign Service specialist and support personnel (FPs) are more flexible, inasmuch as they are not tied to an annual examination. Nonetheless, the same basic principle of competitive selection applies in the FP categories as for FSOs, and candidates are examined for qualifications specific to the field they wish to enter. The State Department regularly hires secretaries, communications specialists, and security officers as FPs, and entrants in these three fields are grouped into classes several times a year. Hiring in other FP career fields, such as physicians, nurses, and medical technologists, is normally done to fill individual vacancies. In recent years, the State Department has also offered a few opportunities to outside candidates in the general services, personnel, and budget and fiscal fields. As is the case with FSOs, the test of qualifications must be supplemented by both physical and suitability examinations before an appointment can be offered.

Toward a More Representative Service

Prior to 1924, when the Diplomatic Service was still a separate organization, it was populated almost exclusively by young men of independent means who had been educated first at preparatory schools and then at Ivy League universities. They thought of themselves as an elite and were untroubled by the modest salaries paid them by the government. Although most of them were serious professionals, there were a few who deserved being called, as one ambassador put it, "the boys with the white spats, the tea drinkers, the cookie pushers."[3] Inevitably, the combined effect of the few "cookie pushers" and the very real predominance in the Service of the wealthy and socially prominent produced a general image of the Diplomatic Service as a citadel of privilege—and a fairly useless one at that.

In the wake of the Rogers Act, the 122 officers of the Diplomatic Service were joined in the newly unified Foreign Service by over four times as many of their consular colleagues (511 to be exact), and this consolidation brought with it gradual change in the character of the FSO corps. Members of the old Consular Service, whose salaries were substantially higher than those of diplomatic personnel, were drawn from a far broader stratum of society and only seldom had private incomes. Nonetheless, the image of the Foreign Service as an elite corps persisted even after the merger, as the ex-diplomats continued to set the tone for the unified Service.

The process of change that began during the 1920s and 1930s accelerated after World War II. The character of the FSO corps was substantially altered when the Wristonization program of the mid-1950s tripled its size, and the expansion of the FSR and FSS groups offered further opportunity to broaden the base of the Service as a whole. Despite these developments, however, the FSO corps remained predominantly white and male until the 1970s, when a deliberate effort to recruit more aggressively for qualified women and minorities began to show results.

The search for qualified minority candidates started in earnest in 1967, when the State Department established its first affirmative action hiring program for minority junior officers (the Affirmative Action Junior Officer Program, or AAJOP). Six minority officers were hired during the first year of the program's existence, all of whom were still in the Service at the time of writing. Between 1967 and 1983, a total of 417 minority junior officer candidates entered the Service through the AAJOP, of whom 80 percent remained on the rolls in 1984. Equally important, the number of minority candidates applying—and succeeding—through the regular examination process grew steadily, as a result both of more vigorous recruitment efforts and of the presence of a growing number of minorities already in the Service to act as role models for new applicants.

A second affirmative action program was added in 1975, this time covering women as well as minorities. As late as 1971, female officers were forced to resign from the Service upon marriage (no law or regulation said so, but the department's policy simply had never been challenged). That anachronistic requirement further complicated recruitment of qualified women into a Service already known for its generally negative attitude toward women officers. Following the repeal of this requirement, active recruitment of women was stepped up along with the effort targeted at minority applicants, with the result that the number of women entering at the junior levels of the FSO corps began a steady rise.

Until 1975, the attempt to attract both minorities and women was focused entirely on the entry levels of the FSO corps. While the lowest grades of the Foreign Service were gradually becoming more representative of U.S. society, the slow operation of the promotion process in the normal career progression of these new recruits meant that years would be needed before the middle and upper levels of the Service approached a representative character. The 1975 program, which offered appointments directly into mid-level ranks (the equivalent of today's FSO-3 through FSO-1), was intended to ameliorate this situation—even though it was recognized that there could be no miracle cure since the basic policy of hiring at the bottom would remain unchanged. With an initial goal of 100, the mid-level program had in fact taken in 156 officer candidates by the end of 1983 and will reach nearly twice its original target before being phased out in 1987.

Nothing more dramatically illustrates the changes brought about by this multifaceted effort than comparative statistics for the FSO corps. In 1968, shortly after the AAJOP was inaugurated, minorities accounted for only 2 percent of all FSOs; by the end of 1984, they represented over 12 percent of the total. The rise in the proportion of women has been equally striking. In 1971, when the requirement for resignation upon marriage was lifted for female FSOs, women made up only 5 percent of the FSO corps; by the end of 1984, the figure for women was over 18 percent, more than a threefold increase. Even more striking is the shape of the future Foreign Service as foretold by the figures at the junior officer levels, where minorities constitute almost 20 percent of all FSOs and women nearly 30 percent.

Despite these impressive figures in the lower grades, however, women and minorities each represented only slightly more than 3 percent of the senior officers at the end of 1984. The Foreign Service has come a long way since it launched the AAJOP in 1967, but the FSO corps is still several years away from being truly representative at all levels.

Although the FSO category has attracted the lion's share of attention, the State Department has also stepped up its efforts to achieve a better balance among Foreign Service specialist and support personnel, whenever feasible. No special affirmative action programs have been introduced, but high priority has been attached to recruitment efforts aimed at stimulating interest in FP careers among women and minorities. The result has been a steady rise in minority representation in most of the specialist categories, as well as a jump in female representation in those fields that previously had been almost exclusively male. As examples of the former, minorities by the end of 1984 accounted for nearly 9 percent of Foreign Service secretaries, 12 percent of communicators, and 17 percent of budget and fiscal officers. Under the latter heading, by 1984 women represented over 11 percent of all communicators and over 7 percent of general services officers, both traditionally male preserves. (As an interesting sidelight, the Service had also succeeded in recruiting ten male secretaries, but they still represented less than 1 percent of the total secretarial resources of the Foreign Service.)

Today's Foreign Service personnel reflect the diversity of the United States in a variety of other ways. Geographically, a 1983 survey shows that they grew up in all parts of the country. Apart from those who were raised overseas or moved too often to identify with any single region, roughly 35 percent came from the Northeast, 25 percent from the Midwest, 13 percent from the West Coast, and 11 percent from the South—almost exactly proportional to the distribution of the adult population of the United States. The same survey also showed considerable diversity in the educational institutions attended. At the time of entry into the Foreign Service, only 13 percent of the personnel had degrees from Ivy League schools, once the principal source of FSO recruits, while the remainder had obtained degrees from over two hundred and fifty colleges and universities throughout the country.

Career Candidates

Whether hired as FSOs or FPs, all new Foreign Service appointees begin their careers as probationers. Their initial appointments, normally for four years, provide a period during which the candidate's abilities and aptitude for the Foreign Service can be tested, and the candidate can decide whether he or she has picked the right career.

Foreign Service specialists (FPs) who join the State Department's ranks are hired for a specific career field (such as secretarial or communications) and generally begin work almost immediately in their designated specialties. New FPs are given a formal orientation to the work of the department and the Foreign Service, and they may also receive language training if it is required for their first post abroad. After they have completed two years in the Service, with regular written evaluations of their performance and potential, they are eligible for career tenure. The final decision on the qualifications of each candidate is made by yet another of the Service's ubiquitous independent boards. The Commissioning and Tenure Board, composed of career members of the Service, judges each candidate individually on the basis of his or her file since entering the Service and then determines whether the candidate shows sufficient ability and promise to be worth having in the Service for a normal career span. A candidate not granted tenure when first looked at by the board is reconsidered annually for the balance of the four-year limited appointment. Since the initial selection of candidates is done with great care, the vast majority of FP probationers attain career status before their initial appointments expire.

Essentially the same procedure applies to the FSO corps, except that FSO entrants are subject to a more structured career candidate program that is intended to expose them to a variety of work experiences during their probationary years. All entering FSO candidates are required to perform consular duties for a minimum of one year, regardless of the career field in which they have been hired, and are expected to work in at least two of the four FSO fields before being evaluated for tenure. In addition, would-be FSOs—unlike their FP colleagues—must demonstrate a working knowledge of a foreign language before they can achieve career status.

Because of the requirements for both language competence and diversified work experience, most FSO candidates spend from three to nine months in training before proceeding to their first assignments. All new entrants into FSO ranks are given a seven-week orientation course, and in addition receive three weeks of specific training in the consular functions all of them will be asked to perform. Candidates who do not enter the Service with a sufficient level of language competence (and only about one-third of new entrants meet the Foreign Service language standard) spend another three to six months either improving existing language skills or learning new ones to prepare for their first overseas posts. Finally, candidates who are expected to have responsibilities in the administrative field on their initial assignment receive additional training in that specialty.

The first tour abroad for an FSO career candidate will be for either eighteen months or two years, depending on the job to be done. If the candidate is able to work in two different functional areas at the same post, usually for one year in each,

Language training and area studies at the Foreign Service Institute.

then the assignment is made for two years. If circumstances are such that the candidate must remain in a single functional area for the entire tour (most often in consular work), then the assignment will be for eighteen months. The relatively short tours of duty mean that most candidates can be evaluated at more than one post before a final tenure decision has to be made. With only rare exceptions, the first tour will be overseas. Ideally, the second tour should also be abroad, but in recent years a number of candidates seeking experience in the political or economic fields have had to serve their second tours in Washington because of a shortage of junior-level positions abroad in those career areas.

As in the case of FP candidates, career status for an aspirant FSO depends on the judgment of a Commissioning and Tenure Board. A performance file goes before the board for the first time when a candidate has completed thirty months of service. Since most candidates will have spent up to nine months in training, many files at this point reflect little more than a year of on-the-job experience and seldom extend beyond the first post. Thus, it is not surprising that only about one-fourth of the FSO candidates are granted tenure at this initial review. The record is far better when the files again go before the board a year later, with the possibility of yet a third look if necessary before the candidate's four-year appointment expires. Overall, the success record for FSOs, like that for FPs, reflects the care with which they are initially selected, and about 95 percent of all career candidate FSOs reviewed by the board are offered tenure—and with it a full career in the Foreign Service.

FSO Careers

Once tenured and in possession of the FSO commission that comes with career status, the new FSO is assured at least twenty-two years on the State Department payroll, subject to being terminated for misconduct, substandard performance, medical disability, or the individual's own decision to resign. (In fact, the number of voluntary resignations each year among FSOs is under 5 percent of the total corps, much lower than at comparable professional levels in most private businesses.) Tenured at the FSO-4 level, the new officer will take an average two years for promotion to FSO-3, and five years thereafter for each of the next two steps through the mid-level ranks to FSO-1.

The kinds of work an FSO will do during those years depend to a considerable extent on the "cone"—that is, the FSO functional field—into which he or she was initially hired. For many years, all FSOs were considered "generalists" and thus, at least in theory, capable of working equally well at any of the jobs normally performed by the FSO corps. Operating under this premise, some officers in fact became the proverbial "jacks of all trades, masters of none." They gained a wide variety of experience working in turn in several functional areas at successive posts, and thus reached the senior ranks without ever acquiring an in-depth knowledge of any single FSO field. Most, however, found a comfortable niche and stayed in it. A few FSOs devoted two years or more to the study of difficult languages and became specialists in the politics of a particular area; others honed their skills in more general political reporting and analysis. Some devoted their careers to consular work, becoming expert in the complex legislative and regulatory framework within which consular policy and decisions are made. Still others opted for economic and commercial work while a handful of generalist FSOs sought career satisfaction in the administrative field.

This self-selection approach produced a number of able senior officers, but it had clear shortcomings. The individuals recruited into the State Department's FSO ranks all tended to have the same general liberal arts background, and most wanted to perform the traditional diplomatic tasks associated with work in the political field. Yet the need of the Service was for a mid-level corps that was spread across the four functional areas, and thus included within its ranks officers with strong skills appropriate to the economic, consular, and administrative fields as well as to the political. It was to meet this broader need that the cone system was introduced in 1963, and all FSOs are now apportioned among the four functional areas, or cones, in proportion to the number of positions requiring each set of skills. Those already in the Service were assigned to the cone for which they had the greatest experience, and new recruits are hired for service in a designated cone in accordance with the procedures outlined above.

Although the introduction of the cone system made it easier to match skills and requirements, it did not put an end to the continuing debate about the way FSO careers should be structured. Should FSOs spend their mid-level years becoming truly expert in their primary field, so that when they reach the senior levels they will be able to compete equally with their expert counterparts in other agencies and other governments? Or should they be given a wide range of jobs and training in management skills to prepare them for future leadership positions? The cone system, by its very nature, places principal stress on the single functional area into which the FSO has been hired. Yet by remaining primarily within that single area, the FSO may reach the Senior Foreign Service with neither the managerial abilities nor the breadth of outlook needed for many top-level jobs.

There has never been an easy answer to this "generalist" versus "specialist" debate, which by its nature can never be fully resolved. Clearly, the Service needs both kinds of skills at the senior levels—a view that is reflected in the 1980 Foreign Service Act definition of the SFS as the corps of both leaders *and* experts.[4] The State Department, however, has never quite decided how to assure the correct balance between its "leaders" and its "experts," or precisely what kind of career development is needed for FSOs destined to fill either of these roles once they reach the SFS.

In consequence, the careers of State Department FSOs passing through the mid-level grades between achieving tenure and competing for entry into the SFS show an almost infinite variety since the initiative still remains largely with the individual officer. In theory, the department encourages all its FSOs to seek both depth of knowledge in their own cones and the broadening effects of out-of-cone experience, with the latter coming either from work in another of the functional areas normally open to State FSOs or from an assignment entirely outside the department. (As noted in Chapter 3, these outside assignments can include work in nongovernmental organizations as well as in other agencies within the U.S. government.) In addition, the State Department's list of ideal mid-level experiences would include dealing both with substantive policy issues (generally viewed as falling largely in the political and economic fields) and with the management of resources, usually meaning either subordinate staff or operational budgets (experience available most often, but not exclusively, in the consular and administrative fields). An attempt to embody this kind of career guidance in a set of rules making varied experiences a prerequisite to entry into the SFS was attempted in 1980 but was quietly shelved when it proved impossible to assure that all FSOs would have an equal chance at the assignments they needed to qualify for the SFS under such a plan.

Given these circumstances, the newly tenured State Department FSO has a great deal of leeway in shaping his or her own career. Officers who have had little or no experience in their own cones while in the career candidate program will be advised by the department's career counselors (FSOs like themselves) to seek early in-cone assignments, since promotion through the middle grades depends largely on demonstrated skill within the officer's cone. If a record of in-cone performance has already been established, the counselors will probably suggest a broadening experience—work in another cone or outside the department. Ultimately, however, the choice lies to a great extent with the individual officer, whose preferences carry considerable weight in the assignment process agreed to between the State Department and the employee union.

Another option open to mid-level FSOs is to spend a year or two in one of the long-term training programs offered by the State Department. On first entering the Service, each career candidate FSO will have spent from three to nine months in training—orientation, instruction in consular or other skills, and perhaps language study. This training is given at the Foreign Service Institute (FSI), a school operated by the State Department but open to all agencies of the U.S. government. The present institute was set up by the Foreign Service Act of 1946, but it is the direct descendant of a Foreign Service School that was established in 1925 under the authority of the Rogers Act. FSI has for many years been best known for its outstanding language instruction, using techniques developed at the institute (and widely copied elsewhere) to provide a professional-level working knowledge of most world languages in twenty to twenty-four weeks of intensive teaching. In addition, FSI offers dozens of courses ranging from advanced economics and negotiating techniques to writing and clerical skills and acts as the department's overseer for training given to Foreign Service personnel at other academic institutions.

The institute's mandate was strengthened by the 1980 Act, which, for the first time, formally directed each of the foreign affairs agencies to set up a professional development program that was targeted not only at career candidates but also at mid-career officers.[5] In response to this congressional injunction, FSI developed a five-month program for the State Department's newly tenured FSOs. The new offering, known familiarly as "the mid-level course," is structured to provide four things: a broad look at a number of "global" issues, as well as a sense of the ramifications of the foreign policy process; a deepening of each officer's knowledge regarding his or her cone; exposure to a new field, preferably pointing to a future out-of-cone assignment; and instruction in basic management skills. The course, which all FSOs must take as soon as possible after they are tenured, has been given twice yearly since early 1981 and appears well on its way to meeting the goal of assuring a wider base of common skills at the mid-levels of the FSO corps. At the same time, FSI is working to develop a more advanced management skills seminar for officers newly promoted to the SFS, but this effort had not yet taken final form at the time of writing.

More important than these mandatory training courses, in terms of an impact on an FSO's career, are the long-term programs to which assignments occur only if the individual officer seeks them out. The most familiar of these involve language studies, which have been a feature of Foreign Service life since George Kennan was sent off to learn Russian in the 1920s. Most such programs involve the so-called hard languages, those which require a year or more of study to acquire professional facility. The heaviest demand in this category, not surprisingly, is for Russian, Chinese, Japanese, and Arabic. Although officers are assigned to posts in the Soviet Union after a year's study of Russian, some of them subsequently go on for a second year of language instruction at a U.S. Army facility in Germany. For the other three languages, two years of training is usual before an officer actually goes to work at a job requiring proficiency in the language, and a second year of study is offered at an FSI outpost in a country in which the language being taught is in daily use—in Taichung (on Taiwan) for Chinese, in Yokohama for Japanese, and in Tunis for Arabic. (A second year of training in Korean is available in Seoul, but usually for only one or two officers at a time.) In all, FSI offers instruction in thirty-eight distinct languages (not counting regional variations), over half of which require forty-four weeks of study in order to reach a professional level of proficiency.

Although language instruction is handled directly by FSI, there are also a number of full-year training options available to State Department FSOs that involve study at other institutions. Under FSI supervision, FSOs are assigned to universities and research centers to acquire new skills and knowledge in such fields as African, Latin American, or Eastern European area studies; management techniques; economic analysis; and the policy process. In addition, a fellowship program under the auspices of the American Political Science Association offers a year of work on Capitol Hill, and with it, new insight into the congressional role in foreign affairs.

The opportunities that are available to the newly tenured FSO are therefore varied. The selections actually made by each officer will depend on a combination of factors: individual preference, the availability of the option desired (some are subject to fierce competition—an average of fifty applicants per year, for example, for ten openings on Capitol Hill), and the inevitable element of pure chance. There have been, for example, cases of relatively junior officers performing routine duties at out-of-the-way posts whose career paths have been dramatically altered by events as major as a sudden political upheaval that focuses Washington's attention on their work or as minor as the visit of a senior official who is sufficiently impressed to become a mentor to a promising young FSO.

The way career opportunities work out in practice is hinted at in Figure 4.1. Drawn from an internal publication targeted at the State Department's own employees,[6] the figure shows a

Career Path
Foreign Service Officer

There are many combinations and sequences of assignments which a Foreign Service Officer's career may take. The types of assignments and movements shown here are designed as an example or illustration of what a typical career pattern might be. They are not to be construed as a master plan or one that will be followed by any given officer. There are many combinations of assignments which could be pursued from entrance into the Foreign Service to the senior levels. This presentation is illustrative only.

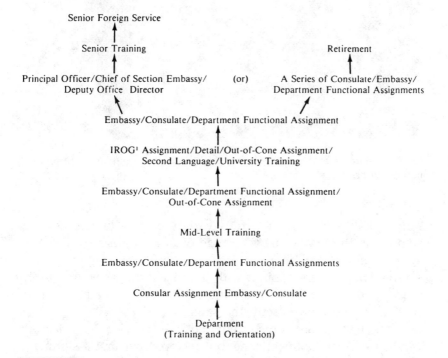

Senior Foreign Service

Senior Training   Retirement

Principal Officer/Chief of Section Embassy/   (or)   A Series of Consulate/Embassy/
Deputy Office Director   Department Functional Assignments

Embassy/Consulate/Department Functional Assignment

IROG[1] Assignment/Detail/Out-of-Cone Assignment/
Second Language/University Training

Embassy/Consulate/Department Functional Assignment/
Out-of-Cone Assignment

Mid-Level Training

Embassy/Consulate/Department Functional Assignments

Consular Assignment Embassy/Consulate

Department
(Training and Orientation)

---

[1]International Relations Officer General

Figure 4.1 *Source:* U.S. Department of State, *Career Mobility Handbook* (Washington, D.C.: U.S. Department of State, 1983), pt. 4, p. 5.

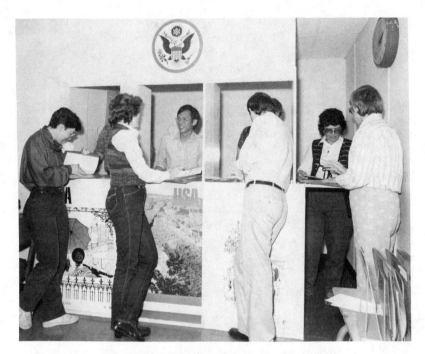

Consular training at the Foreign Service Institute uses role-playing to prepare junior officers for visa work.

sample FSO career path with a variety of possibilities at each step along the way—just the range of options discussed above. To supplement the chart, it may be helpful to examine a few sample FSO careers, though with the caveat that they are purely illustrative and provide no assurance that any other FSO career path will ever look exactly the same.

Our first junior officer entered the Service as a career candidate in the political cone, but received her first assignment abroad as a visa officer at a consular post on the U.S.-Mexican border. After eighteen months, she had the good fortune to land one of the relatively few overseas jobs involving political work at the junior level, a position at a medium-sized embassy in Europe where her two-year tour was split between the political section and a stint as an assistant general services officer. Tenured during her second tour, this new FSO went through the five-month mid-level course at FSI and then took another assignment that allowed her to hone her political skills, that of desk officer in Washington for the European country in which she had recently served. On the basis of her strong performance, she was selected to work in the State Department's Executive Secretariat, providing staff support to the secretary of state and his senior colleagues. There, she again attracted favorable notice, and after only a year, she became a staff assistant to one of the under secretaries of state.

After completing slightly over four years in Washington, our young officer (having been promoted once to FSO-3 and about to receive a further promotion to FSO-2 because of her exceptional work) went abroad again, this time for a three-year tour in the political section of yet another embassy in Europe. In search of management experience, she next tried for a position as head of a small consular post or of the political section in an embassy. Since she had not served recently at a hardship post (her two previous overseas tours having been in Western Europe) and since she was still somewhat junior for the level of responsibility she was seeking, she asked to be assigned to a post in one of the less desirable areas—which generally attract fewer applicants—and got one of her top choices, going via Spanish language training to head the political section of a medium-sized embassy in Latin America.

Three years and another promotion later, our FSO-1 returned again to Washington and a job outside her own cone as an assignment officer in the Bureau of Personnel. After two more years, she went back to her "home" in European affairs to work on the problems of the NATO alliance, and she had enough seniority to be on the threshold of entry into the SFS.

Our second officer also entered the Service in the political cone, but he followed a different career path by opting to study a difficult language. After service as a career candidate in a consular position abroad, he returned to Washington for his second tour in order to work at a job in the political field. Tenured during his stay in Washington, he went on to the mid-level course at FSI and then was accepted into the two-year program of Chinese language and area studies. Following one year at FSI and another on Taiwan learning Chinese, our officer (now an FSO-3) was assigned for two years to the political section of the consulate general in Hong Kong and for another two years to one of the consulates on the Chinese mainland—a total of six years of deep immersion in Chinese affairs.

By this time, both the officer and his counselor recognized the need for a break in his intensive involvement with China, so the officer sought and received an assignment to the one-man political/economic section of a small embassy in Africa. With that behind him, and newly promoted to FSO-2, he was ready to return to Washington and to Chinese affairs, but he was unable to land a job in the department directly in his field. What was available was a position running a refugee relief program targeted at Southeast Asia, for which his knowledge of China was indirectly relevant and which gave him valuable experience in program management. Since his day-to-day work kept him in close touch with the East Asian Bureau, which cast a benevolent eye on his performance, he was able to move after two years to the kind of position he had sought initially in Washington, in the office handling U.S. relations with China.

Although this second tour in the department gained him further promotion to FSO-1, he had a falling-out with the bureau's senior officials, who declined to support him for the political position he wanted overseas in their area of responsibility. Without such backing, the best he could do was to draw on his refugee experience and to compete successfully for a field post as refugee coordinator at an embassy in Southeast Asia. By the time he had completed three years in this position, he had drifted somewhat away from his initial focus on Chinese affairs but had become one of the department's most knowledgeable officers in refugee affairs—and in the process had acquired the seniority to compete for the SFS.

Both of these examples are of officers who opted to work whenever possible in the political field into which they were hired, and neither was assigned outside the State Department. Yet even with these major parallels—which are by no means universal for political cone officers—their careers diverged significantly. One officer, with a particularly strong record, was able to remain on her chosen career path; the other, with a blemish on his slate, was forced at least temporarily onto a different track. In all likelihood, he would later go back to Chinese affairs, once the senior officials who had blocked his assignment themselves moved on, but the detour would probably have put him behind his colleague on the road to the top.

Given such variations even within a single cone, it should come as no surprise that career paths in different cones bear even less resemblance to one another. Our third career candidate entered the Service in the administrative cone, and had the luck to go overseas after five months of language training to a rotational position in which he could meet the requirement for consular experience and also make a start in his own field with a year as a budget and fiscal officer. With his mandatory consular stint behind him, and having already shown promise in the administrative field, our candidate was able to move on to a second post as the sole administrative officer of a small consulate—and to both tenure and a promotion to FSO-3.

The mid-level course next called him back to Washington, but his administrative skills were by now in sufficient demand that he was able to achieve his first choice and return immediately abroad to a post as general services officer at a medium-sized embassy. With his prior budget and fiscal work experience, this post gave him the second leg of the administrative triad, and he next returned to Washington and a tour as personnel officer in a regional bureau in order to gain experience in the third principal administrative subspecialty.

Well grounded in the major elements of his cone, and promoted meanwhile to FSO-2, he next opted to step outside the administrative field for awhile to seek a broader range of experience. One route might have led him to the Executive Secretariat, as it did our first young FSO; another could have involved competing for a position as desk officer for one of the countries in which he had served or working in an "interfunctional" area (that is, one not limited to individuals with any specific cone background) such as human rights or refugee policy. The one he chose was an assignment to work in the office of a midwestern governor who had asked the department for an FSO with overseas experience to set up a program to coordinate the growing number of foreign contacts being made by state officials. Like all assignments of this kind, it was initially made for one year, but it was extended for a second year when the governor asked his FSO assistant to stay on.

After two years, however, it was time to return to more traditional Foreign Service pursuits, and our mid-level FSO stopped off in Washington to learn a new language and then went overseas again to serve as administrative officer at a consular post. Secure in his own field and still desirous of broadening his experience, he next competed successfully for the post of deputy chief of mission (the number-two officer) at a small embassy in the Caribbean. He did well in this demanding position, which won him promotion to FSO-1 and resulted in his being sought out for further assignments both in Washington and abroad. Partly for family reasons (his oldest child was about to enter high school), he chose to return to Washington and the State Department for successive two-year tours, working first as a bureau budget officer and then as a special assistant in the Bureau of Administration. At this point, he too was looking ahead to the SFS.

All three of these officers, having been promoted at a steady rate through their mid-level years, had now arrived at the threshold for entry into the Senior Foreign Service. As FSO-1s, they thereby automatically became candidates for yet another training program—a year at the National War College or an equivalent institution, which was intended to give them a better foundation for subsequent service at senior levels. Each year, all FSO-1 officers due for transfer are rank-ordered for this training, and those judged most likely to achieve SFS rank receive the prestigious training assignments. Although this training is not a prerequisite to promotion into the SFS, selection into the program is an official vote of confidence in the chosen candidate's future prospects.

Unlike the military services, in which retirement at the rank of colonel or navy captain is usual and promotion to general or flag rank the exception, most FSOs historically have, in fact, reached the senior grades before retiring. Recently, however, the department has begun dropping strong hints that this "norm" may be changing. As the department's own illustrative FSO career chart shows (see Figure 4.1), retirement at the FSO-1 level is now one of the acceptable career outcomes. Indeed, the handbook containing the chart makes this assumption explicit by observing that FSOs "usually will end their careers at the FSO-1 level and retire."[7]

This message has not yet reached most of today's FSOs, who still look to the SFS as the "normal" summit of their careers. They continue to have the long-held view that a career which ends in retirement below senior rank somehow has been less than successful—an unwarranted stigma that has needlessly hurt many officers who left the Foreign Service with a rank equivalent to colonel but enjoyed none of the sense of satisfaction felt by most retired military officers after completion of an honorable career. If the Foreign Service "norm" is in fact changing, both time and effort will be required to modify FSO attitudes to the point at which retirement at FSO-1 can be accepted without bitterness or a sense of failure.

For those FSOs who do make it into the Senior Foreign Service, the route by which they reached the SFS threshold will have considerable influence on the way their careers develop at the senior levels. An officer whose experience has been narrowly focused in a single field may find it hard to compete successfully for one of the major program direction positions— consul general, deputy chief of mission, or ambassador abroad and office director or deputy assistant secretary in Washington. Although some jobs of this kind demand an in-depth knowledge of a particular subject (for example, those which might require strong skills as a financial economist or detailed knowledge of visa law and regulations), the advantage in competing for program direction positions normally will lie with the officer who has a broad range of experience and who has already demonstrated some competence as a manager. Officers who have stayed within a relatively narrow field are more likely to occupy the senior positions in their own fields, most commonly as heads of the appropriate sections at the larger posts abroad or in equivalent jobs at home.

As is so often the case in describing the workings of a personnel system, however, the human factor can change the equation. Personal chemistry and personal confidence play an increasingly important role in the assignment process as officers rise through the ranks, and at SFS levels, they not infrequently override all the well-considered elements that might otherwise seem to dictate a particular posting. Ambassadors, for example, traditionally have enjoyed something close to carte blanche in selecting their deputy chiefs of mission, who clearly must enjoy the full confidence of their bosses in order to function effectively as alter egos. An ambassador whose own background is in the political cone (as is often the case) might be well advised to select a deputy whose skills complement, rather than duplicate, his or her own. If, however, the ambassador is determined to choose another political officer with whom he or she is particularly comfortable, logic and good advice are often resisted.

Similar considerations affect nearly all assignments to the more sensitive senior-level positions. Each assistant secretary has the same degree of freedom of choice in picking his or her deputies in Washington as an ambassador enjoys in picking a deputy for a mission abroad, and often claims the same freedom in selecting office directors and even key desk officers within the bureau. Clearly, officers with whom an assistant secretary (or an ambassador) will work closely should enjoy that official's personal confidence. When these senior officials get their way, however, the result sometimes is the assignment to key jobs of officers who are less than ideally suited for them in terms of skills or experience while better qualified candidates are passed over.

Much the same is true of the process by which career officers are selected for ambassadorial posts. A high-level committee chaired by the deputy secretary of state looks at nominees not only from the Department of State but from all the foreign affairs agencies and makes recommendations to the secretary and then to the president. The candidate put forward by the department for any given post will not necessarily be chosen on the basis of experience and skills most appropriate to the job. Some career officers are proposed at the behest of powerful patrons, either within the foreign affairs community or outside of it; some are officers the secretary of state or the White House wants to move from a senior position in Washington, but in such a way as to avoid any appearance that they are being punished (one of the elder statesmen of the Foreign Service, Loy Henderson, became ambassador to Iraq in just this way when President Roosevelt ordered him removed from his job in the department in 1943, and Thomas Enders went to Spain in 1983 under essentially similar circumstances); and others are simply officers whom the department's senior managers feel are "owed" something for past service or loyalty.[8]

The deputy secretary and his or her colleagues on the selection committee pay particular attention to the views of the assistant secretary responsible for the area in which the new ambassador is to serve. For as with any senior position, a relationship of confidence between an assistant secretary in Washington and an ambassador in the field is important to the smooth functioning of the foreign policy process. The role permitted the assistant secretaries normally confers an extra advantage on candidates who come from the regional bureau or are otherwise known personally to an assistant secretary, and it is sometimes an uphill battle to ensure that qualified officers serving elsewhere in the department, in other agencies, or overseas are given equal consideration.

FP Careers

As Figure 4.2 suggests, Foreign Service specialist and support personnel (FPs) follow career paths that are very different from those of their FSO colleagues. For although FSOs are encouraged to seek breadth and variety in their work experiences, FPs normally remain in the specialized fields for which they are initially hired and thus follow essentially vertical career paths. Career mobility programs offer FP (and Civil Service) employees the possibility of lateral and upward movement, but relatively few FP personnel in fact leave the fields in which they are expert to seek greener pastures.

Secretaries make up one of the two largest occupational groups in the FP category. Like most FP personnel, they can expect to spend the bulk of their careers overseas, where roughly 80 percent of the State Department's 950 Foreign Service secretaries will be serving at any given time. Secretaries enter the Service at the FP-9 or FP-8 level, depending on their qualifications at the time of appointment (most entrants have had extensive experience in the private sector or elsewhere in government),

Career Paths

Foreign Service Personnel
(Noncommissioned Specialists and Secretaries)

There is no set sequence of assignments that the Foreign Service specialist or secretary must follow. The types of assignments and movements shown below are designed as an example or illustration of what a typical career pattern might be. They are not to be construed as a master plan or one that necessarily will be followed by any given employee. This presentation is illustrative only.

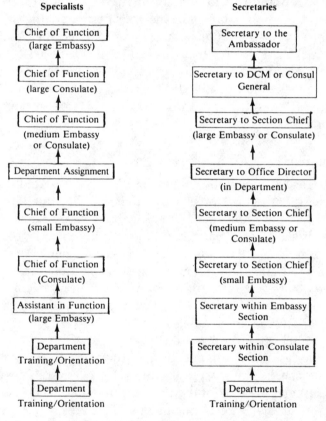

Figure 4.2 *Source:* U.S. Department of State, *Career Mobility Handbook* (Washington, D.C.: U.S. Department of State, 1983), pt. 4, p. 6.

and they can be promoted to a maximum grade of FP-4. On the hypothetical career path shown in Figure 4.2, for example, the ambassador's secretary (at a large embassy) would be an FP-4 and the deputy chief of mission's secretary an FP-5, with the other positions graded accordingly. Especially at the more senior levels, Foreign Service secretaries commonly double as staff assistants to their bosses, handling everything from office management to protocol in addition to their basic secretarial responsibilities.

Taken as a whole, the total number of FP personnel in the communications field roughly matches the number of Foreign Service secretaries. Communications, however, spans a far wider spectrum of both functions and grades. Specialists in the communications field normally enter the Service at the FP-8 level, though personnel who qualify as communications technicians (that is, who have the skills to repair and maintain equipment rather than simply to operate it) are hired at FP-6. Most communicators work their way through positions of increasing responsibility to the FP-4 level (FP-3 for the technicians), but a number of supervisory opportunities are available in the communications field up to and including the Senior Foreign Service. As is the case with secretaries, communicators can expect to spend approximately 80 percent of their careers overseas.

One communications subspecialty deserves special mention because it represents a way of life that is unlike any other in the Foreign Service. The department's diplomatic couriers, roughly seventy in number, escort diplomatic pouches containing material that is both sensitive and urgent between Washington and U.S. posts abroad—an occupation that keeps most of them on the go for the better part of their service. Diplomatic couriers are the modern practitioners of a profession that dates back at least to ancient Egypt, and has been a career element of the U.S. diplomatic establishment since 1934. Working out of regional centers in Washington, Bangkok, and Frankfurt, couriers average nearly two hundred thousand miles of travel annually, and not surprisingly, many seek to move on to other kinds of work after a few years of serving under these demanding conditions. Advances in telecommunications have had little effect on their workload, and there is no indication that any technical marvels presently in sight are likely to put them out of business.

The third major group of FPs consists of the State Department's security officer force, nearing five hundred strong. Security officers have been around for years, but in the past they concentrated largely on protecting classified material, investigating prospective employees, and guarding visiting dignitaries. As threats and attacks on diplomatic personnel have multiplied in recent years, the security workload has grown apace, and major new responsibilities for the protection of U.S. diplomatic and consular installations abroad have been added to the existing duties. Security officers have become increasingly expert in everything from installing and maintaining sophisticated protective devices to evaluating and combating potential terrorist threats—and many have had some dramatic experiences along the way. One security officer, for example, cleared a ticking bomb from an embassy lobby moments before it exploded, and others have guided the defense of posts under mob attack.

The career pattern for security officers differs from that of most other FP personnel. Newly hired security officers, who enter the Service primarily at the FP-6 or FP-5 level, spend their first few years in the United States rather than overseas. During the course of their careers, they will normally serve longer at home than abroad, with tours spent both in Washington and at field offices in other U.S. cities. The career path for most security officers leads upward to FP-3 and for many to FP-2. As in the case of communicators, however, there are a number of supervisory positions available at the more senior ranks, including several within the SFS.

The remaining FP fields involve smaller numbers of people, but they include functions that are equally essential to the effective operation of the State Department and posts abroad. Foreign Service medical personnel, for example, serve both in Washington and overseas, providing a range of services from routine physical examinations to preventive medicine and emergency care. Doctors are recruited at the FP-1 level and normally serve at SFS ranks for the bulk of their careers; nurses and medical technologists follow career paths through the mid-level grades. Personnel in the administrative subspecialties—such as personnel, budget and fiscal, general services, or building maintenance—also are found primarily at the middle grades, and in the course of their Foreign Service careers, they can expect to spend about 80 percent of their time at posts abroad.

The Director General

It is commonly said of the State Department, which is responsible for few operational programs, that people are its principal resource. The management of that resource is in the hands of the department's Bureau of Personnel, headed by a career member of the Senior Foreign Service with the dual title of director general and director of personnel. In the immediate aftermath of the Foreign Service Act of 1946, which created the position, the director general personally held the authority to administer the Foreign Service. The Hoover Commission noted that this situation was anomalous, since the director general's authority under the statute was independent of the secretary of state. A 1949 amendment remedied the situation by placing the director general clearly within the department hierarchy, and the incumbent of the office has since exercised authority by specific delegation from the secretary and from the under secretary for management.

The scope of the director general's responsibilities originally covered only the Foreign Service component of the department's workforce, and even then it nominally involved only the setting of policy while a deputy held the separate title and authority of director of personnel. In practice, of course, the director general was the boss and gave the orders, but this further anomaly was not corrected until the two titles (and their authority) were formally combined in 1975.

Since that date, the director general and the Bureau of Personnel have been both policy-makers and managers in the field of personnel. All the elements of the Foreign Service personnel system, from recruitment through career planning to retirement, are within their purview. For the State Department, the director general holds delegated authority to run the system directly; for the other foreign affairs agencies, the director general is the focal point for the effort to achieve maximum compatibility among the several personnel systems. Since the adoption of the 1980 Foreign Service Act, the director general has chaired regular meetings of the personnel directors of the foreign affairs agencies and, in late 1983, also assumed the chair of the Board of the Foreign Service. The latter body, established by the 1946 Act and reaffirmed in 1980, has a mandate "to advise the Secretary of State on matters relating to the Service."[9] Its membership includes, in addition to the foreign affairs agencies, other organizations that have an interest in the Foreign Service such as the Department of Labor, the Equal Employment Opportunity Commission, the Office of Personnel Management, and the Office of Management and Budget, and the board has sought to encourage increased compatibility within the foreign affairs community.

The United States Information Agency

Recruitment and Hiring

The State Department and USIA hire their FSO personnel through the same examination and employment process. Thus, the approximately fifty career candidate FSOs USIA adds annually, like those in the State Department, are survivors of the annual Foreign Service exam and the subsequent oral assessment and have been offered appointment on the basis of their high standing on the functional register for information and cultural affairs. Their initial training is very similar to that offered their State counterparts; indeed, part of it is conducted jointly by the two agencies. It also includes orientation to the agency and necessary language instruction for the first post of assignment (or in one of the agency's six principal working languages— French, Spanish, Portuguese, German, Chinese, and Arabic) along with a heavy dose of course work on contemporary policy issues.

Like the State Department, USIA has also made an effort to ensure a more representative Foreign Service. For a number of years, USIA was the most successful of the foreign affairs agencies in attracting qualified women and minorities to its ranks, and it has maintained that record by actively recruiting candidates in these categories (including a Comprehensive Minority Recruitment and Training Program, or COMRAT, which is similar to the AAJOP program of the State Department). As of mid-1984, minorities and women each represented over 7 percent of the employees at the SFS level in USIA, and they made up 12 percent and 22 percent, respectively, of the mid-level staffs. As is the case with the State Department, their numbers in the junior officer ranks—17 percent minorities and 38 percent women—suggest that these groups will be even better represented in USIA's future FSO corps.

USIA operates independently of the State Department in recruiting and hiring its FP personnel. Apart from a common requirement for able secretaries, USIA generally seeks specialists in fields different from those required by State. In recent years, USIA has sought FP personnel in the areas of radio engineering, English-language teaching, library science, and general administration, though its ranks also include such specialties as exhibits manager, audio-visual producer, and Voice of America correspondent. Although USIA traditionally did its own testing of the qualifications of FP candidates, it has recently turned this task over to the Board of Examiners, which performs this same function for the State Department and also handles FSO examinations for both agencies.

The USIA career candidate programs operate in essentially the same way as those of the State Department. Commissioning and tenure boards evaluate the performance of newly hired personnel during their initial assignments and decide whether to offer them career status; if the boards render negative decisions, candidates are separated from the Service at the expiration of their four-year limited appointments.

Insofar as possible, first tours for USIA FSOs are in special training positions overseas, to which they are assigned for tours of about twelve months. These give them the opportunity to experience—and be tested in—a wide variety of agency operations, and in many cases to serve in other sections of the mission as well. From these initial tours, candidates move on to regular tours of from two to four years, usually in a number-two position in either information or cultural affairs. As is the case with their State Department counterparts, tenure comes after an average of about three and a half years of service.

USIA Careers

Unlike their State Department counterparts, FSOs on the USIA rolls are not divided among several cones. They do, however, tend to specialize through their mid-career years in one of the two primary functional areas for which the agency is responsible—that is, either in informational or in cultural affairs. To the extent possible, all USIA FSOs are given an opportunity to gain experience in both areas by serving overseas during their first tours after tenure as both assistant cultural affairs officer and assistant information officer. Thereafter, USIA officers generally remain in one function or the other until the promotion process brings them to a high enough rank that they can compete for a position as deputy public affairs officer (DPAO) or public affairs officer (PAO). In the past, officers in the information field garnered a disproportionate share of these career-enhancing jobs, but executive positions today are more evenly shared by officers from both the information and the cultural fields.

Within USIA, the major DPAO and PAO positions overseas and the senior positions in the agency at home are the normal career summit for FSOs. The SFS officers in USIA, like those in the other foreign affairs agencies, can also aspire to appointment as chiefs of mission, but nearly all of these positions that are held by career officers normally have gone to State Department members of the SFS. At any given time, chief of mission ranks will usually include two or three officers from USIA, but most of that agency's FSO careers are limited to positions within USIA's own structure.

The careers of specialist and support personnel (FPs) are much like those of their State Department counterparts, though the USIA FPs form a much smaller group—only some three hundred in all. Here again, the largest component comprises roughly seventy Foreign Service secretaries, with the balance spread across fourteen other specialties. Several of these—such as radio and power plant engineers, librarians, and English teachers—are unique to the needs of USIA, so personnel in these fields will necessarily spend their careers entirely within their own agency. In those functions shared by several of the foreign affairs agencies, such as secretarial or general administrative, USIA's FP employees sometimes have the opportunity to trade jobs with comparable personnel from one of the other agencies.

The Agency for International Development

Recruitment and Hiring

Until recently, AID differed from the other foreign affairs agencies because it utilized only two of the three available categories of career appointment for the U.S. citizens on its Foreign Service rolls. At the top, AID had approximately two hundred and fifty career members of the Senior Foreign Service, but all of its seventeen hundred U.S. employees below the SFS level held FP rather than FSO appointments. As noted in Chapter 3, however, AID began commissioning tenured FP personnel as FSOs in 1984, at grade three and above (nearly eight hundred to date), and plans to use all three appointment categories in the future to meet its needs.

AID also differs from both State and USIA in its hiring practices. Although those agencies hire career personnel almost exclusively at the entry level, AID in recent years has offered roughly two-thirds of its initial appointments at the mid-level (for AID, pay grades FS-4 through FS-2) and expects to continue this pattern. This variance from the practice of the other agencies results in large part from the fact that AID's need for professional staff varies from year to year and from country to country, depending on the nature of the projects and programs for which AID is responsible at any given time. One presidential administration may emphasize agricultural development, for example, in which case AID's most urgent need will be for agricultural economists and experts in related fields. Should the next administration shift its priority to infrastructure projects, however, engineers rather than agronomists would suddenly be more in demand.

Today, AID hires approximately one hundred new Foreign Service personnel each year into twenty-six distinct functional categories, which are grouped under the four broad headings of program direction and development, program operations and management, program support (encompassing such professional-level administrative personnel as auditors, financial managers, and commodity procurement specialists), and administration (clerical and administrative support personnel). New recruits enter either at the mid-level or, at the junior level, into AID's International Development Intern (IDI) program; in either case, they come into the Foreign Service as career candidates under five-year limited appointments and are reviewed for permanent tenure by independent boards after they have completed a minimum of three years of service, at least two years of which must be overseas.

Mid-level entrants, who are hired to meet specific needs abroad, receive individualized orientation and training in Washington before going to their first posts. The twenty-five interns who enter each of the twice-yearly IDI classes receive formal group instruction consisting of orientation to AID; an introduction to program design, implementation, and management; and other topics broadly related to the foreign assistance program. This instruction is followed by on-the-job training and necessary language instruction in Washington before they proceed abroad. Because IDIs are hired to work in specific functional areas, they are assigned to positions in their own fields, but they are given opportunities during their initial overseas tours to become familiar with all aspects of AID mission operations.

The list of functional specialties for which AID hires is a varied one. It includes experts in such fields as accounting, contracting, computers, economics, engineering, family planning, and nutrition; specialists in agriculture, energy, public health, regional planning, and urban/rural development; and qualified secretaries and project development officers. For most of these positions, the agency seeks candidates with at least a master's degree in a related area and a minimum of three years of work experience; new recruits for mid-level positions will normally have worked at least five years in their fields before joining AID. The program support field (that is, professional-level administrative personnel) is filled through mid-level hiring and thus is not included under the IDI program.

In addition to the new career personnel it hires each year, AID regularly employs a number of technical specialists on limited appointments to meet needs that are associated with specific projects or programs. The agency in recent years has also resorted increasingly to contracts with private organizations for support services in connection with individual projects. The resulting flexibility has enabled AID to bring greater stability to its planning for the career Foreign Service.

AID Careers

Like its counterpart foreign affairs agencies, AID offers career opportunities to personnel in most of its functional fields up to and including the SFS level. In addition to a number of senior positions in the agency in Washington, AID personnel normally compete at the SFS level for jobs as director or deputy director of the roughly sixty AID missions abroad. Historically, the lion's share of these executive positions has gone to officers who have come up through the ranks in the program direction and development specialties—that is, as program analysts, economists, or project development officers. Because of the nature of their work, individuals in these fields tend to be heavily engaged from the start of their careers in the kinds of policy and program issues that are standard fare at the senior levels. As a result, they reach the SFS with more experience that is directly relevant to the work of a mission director than their colleagues in the more specialized fields, whose careers tend to be spent predominantly in their own functional areas. It thus is not surprising that officers who have worked in program direction and development functions normally enjoy an advantage in competing for the most prestigious senior jobs.

Senior AID officers, like their USIA counterparts, are sometimes proposed as candidates for positions as chief of mission. Here again, however, the nomination of AID officers is relatively rare, and the apex of most AID careers is normally a senior position within the agency's own structure.

The Department of Commerce:
The Foreign Commercial Service

Recruitment and Hiring

When FCS began operations in 1980, it was faced with the task of hiring a new staff quickly in order to meet the responsibilities it had just inherited from the State Department. Its first Foreign Service personnel consisted largely of the State Department FSOs who were actually doing the jobs that were transferred to FCS; they were simply retained in their positions on detail to FCS until their regular tours of duty ended. But this was only a temporary solution, and FCS began promptly to recruit a career cadre of its own.

FCS looked essentially to three sources for its initial career FSOs: experienced commercial officers on the State Department rolls, Civil Service personnel from the Commerce Department's International Trade Administration (FCS's bureaucratic home), and individuals from the private sector possessing international marketing experience. Those who already held FSO appointments with State retained their career status when they transferred to FCS. The others either became career candidates or, in many cases, joined FCS on limited appointments for a single tour. Nearly all of these first appointees entered the Foreign Service at mid-levels, since they were hired to meet immediate operational needs abroad and necessarily had to come to their jobs fully equipped to begin work immediately.

As noted earlier in this chapter, one of the functional fields for which candidates are tested in the Foreign Service examination is commercial affairs. In 1985, FCS will hire its first group of career candidates through the examination process, as its personnel system begins to stabilize after the hectic initial recruitment. In the future, FCS expects to maintain its FSO strength at approximately two hundred entirely through career candidate appointments at the entry level—the basic pattern followed by State and USIA—and will resort to mid-level appointments only if there is a sudden need for additional personnel.

The candidates who survive the double hurdle of the written and oral examinations (an estimated five or six each year), like their counterparts in the other agencies, will receive appropriate training before proceeding to posts abroad. They too will be subject to evaluation by an independent board during the period of their initial limited appointments, with career status dependent on satisfactory performance at their first posts.

FCS Careers

Once tenured and commissioned, FCS officers should be able to look forward to careers much like those of their State Department colleagues who once performed the same functions. However, there will be one noticeable difference, if current FCS plans are maintained: FCS officers can expect to spend about 80 percent of their careers overseas, compared with an average of 60 percent for FSOs on the State Department's rolls. Apart from this difference, however, career progression through the middle grades should give FCS officers an opportunity to perform the full range of commercial work, possibly including service in an Export Development Office as well as in an embassy or a consulate. At the senior levels, FCS members of the SFS will normally serve in management positions in Washington or, most often, as counselors for commercial affairs at major posts abroad. Like senior officers in AID and USIS, FCS officers at the SFS level may also be candidates for chief of mission positions, but such nominations will be the exception to the general rule that FCS careers are confined for the most part to the agency's own positions.

The Department of Agriculture:
The Foreign Agricultural Service and
the Animal and Plant Health Inspection Service

Recruitment and Hiring

The Department of Agriculture is unique among the foreign affairs agencies in its method of hiring Foreign Service personnel. Unlike the other services, which recruit almost entirely from outside the ranks of government, both FAS and APHIS select only individuals who have had some previous Civil Service experience—normally with the Department of Agriculture. The average entrant into the FAS Foreign Service component will have worked several years as a Civil Service employee with FAS in Washington, usually as an agricultural economist or an agricultural marketing specialist; APHIS requires a minimum of two years of experience in Civil Service positions related to the service's responsibilities.

Like FCS, the two Foreign Service components of the Department of Agriculture are relatively small. FAS has about two hundred career personnel who are U.S. citizens (including approximately twenty Foreign Service secretaries), and APHIS currently employs slightly over a hundred (with only a single career secretary). Both services manage their own recruitment and examination procedures. FAS normally has a single "window" each year for its professional recruitment, annually soliciting applications for review by a series of panels, which evaluate and rank-order the candidates. The best of the applicants undergo an oral examination; if successful, their names are placed on a roster similar to the rosters maintained by the Board of Examiners for State, USIA, and FCS. In FAS, however, appointments are offered individually, rather than in classes, as appropriate overseas vacancies occur. Here again, there is a time limit for remaining on the roster of eligible employees, and a candidate who is not offered an appointment within two years after qualifying will be dropped from the list.

APHIS follows an essentially similar procedure, except that its announcements of potential openings are not keyed to an annual schedule but are made in anticipation of vacancies in one or another of the service's functional fields. Unlike FAS, which has a single cadre of FSO professionals, APHIS personnel (all of whom receive noncommissioned FP appointments) specialize in any one of several areas. Nearly one-fourth of the APHIS Foreign Service workforce comprises doctors of veterinary medicine, and another one-fourth works in general administration or one of its subspecialties (such as personnel, budget and fiscal, or procurement and supply work). The remainder of the workforce includes entomologists, plant protection and quarantine (PPQ) officers (whose degrees are usually in biology, entomology, or animal husbandry), biological and animal health technicians, and even a few airplane pilots and information specialists.

As in the other foreign affairs agencies, FAS and APHIS recruits into the Foreign Service initially receive limited appointments and must be recommended for career status by independent tenure boards. Both services send career candidates abroad for their first jobs in order to test them promptly under the conditions of overseas service. FAS candidates are normally assigned to their first posts for a two-year tour. At the end of this period, those whose performance has been strongest may move on to serve as agricultural attachés at small posts, but most remain at their initial posts for a third or even a fourth year before graduating to run their own shops. Many APHIS personnel serve initially in one of the service's programs in Mexico (these programs encompass 70 percent of APHIS employees overseas), in Central or South America, or in the Caribbean and can expect to spend a large part of their careers in those areas.

FAS and APHIS Careers

Historically, FAS has been the most self-contained of the foreign affairs services. Its personnel perform a specialized function that has no counterpart elsewhere in the Foreign Service system, and thus their careers are appropriately limited entirely to service in their own field. The personnel interchange that occurs regularly among the other agencies has not attracted FAS employees, nor do the other agencies have personnel who are qualified to fill FAS positions. In consequence, career members of the FAS Foreign Service can expect to spend their careers in FAS headquarters in Washington and in positions abroad as agricultural attaché and counselor for agricultural affairs, moving to positions of increasing responsibility within the FAS structure as they climb the promotion ladder.

Although APHIS is new to the Foreign Service, the career pattern of its pre–Foreign Service days suggests that its personnel can expect to follow the FAS example in spending virtually all of their careers directly engaged in the service's own activities. APHIS and FAS differ in one important respect, however, since

APHIS expects its Foreign Service personnel to spend about 80 percent of their careers abroad while FAS anticipates that careers will be divided almost evenly between domestic and overseas service.

Notes

1. Quoted in Martin Mayer, *The Diplomats* (New York: Doubleday and Company, 1983), p. 148.

2. U.S. Department of State, *Foreign Service Careers*, Department of State Publication 9202 (Washington, D.C.: U.S. Department of State, 1984), p. 11.

3. Hugh S. Gibson, testifying in 1924 before the House Foreign Affairs Committee, as quoted in Tracy Hollingsworth Lay, *The Foreign Service of the United States* (New York: Prentice-Hall, 1925), p. 240.

4. PL 96-465 (22 USC 3927), sec. 103(3).

5. Ibid., sec. 703.

6. U.S. Department of State, *Career Mobility Handbook* (Washington, D.C.: U.S. Department of State, 1983), pt. 4, p. 5.

7. Ibid., pt. 4, p. 3.

8. The process, and its impact on the individuals involved, are discussed in Martin F. Herz, *215 Days in the Life of an American Ambassador* (Washington, D.C.: School of Foreign Service, Georgetown University, 1981), pp. 83–90, and in the same author's article, "View from the Top," *Foreign Service Journal* 60:6 (June 1983), p. 27.

9. PL 96-465, sec. 210.

5

THE FOREIGN SERVICE
AT HOME

Many writers and speakers are disposed to put the blame for a weak
and unintelligent diplomacy on the agent, but . . . the real responsibility
necessarily rests with the government concerned.
                                                    —Sir Ernest Satow, 1917

In the early days of the Diplomatic and Consular Services, the
very idea of the Foreign Service at home would have seemed
inherently contradictory. The handful of early career members
in these separate services were appointed to posts abroad and
were expected to remain outside the United States if they wished
to stay on the public payroll. A few rare individuals did serve
first overseas and then later in the State Department in Washington, but in order to do so they had to resign from the
Diplomatic Service or the Consular Service and be given a
domestic appointment before they could take up their new duties
in Washington. A further damper to personnel interchange
between the domestic and overseas complements lay in the fact
that Diplomatic or Consular Service personnel who agreed to
serve in Washington were appointed only as clerks, which
usually meant a pay cut of about 50 percent.

By the early twentieth century, the State Department had
recognized the value of including on its Washington staff at
least a few officers with a first-hand experience of conditions
abroad, and had begun to bring in a small number of its overseas
personnel via the cumbersome resignation and reappointment
route. The first step in the direction of a more regular interchange

came with a 1909 appropriations act that provided funds for the salary of a single "resident diplomatic officer" in Washington so that the secretary of state might always have available an adviser with field experience. Six years later, the 1915 legislation that gave a statutory base to the merit system in the Diplomatic and Consular Services also made it possible for any consul or diplomatic secretary to be assigned to the Department of State for three years without loss of grade, class, or salary.[1] Under this authority, three diplomatic secretaries and three consuls were assigned to the department in 1915, and a number of additional personnel were added during the next few years to help the department cope with the extra demands arising out of World War I and its immediate aftermath. By 1924, when the Rogers Act established the unified Foreign Service, there were twenty diplomatic secretaries and thirty-two consuls serving in Washington, about 8 percent of the total register of officers.

The proportion of FSOs in the department fluctuated over the next thirty years, reaching a high of 15 percent at the end of World War II and slipping gradually back to 10 percent by 1954. The relatively small number of FSOs with domestic experience was cited by each of the postwar study commissions noted in Chapter 2 in support of their recommendations for greater integration of domestic and overseas personnel. At the time of the Wriston Committee (1954), 43 percent of the FSO corps had less than one year's duty in the United States and between one-third and two-thirds of the officers in the top three grades had fewer than three years of domestic service. This situation led the Wriston Committee to describe the Foreign Service as "a service in official exile"—and helped persuade then–Secretary of State Dulles to proceed with the expedited timetable for integration proposed by the committee.

In the wake of Wristonization and the consequent opening up of a larger number of domestic positions for FSOs, service at home became a much more normal and accepted part of Foreign Service careers. The Foreign Service Act of 1980 requires assignment to duty in the United States "at least once during each period of fifteen years that the member is in the Service,"[2] a change from the mandate of the 1946 Act calling only for three years at home during the first fifteen years of total service.

In practice, very few members of the Service need to be reminded that they have to come home at least once in every fifteen years. Among the State Department FSOs, whose average careers are split 60 percent overseas and 40 percent in the United States, only officers in the consular cone are likely to spend a significantly larger part of their service abroad. In State's FP ranks, the percentage of overseas service is often greater, and it does sometimes happen that an employee has to be brought reluctantly back for a tour in Washington. Secretaries and communicators, for example, spend an average of 80 percent of their careers abroad, and this pattern is not uncommon in several other specialist fields.

The tasks performed by Foreign Service personnel on domestic assignments vary from agency to agency, reflecting not only the different agency missions but also the size of the Foreign Service contingent in each agency in relation to its Civil Service workforce. Each of the foreign affairs agencies exercises its responsibilities in Washington through a mixture of Civil Service and Foreign Service personnel. The former provide continuity and expert knowledge in a particular area, and the latter bring first-hand experience of the foreign countries and cultures with which the agency deals. Despite occasional jealousies and misunderstandings between personnel in the two distinct systems, the overall balance sheet for this mixture is overwhelmingly positive—a blend of complementary strengths that neither component could provide alone.

The Department of State

The largest single group of Foreign Service personnel serving in domestic assignments belongs to the State Department— about three thousand of State's approximately nine thousand Foreign Service employees. Although they are outnumbered by the four thousand plus Civil Service employees of the department, nearly half the Civil Service personnel are secretaries, and the remainder are concentrated in a relatively few areas (with the largest group in administrative services). In consequence, the majority of State Department positions involved most directly

FSOs in the Operations Center monitor events worldwide and help coordinate the U.S. government's response.

in foreign policy issues are staffed by Foreign Service personnel, with only a leavening of Civil Service employees to provide necessary continuity.

The Foreign Service staffing within the State Department begins at a quite senior level, with at least one and sometimes more of the seven "principal" positions being filled by a career officer. On the department's famed seventh floor, the seat of power, the secretary of state is flanked by his alter ego, the deputy secretary; by four officials with the rank of under secretary; and by the counselor. The four under secretaries each have specific functional responsibilities—political affairs; economic affairs; management; and security assistance, science, and technology—and the counselor tends to be something of a utility infielder, dealing with specific policy issues as they are delegated by the secretary. In most government departments, positions at this level would be filled entirely by outside appointees chosen by the incumbent administration. At the State Department, however, the position of under secretary for political affairs has long been reserved for a career officer, and FSOs also have served in recent years as deputy secretary, as counselor, and as under secretary for management.

Below the seven principal positions, the State Department is divided into a complex of bureaus and offices headed by assistant secretaries or officials of equivalent rank. The oldest part of the structure, dating from 1909, comprises the five bureaus that deal directly with the posts abroad and the foreign embassies in Washington—the so-called regional bureaus for Europe, the Near East and South Asia, the American Republics, East Asia and the Pacific, and Africa. For many years, the business of the department was handled entirely by four regional bureaus (Africa did not become a separate bureau until 1959) and the offices responsible for consular affairs and for administrative support. Only with the growing complexity of foreign policy issues in the years during and after World War II did the department create additional organizational elements to help deal with its new problems. Today, these functional bureaus cover subjects ranging from economic and politico-military affairs to science, narcotics, and human rights—many of which are total newcomers to the foreign policy world.

Within the five regional bureaus and in most of the functional bureaus as well, the career Foreign Service is well represented. FSOs are frequently called on to serve as assistant secretaries, positions subject (like those of the seven principals) to presidential appointment and Senate confirmation and filled in most government departments by political appointees from outside career ranks. For career officers at this level, finding the right balance between their nonpolitical career status and the demands of the incumbent administration can be a tricky business.[3] Every new administration is determined to make its mark on foreign affairs as well as on domestic issues, and tends initially to be uneasy with the professionals who have been faithful servants of the preceding administration. Elected officials seeking visible change, but inexperienced in foreign policy, quickly grow impatient with career personnel who emphasize the importance of consistency in dealing with other nations and may conclude that career employees are unsympathetic to administration goals.

In this delicate situation, the role played by career Foreign Service personnel in senior positions can be critical to overcoming the new administration's inevitable suspicion of the Service as a whole. For it is the senior cadre that is most immediately visible to the newcomers in the White House and to the political appointees at the top of the State Department and the other foreign affairs agencies, so it is their sensitivity to the political concerns of the new administration that will be seen and registered. To the extent that they can bridge the cultural gap between the career bureaucracy and the elected leadership, they can greatly speed the process of gaining an administration's acceptance of the Foreign Service as a professional body that loyally supports and implements the policy decisions of the president and the secretary of state.

Loyalty and Dissent

The issue of loyalty deserves special attention, for it has been much debated within the Foreign Service. The argument runs along these lines. The Foreign Service, its members all acknowledge, is an instrument for carrying out the policies chosen by the nation's elected leaders, to whom it has promised its loyal support. But what if a particular policy appears morally wrong in the eyes of a member of the Service? At what point does the member's sense of obligation to a higher morality outweigh the loyalty owed to the president and his colleagues? The question is not a new one, for there are documented cases of career FSOs seeking to sabotage presidential policy decisions during the 1930s by careful leaks to the press.[4] The issue became a major one during the period of U.S. involvement in Vietnam, when many members of the Foreign Service shared with millions of fellow citizens a sense of moral discomfort at the U.S. role there. Some career personnel resigned in protest; others swallowed their concern and simply avoided direct involvement with Vietnam policy issues, and a few may have salved their consciences while working on Vietnam issues by secretly leaking inside information to congressional and other domestic opponents of U.S. intervention.

In January 1969, in an attempt to provide a disciplined alternative for Foreign Service personnel who are unhappy with a particular policy, the State Department established a "dissent channel" through which employees can submit alternative policy proposals to the direct attention of the seventh-floor principals. Any employee, at home or overseas, may send a message through this channel. An ambassador in the field may add his or her comments, but may not block transmission of the dissenting views. All recommendations sent through the dissent channel go to the Policy Planning Council, a body that is responsible directly to the secretary of state. The council evaluates dissent channel proposals on the secretary's behalf, reports its findings to the appropriate senior officials of the department, and responds to the drafter of the initial message. This is not a hollow exercise, since policy has in fact been changed more than once as the result of a dissent channel message conveying events or trends that an ambassador had chosen not to report.

Naturally, some dissent is based on incomplete or inaccurate information about the situation that troubles the dissenter or about the reasons underlying the policy to which he or she objects. When this is the case, the dissent channel can serve an important purpose simply by providing the dissenter with a fuller understanding of why a particular policy was adopted. Simply knowing the whole story is sometimes enough to persuade a dissenter that the policy in question is more justified than at first appeared to be the case.

Even with the dissent channel available as an in-house mechanism for employees troubled by a given policy, there have still been occasions when career Foreign Service personnel have felt it necessary to take more dramatic action to make their views known. The highly public resignations of several FSOs at the time of the Cambodian bombings in 1971 and the congressional testimony on El Salvador by Ambassador Robert White in 1981 have been among the most visible examples of this type of action, and these cases are frequently cited in the still-open debate about the proper limits of dissent. In recent years, and particularly in the wake of Ambassador White's action at the start of the Reagan administration, the Service has once again been seeking to reach a consensus to which all its members can subscribe. If, however, the career Foreign Service is to win and hold the trust of successive administrations, its members must at all times be publicly loyal to the policies adopted by the president and his cabinet. A member of the Service who is morally troubled by an individual policy basically has two options. The first is to remain in the Service and limit his or her expressions of unhappiness with the policy to established channels within the department and, if conscience demands, ask to be assigned to a position that does not involve work in the area that causes concern. The second option is to resign from the Service, and thus be free to speak out as a private citizen in opposition to established policy.

As the continuing debate suggests, a consensus has not yet been universally accepted. A minority within the Service still argues that leaks to the press in an effort to sabotage a distasteful policy are morally justified. Such tactics are used regularly by political appointees, they contend, both to undermine opponents and to build support for their own positions, and thus should be legitimate weapons for career personnel as well. Unfortunately, this argument overlooks the critical difference between career and noncareer officials, since only the former face the challenge of proving their loyalty anew to each incoming administration. When there is a damaging leak, the instinct of any president is to trust his own appointees and to assume that the leak has been perpetrated by career officials still longing for the previous administration. The president will almost always be wrong in making such an assumption, but if leaks are occurring in the foreign affairs field, he need be proved right only once for the reputation—and with it, the effectiveness— of the entire Service to suffer. Whatever the presumed moral justification, the cost to the Service of such individual gratification is too high for most members to accept.

The Foreign Service at Work

When a member of the Foreign Service reports for duty in the State Department, he or she becomes part of a foreign policy apparatus that extends well beyond the foreign affairs agencies. Since World War II, foreign policy has become the daily concern not only of a large number of executive-branch departments but also of the Congress. Once the Department of State was free to act virtually alone, but its role has now become that of a coordinator in the foreign policy field—and even that role is often shared with the National Security Council. As a result, the work of FSOs serving in Washington has become more complex than ever before. In order to play an effective part in the policy-making process, they need to take into account the many interests that affect each issue, including domestic political factors, and the interrelationships among both policies and their proponents. The traditional Foreign Service skills of reporting and analysis must be supplemented by new conceptual and bureaucratic skills in order to ensure successful performance in this demanding setting. Although the training programs described in Chapter 4 seek to impart these extra skills, they are still acquired largely through on-the-job experience.

On most policy issues involving U.S. relations with one country or a group of countries, the principal coordinating role continues to be played by the regional bureau responsible for the area. Each of the regional bureaus is subdivided into offices that handle policy questions relative either to a single nation or to a group of nations, usually geographically contiguous (for example, northern Europe, East Africa, or the Caribbean); one or more offices dealing with regional affairs; a public affairs office; and an office headed by an executive director responsible for administrative support both to the bureau at home and to its overseas posts. The regional offices incorporate individuals with special skills in such fields as labor, politico-military affairs, and economic development while the public affairs office works with the department's overall Bureau of Public Affairs to ensure that accurate information on U.S. policy in the region is made available to the media and to the public. The executive director and his or her staff manage the bureau's resources of money and personnel and work to ensure that staffing, housekeeping, and general welfare are well looked after both in Washington and abroad.

The offices directly responsible for bilateral relations with other nations have evolved from a system of country directorates introduced in 1966 to upgrade the level of the officers who, in the words of then–Secretary of State Dean Rusk, "brood twenty-four hours a day on the problems of a particular country."[5] Prior to that date, U.S. relations with each of the world's nations were presided over by a desk officer, who was several layers below the assistant secretary responsible for the region. Since these desk officers were relatively junior in grade, they tended to find themselves increasingly shunted aside in the status-conscious bureaucratic process through which policy decisions were reached. The solution adopted at the time was to replace the desk officers with country directors of sufficient rank to have an effective voice in the policy process. Not surprisingly, this organizational change, like so many others, failed to provide a magical cure for the ills it was intended to address, and the pendulum has swung partway back to produce the structure of offices within each bureau that we find today.

Almost without exception, the positions of office director, deputy office director, and desk officer are staffed by FSOs, many of whom have had first-hand experience in the countries with which they are asked to deal. Along with the assistant secretaries and deputy assistant secretaries to whom they report, they are the normal point of contact on policy matters for both the foreign embassies in Washington and the U.S. diplomatic and consular posts abroad. The level of contact in either case depends on the circumstances, the issues, and the importance (self-assigned or otherwise) of the ambassador in question. In the case of the foreign embassies in Washington, discussion of relatively routine matters is likely to occur between the desk officer and an embassy official at the counselor level. On issues of greater weight, the office director may deal either with the foreign ambassador involved or with his or her immediate deputy, and a prudent office director will seek to maintain a regular dialogue at this level in order to ensure that the channel will be readily available when needed. If a foreign ambassador judges that an issue is of particular importance, he or she will normally seek to deal directly with the assistant secretary or the appropriate deputy assistant secretary rather than with the office director. Although the substantive outcome may be no different, the ambassador can at least report that his or her demarche was effected at a suitably high level, and thereby perhaps gain some credit even in a losing effort.

Most communications between the foreign affairs agencies and the U.S. diplomatic and consular posts abroad take the

Today's communicators operate sophisticated equipment to link Washington to even the most remote posts—in this case, the Sinai Field Mission.

form of cables, which are exchanged at the rate of about three million a year. These are supplemented by periodic visits of department officials to posts abroad and consultations in Washington for chiefs of mission; by instructions conveyed to posts in the pouches carried by diplomatic couriers or in unclassified pouches, which are routinely sent as air cargo; and by written reports sent from the posts to Washington when the pouches are returned. Except for a few of the most sensitive telegrams and written reports, incoming messages are reproduced in the State Department's Office of Communications (which provides the link to posts abroad for all the foreign affairs agencies) and disseminated to a wide range of interested departments and agencies.

Since most cables are automatically distributed to a multitude of readers, something was needed to provide a channel for discreet communication on issues that do not justify applying the special classifications used for particularly sensitive subjects. The answer is "the official-informal letter," a hybrid that has official standing but offers the possibility of discreet exchanges of view because it goes only to its addressee. Correspondence that goes through this channel may be at any level from office director to ambassador or from desk officer to embassy section chief, and the subject matter may concern anything from scraps of information too fragmentary for a formal report to a request for assistance from the desk officer in securing administrative support from another office or agency. Ideally, a relationship of trust and confidence between the ambassador and an office director or a desk officer will permit them to work effectively as a team in securing approval of policy initiatives on which they agree. More than one desk officer, knowing that a key interagency meeting was about to be held, has quietly suggested to his or her ambassador which arguments from the embassy would be most helpful in pursuing their mutual objectives. This kind of collaborative effort has succeeded often enough to remain a favorite weapon in every desk officer's armory.

As the above discussion suggests, the most challenging work done by office directors and desk officers normally involves neither foreign embassies nor U.S. posts abroad but the bureaucratic machinery through which foreign policy is formulated in Washington. The number and nature of the players vary from issue to issue, but the complexity of the process is vividly illustrated by the fact that some telegrams sent from the State Department on particularly sensitive or controversial issues may end up with as many as twenty or thirty separate clearances. Although some of these may represent nothing more than an office or agency asserting its right to be consulted, others reflect the difficult process of negotiation and compromise that often precedes agreement on a new policy direction.

The Policy-Making Process: A Case Study

To illustrate the trials and tribulations of a desk officer who is seeking consensus on a policy issue, it may be helpful to track a hypothetical case through the bureaucratic process. The

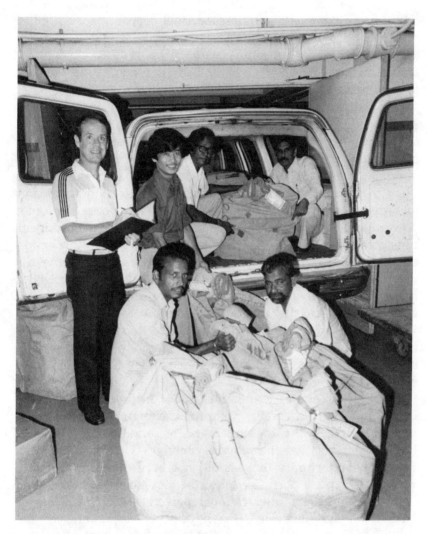

Diplomatic pouches arrive in New Delhi.

scenario begins in the capital of a friendly African nation, small but prosperous, where the country's president has asked the U.S. ambassador to call at the presidential mansion for one of their periodic *tours d'horizon*. (It should be noted at this point that regular meetings between U.S. ambassadors and the chiefs of state to whom they are accredited are not uncommon in many of the smaller countries of the world. In Washington and other major capitals, an ambassador will probably see the chief of state only when presenting his or her credentials and at an annual reception for the diplomatic corps; only rarely will an ambassador do business directly with a secretary of state or foreign minister.)

As the late afternoon conversation proceeds, the president says he is growing increasingly concerned about the intentions of two neighboring states, which have been receiving economic and military assistance from Communist countries. "Our neighbors," he says, "are jealous of our hard-earned prosperity, and I fear they may resort either to subversion or to open aggression in order to acquire our riches." Although the former colonial power has been providing some military assistance, the president considers it inadequate to meet the threat he sees developing on his borders, and he has been unable to persuade the ex-metropole to augment its small military aid program. Under these circumstances, he continues, he is turning to his great and good friend, the U.S. ambassador, to plead his case in Washington and to obtain from the U.S. government the equipment and training his country so desperately needs for self-defense against the predatory designs of his Communist-supported neighbors.

Back at his embassy, the ambassador incorporates the president's request in a careful cable to Washington. He adds to it his own judgment that the threat is not as serious as the president has alleged, but that the request nonetheless offers the United States an opportunity that should not be lost. As in so many newly independent African states, the local scene has long been dominated by the former colonial power, and U.S. businesses have been systematically frozen out. By responding to the president's appeal, even in a limited way, the United States can help him move away from dependence on the ex-metropole and perhaps open up a potentially lucrative market for U.S. firms. On balance, the ambassador therefore recommends a positive response.

When the desk officer comes to work the next morning, the ambassador's cable is waiting for him. Copies have already been distributed to other interested offices both in the State Department and in other government agencies, so it is important for the desk officer to move quickly in order to establish his office's central role in the decision-making process. The desk officer's first stop is in an adjacent office, where he has a preliminary discussion with the office director, who shares his initial view that the president's request for military assistance should be pursued. They agree on two initial steps: the desk officer will walk down the hall to get the views (and, it is hoped, the support) of the bureau's regional affairs office, which numbers among its responsibilities the coordination of African Bureau action with regard to all military assistance programs on the continent, and the office director will then raise the request the following morning at the assistant secretary's weekly staff meeting.

As these first steps suggest, in all but crisis situations the normal process by which a policy develops involves a series of concentric circles. The "action officer," the individual with primary responsibility for shepherding the issue to decision, begins within his or her own bureau, and usually will not go beyond its confines until the assistant secretary or one of that person's deputies has committed the bureau to a preferred outcome. In our hypothetical case, the desk officer first gains the concurrence of the colleague responsible for military assistance, and the office director then presents the issue the next day to the assistant secretary as a joint recommendation from the ambassador and from two offices in the bureau.

Once the blessing of the bureau's leadership has been secured, the process can proceed to the second concentric circle in an effort to transform the "bureau position" into a "department position." Again, there normally will be no formal consultation with other departments and agencies until the State Department is prepared to speak with a single voice. In a case involving military assistance, there will be two stops of particular importance: the Bureau of Politico-Military Affairs, which has a department-wide coordinating role in this field similar to that played at the bureau level by the regional affairs office, and the Office of the Under Secretary for Security Assistance, Science and Technology, which makes the final decisions for the Department of State on all requests in this area. Other offices consulted may include such bureaus as European Affairs, for a reading on whether the former colonial power will be upset by the proposed U.S. program in a country of interest to them; Intelligence and Research, for an independent appraisal of the threat alleged by the president; Human Rights, to determine whether there are any serious problems in this area that would argue against going ahead with military assistance; and Legislative Affairs (formerly known as Congressional Relations), for a reading on probable congressional reaction to a request for funds.

The small proposed program proves noncontroversial, and agreement in principle to respond positively to the president's request is easily obtained within the State Department. The time has now come to move to the third circle in the policy process, and the net thus spreads across the Potomac River to the Department of Defense. Since the members of both the African Bureau and the Bureau of Politico-Military Affairs are in daily contact with their opposite numbers in the Pentagon's Office of International Security Affairs and Defense Support Assistance Agency, the possibility of a new military assistance program may already have been the subject of informal discussion. Working through the Bureau of Politico-Military Affairs, the desk officer secures formal concurrence in principle from Defense. With it, however, comes a question: what kind of assistance does the president want—or need? What types of equipment, how soon, and at what cost? Since the small U.S. embassy in the country has no one qualified to make such judgments, the Pentagon offers to send a survey team from the appropriate regional command (in this case, European Command, or EUCOM, in Stuttgart, West Germany) for an expert on-the-spot assessment.

Now it's the desk officer's turn to draft a telegram, instructing the ambassador to tell the president that the United States is prepared to help meet his needs but that a survey team will have to be sent before any specifics can be discussed. The cable also contains appropriate cautionary language from the Pentagon about the long lead times for delivery of equipment and the likelihood that the country's prosperity will make it ineligible for grant assistance, but the desk officer knows full well that these caveats are less likely to register on the president than the basic "yes" to his request. Duly cleared by all interested offices, and signed personally by the assistant secretary, the cable goes on its way. The ambassador delivers the message, the survey team visits the country and makes its report, and the stage is then set for step two in the overall policy process.

The survey team has come back with an ambitious proposal for a military assistance program costing over twenty million dollars. Unfortunately, however, all available funding—whether for grant assistance or for loan guarantees—has already been committed to programs for other countries, so a new program can be started only by shaving the assistance being given to someone else. At this point, it is time for one of the ubiquitous meetings that provide the forum for much of Washington's decision-making.

An FSO serving in the State Department can expect to spend a good part of his or her time at meetings, some regularly scheduled and some called to deal with a specific issue. The periodic meetings spread downward from the top. The secretary of state meets several times weekly with the deputy and the under secretaries and monthly with all the assistant secretaries; the last, in turn, meet from one to three times a week with their office directors, who will usually then meet at least as often with their own staffs to pass on the news from the front office. These in-house sessions are supplemented by gatherings of personnel from various bureaus of the department or from several agencies that work on common problems—anything from debt renegotiation or immigration policy to scientific exchanges or narcotics interdiction. Such meetings are held at regular intervals to coordinate activities.

This time, however, there is no convenient scheduled meeting to provide a forum for discussion of the pending military aid proposal, so the office director takes the lead in assembling interested colleagues from the Pentagon and elsewhere in the department. The desk officer, in consultation with the specialists in the Bureau of Politico-Military Affairs and the Defense Department, has prepared a discussion paper containing a series of options for both grant and loan programs ranging from five million to twenty million dollars, with the pros and cons of each. At the meeting, the decision is made that the symbolic value of a rapid response to the president's request is more important than the size of the program; thus five million dollars this year is preferable to a promise of a larger amount two or three years hence. The participants also agree that the country's prosperity makes it ineligible for a grant program, but that a program involving guaranteed loans will serve the essential purpose of demonstrating U.S. support. A larger program for another African country will be stretched over an extra year, thus freeing the five million dollars that is needed for a quick start on the new program, and the Defense Department's recommendations on the specific equipment to be offered gain quick acceptance.

Working with their military and Civil Service counterparts in their own department and at the Pentagon, and with their FSO colleagues in other bureaus at State, the FSOs in the regional bureau have successfully taken a recommendation from an ambassador in the field and translated it into a policy decision that commits the U.S. government to a specific course of action. The example chosen, involving only one government agency outside the State Department, is a relatively simple one. FSOs working in Washington are often caught up in far more complex interagency negotiations on policy issues. Officers in the Bureau of Consular Affairs, for example, may be asked to help develop a consensus on immigration policy, a politically delicate topic of interest to a host of agencies in the executive branch, to the Congress, and to a wide range of influential groups in the private sector. FSOs in the Bureau of Economic and Business Affairs may find themselves trying to draft instructions for the U.S. delegation to a forthcoming conference on civil aviation or trade policy, either of which involves a number of government agencies and private organizations. The Bureau for Refugee Programs handles issues of vital concern to state and municipal governments as well as to federal agencies; the Bureau for International Narcotic Matters coordinates closely with the Department of Justice and local law enforcement agencies; and the Bureau of Administration deals with dozens of agencies for which the State Department provides administrative services abroad. In short, no office in the State Department is totally divorced from the bureaucratic mechanism through which interagency policies are hammered out. Wherever an FSO serves in Washington, he or she will have ample opportunity to participate in the policy process.

Beyond the Regional Bureaus

Although the regional bureaus were first on the scene, along with the offices handling consular and administrative affairs, they are now outnumbered on the State Department's organization chart by the functional bureaus and offices, many of which have already been discussed. Several of these have a very direct impact on the Foreign Service. Among them is the Bureau of Personnel, headed by the director general of the Foreign Service, whose responsibilities range from recruitment through retirement and thus affect the career of every member of the Service; the Bureau of Administration, which assures logistic support to posts around the world and includes the Office of Communications, home base of the network that moves over two million words a day between Washington agencies and posts abroad (in 1930, the volume was only two million words a year!); the Office of Medical Services, which monitors the health of members of the Service and their families and provides emergency care at overseas posts; and the Office of the Inspector General, the department's watchdog at home and abroad.

The last of these agencies deserves special mention, for the inspector general and that office's staff are the heirs of a function that dates back to the early nineteenth century. Inspectors were sent from time to time to consular posts in an effort (albeit seldom very successful) to stem the rampant fraud that characterized the early years of consular operations. The inspection function was regularized in 1906 when the position of "consul general at large" was established to check on the work of consular officers abroad, and its responsibility was extended to diplomatic as well as consular posts when a unified Foreign Service was created by the Rogers Act of 1924. The Foreign Service Act of 1946 set up a corps of inspectors along the lines that exist today and charged them with inspecting all overseas posts at two-year intervals. Operating under the 1946 mandate, the Office of the Inspector General looked not so much at the mechanics of post operations as at the manner in which each post (and the supporting bureau in the department) managed the relationship with the country or organization to which it was accredited—an approach that came to be known as a "conduct of relations inspection."

In the wake of the 1980 Foreign Service Act, inspectors now spend somewhat more of their time than in the past on operational details. Although they have not lost sight of their responsibility to evaluate how effectively a bilateral relationship is being managed, the act reflects a new emphasis throughout the federal government on the prevention and detection of "waste, fraud, and mismanagement" (known familiarly by their initials, WFM, commonly pronounced "wiffem"). Thus, today's inspection teams routinely include qualified auditors and administrative specialists who are specially charged with uncovering instances in which government funds are being spent either wrongfully or unnecessarily. Each team continues to be headed by a senior FSO, who has served either as an ambassador or as a deputy chief of mission at a major embassy, and is rounded out by mid-level FSOs (and sometimes a senior secretary) with a wide range of experience. With this membership, the team is well equipped to make informed judgments on all aspects of post operations and on the overall management of the relationship for which the post is responsible.

The objective of each inspection team is not simply to find out what is wrong but to provide assistance to the post in setting things right. Inspection reports are frank to point out operational shortcomings at a post, but they also include specific recommendations for correcting any flaws they have uncovered. Given the wealth of experience that the teams bring with them, they are often able to work with post personnel during their visits to solve problems on the spot. Recommendations requiring longer-term action, or support from the department, are incorporated into the team's formal report, and the post then has several months to take necessary action.[6]

The Other Foreign Affairs Agencies

Foreign Service personnel of the other four foreign affairs agencies (AID, USIA, Commerce, and Agriculture) also spend part of their careers in the United States (see Chapter 4). At both AID and USIA, where the entire agency deals with foreign policy issues, the role played by members of the Service is akin to that of their Foreign Service counterparts at the State Department. As is the case at State, the Foreign Service is most heavily represented in those agency components that deal directly with overseas posts and programs. For example, FSOs dominate the AID and USIA equivalents of the regional bureaus, handling day-to-day policy issues in conjunction with the posts abroad. AID FSOs serving in Washington hold regional bureau positions as director and deputy director, desk officer, and program and project design officer, and their USIA colleagues are similarly assigned.

In AID, which expects its two thousand Foreign Service employees to spend about three-fourths of their careers abroad, there are still relatively few domestic positions beyond the regional bureaus that are occupied by Foreign Service personnel. However, the personnel balance in AID is shifting increasingly toward its Foreign Service component, which, overall, already outnumbers the agency's fifteen hundred Civil Service employees. Under pressure from Congress, AID has been redesignating policy positions in various parts of the agency from Civil Service to Foreign Service, with the objectives of both providing better domestic career opportunities for Foreign Service personnel and assuring a greater degree of input into the policy process from those who have had first-hand experience overseas. In consequence, the range of jobs available in Washington to AID's Foreign Service personnel has been expanding steadily and is expected to continue to do so.

Within USIA, the range is already fairly broad, even though the agency has a total of approximately three thousand Civil Service employees compared to only some thirteen hundred in the Foreign Service (of whom about one-third are likely to be in Washington at any given time). Nonetheless, FSO and FP personnel are well represented in both policy and operational positions in a number of the agency's major components beyond the regional bureaus. The largest single group is found in USIA's Bureau of Programs, which has responsibility for functions ranging from press and publications through exhibits and foreign press centers to basic program development. Foreign Service personnel also hold jobs in the Bureau of Educational and Cultural Affairs, which deals both with visitors from abroad (those who come on their own as well as those invited by the U.S. government) and with such cultural programs as English-language teaching and the dissemination of books published in the United States. In addition, there are Foreign Service positions in the Bureau of Management, in the director's immediate office, and at the Voice of America (though the last is staffed predominantly by Civil Service personnel).

Like the State Department, both AID and USIA offer opportunities for members of the Senior Foreign Service to serve at the policy level in Washington. Career officers at the SFS level have served at times as deputy director in both agencies, and from 1977 to 1981, USIA had career FSOs in both the director and deputy director positions. AID currently has a position designated counselor, and ranked number three in the agency hierarchy, which is reserved for a career officer; USIA experimented with a similar position in the early 1980s but abolished it after two years. At a slightly lower level, the officers responsible for geographic areas in the two agencies (roughly equivalent to the assistant secretaries in the State Department) are often appointed from career ranks; they have the title of director in USIA and assistant administrator at AID.

The situation is somewhat different in the Foreign Service components of the Departments of Commerce and Agriculture as they are small elements of large agencies engaged primarily in domestic programs. The Foreign Commercial Service, for example, totals only about two hundred U.S. employees in a department of nearly forty-eight thousand. Even its parent component in the Department of Commerce, the International Trade Administration, has twenty-three hundred employees, and the United States and Foreign Commercial Service (US/FCS), of which FCS is a part, has over thirteen hundred. Within this structure, FCS clearly exists almost exclusively as the overseas element of the overall operation, an institutional form that helps explain the agency's career pattern, which calls for 80 percent of an employee's career to be spent abroad.

Nonetheless, FCS personnel will normally find themselves in the United States once or twice during the course of their careers. When they do return home for assignment, they normally serve within the small headquarters component of the FCS itself or elsewhere in the International Trade Administration, but they may, in theory, be assigned anywhere within the Department of Commerce (including US/FCS field offices across the United States). FCS headquarters includes four SFS positions reserved for staffing by senior members of the Service who have had experience at major posts abroad. These four regional coordinators are responsible for support to the posts and their activities in designated areas of the world, and thus, they serve in effect as the equivalents (albeit on a smaller scale) of the regional assistant secretaries and bureau heads of the three agencies previously discussed.

The Foreign Agricultural Service, whose personnel will normally split their careers almost equally between Washington and posts abroad, has about eighty domestic positions for its Foreign Service workforce of approximately 200 Americans. Not surprisingly, members of the Service occupy a substantial proportion of FAS headquarters positions and are especially well represented in those jobs in which the responsibilities include overseeing operations at overseas posts. Nonetheless, FAS itself is only a small component of the Department of Agriculture. Its workforce of about 640 Americans (Foreign Service and Civil Service combined) represents less than 1 percent of the Agriculture Department's 110,000 employees; even measured against the 12,000 people who work for Agriculture in the Washington area, FAS employees make up only 5 percent of the total.

The other Foreign Service arm of the Department of Agriculture, the Animal and Plant Health Inspection Service, has only about half as many Foreign Service employees as FAS (there are currently just over one hundred Foreign Service Americans in APHIS). However, APHIS as a whole, including its Civil Service workforce, has a total of nearly five thousand employees, so its Foreign Service component is clearly designed to serve almost exclusively as the overseas arm. After its first two years of operation within the Foreign Service family, APHIS had designated only a handful of domestic positions to be filled on a rotational basis by its Foreign Service personnel and continued to rely on Civil Service employees for nearly all of its needs in the United States. The agency expects to make additional domestic jobs available for Foreign Service staffing over the next few years, however, so tours in Washington will eventually become a regular part of APHIS Foreign Service careers.

Notes

1. William Barnes and John Heath Morgan, *The Foreign Service of the United States* (Washington, D.C.: Historical Office, Bureau of Public Affairs, U.S. Department of State, 1961), pp. 171–172 and 275–276.

2. PL 96-465 (22 USC 3927), sec. 504(b).

3. This section is drawn largely from David D. Newsom, "The Executive Branch in Foreign Policy," in *The President, the Congress, and Foreign Policy* (Washington, D.C.: Atlantic Council, forthcoming).

4. The story of an attempt to undermine policy in 1933 through a deliberate leak is told in Martin Weil, *A Pretty Good Club: The Founding Fathers of the U.S. Foreign Service* (New York: W. W. Norton, 1978), pp. 70–71.

5. Quoted in W. Wendell Blancke, *The Foreign Service of the United States* (New York: Frederick A. Praeger, 1969), p. 72.

6. Additional information on the structure and operations of the State Department may be found in Thomas S. Estes and E. Allan Lightner, Jr., *The Department of State* (New York: Frederick A. Praeger, 1976).

6

THE FOREIGN SERVICE ABROAD

An Ambassador is one official the state cannot do without.
—Abraham de Wicquefort, 1682

. . . we must be equipped for emergencies, and every now and then, even at the smallest and most remote courts, there is a critical need of an American representative to protect American citizens and American interests.
—President Benjamin Harrison, 1889

Although all members of the Foreign Service spend part of their careers in the United States, their natural habitat is in the nearly 300 posts around the world where the majority of them can be found at any given time. These posts include 142 embassies and embassy branch offices, 106 consulates and consulates general, and a number of special missions through which the United States deals with international organizations or conducts complex negotiations. They also include about 50 posts without formal diplomatic or consular status, at which Foreign Service personnel from agencies other than the State Department perform only the specialized functions appropriate to the work of their individual agencies. Posts range in size from the U.S. Embassy in Bangkok, with 190 Foreign Service personnel, 180 other Americans (representing a number of agencies), and nearly 750 total employees; to the minuscule U.S. Embassy in Malabo, Equatorial Guinea, which has only three Americans on its staff; and to several one-officer USIS posts in cities with no other official U.S. presence.

Although many new nations have emerged on the world scene since the 1950s, the total number of U.S. diplomatic and consular posts has actually dropped slightly since 1955, when there were 273. The United States has added embassies in most of the newly independent countries, but that growth in the number of embassies has been offset by a drop from 158 consular posts in 1955 to the 106 of today. Both figures are well below the record high hit in 1920, when the total number of posts peaked at 413—45 diplomatic and 368 consular (see Table 6.1). Much of the latest reduction in consular posts occurred during the 1960s and 1970s, when successive administrations decreed a cut in the number of U.S. officials abroad. Consulates proved most vulnerable to the ax, and only in the past few years has the number of consular posts again begun to increase.

Structure of an Embassy

As the personnel figures for Bangkok and for Malabo suggest, U.S. embassies around the world vary enormously both in size and in scope of responsibility. These differences receive formal recognition in a classification system applied to U.S. missions abroad (all "missions" conduct diplomatic business, but the term includes both embassies, which are accredited bilaterally to another sovereign nation, and special missions that deal with an international organization or handle a major negotiation). Missions are divided into four classes according to the size of their staffs, a fairly reliable indicator of the importance of the work with which each is charged. Under this system, the United States currently has twenty-nine Class I missions, each staffed by more than fifty-four Foreign Service personnel on the State Department's rolls or more than two hundred U.S. employees. Class II missions, of which there are also twenty-nine, have between thirty and fifty-four State Department Foreign Service employees; the sixty Class III missions have twelve to thirty such personnel; and the thirty-four Class IV missions have twelve or fewer employees in this category.

But who are these people who staff the U.S. missions abroad, and what do they do all day? To answer those questions, it

Posts come in all sizes—from Athens (top) to Medan (bottom).

Table 6.1.   Number of U.S. Diplomatic and Consular Posts, 1790–1984

	Diplomatic Posts	Consular Posts	Total
1790	2	10	12
1800	6	52	58
1810	4	60	64
1820	7	83	90
1830	15	141	156
1840	20	152	172
1850	27	197	224
1860	33	279	312
1870	36	318	354
1880	35	303	338
1890	40	323	363
1900	41	318	359
1910	48	324	372
1920	45	368	413
1930	57	299	356
1940	58	264	322
1950	74	179	253
1960	99	166	265
1970	117	122	239
1980	133	100	233
1984	140	106	246

Sources: State, no. 230 (January 1981), p. 27, for figures
through 1980; the 1984 figures are taken from the list of posts
in Appendix B. U.S. missions to international organizations and
the embassy offices in Geneva and Dubai have been excluded from the
total of diplomatic posts to keep the 1984 figures consistent with
those for earlier years.

may be helpful to start by examining the composition of a
medium-sized U.S. embassy—a hypothetical Class II mission in
a developing country that receives both economic and military
aid from the United States.

As Table 6.2 indicates, our example includes personnel not
only from the five foreign affairs agencies but also from the
Peace Corps and the Department of Defense. A number of the
senior personnel, in several agencies, are identified on the chart
by diplomatic titles (counselor or attaché) while the remaining
staff members are listed simply by functional title. However,
most of the other officers will, in fact, have diplomatic titles—
the exact nomenclature depends largely on whether or not they
are members of the Foreign Service.

All Foreign Service Officers receive presidential commissions
as both consular officers and members of the diplomatic service.

Table 6.2. U.S. Staffing at a Hypothetical Class II Embassy

Executive Section
Ambassador
Deputy chief of mission
Two secretaries

Political Section
Counselor for political affairs
Four political officers
Three secretaries

Economic Section
Counselor for economic affairs
Two economic officers
Two secretaries

Consular Section
Consul general
Four consular officers

Foreign Agricultural Service (FAS)
Counselor for agricultural
  affairs
Assistant agricultural attaché

**United States Information
  Service (USIS)**
Counselor for public affairs
Executive officer
Information officer
Asst. information officer
Cultural affairs officer
Two assistant cultural
  affairs officers
Secretary

Administrative Section
Counselor for administration
Two general services officers
Personnel officer
Budget and fiscal officer
Security officer
Two secretaries
Communications supervisor
Two support communicators
Two telecommunications
  specialists
Seven marine guards

Foreign Commercial Service (FCS)
Counselor for commercial
  affairs
Two commercial officers
Director, Export Development
  Office

**Agency for International
  Development (AID)**
Mission director
Deputy director
Executive officer
Controller
Project development officer
Program officer
Agricultural development
  officer
Rural development officer
Health/population officer
Science/technology adviser
Secretary

Non-Foreign Affairs Agencies

Service Attachés
Defense attaché (and
  air attaché)
Army attaché
Assistant air attaché
Administrative officer
Two clerks

Peace Corps
Peace Corps representative
Deputy representative
Physician

**Military Assistance Advisory
  Group (MAAG)**
Commander
Chief, Army section (and
  deputy commander)
Four officer advisers
Chief, Air Force section
Three officer advisers
Administrative officer
Three clerks
Six NCO trainers

Note: The U.S. personnel shown on this chart of a hypothetical mission
would be supplemented in most sections by Foreign Service National (FSN)
employees. In those sections of the mission which show no U.S. secretaries, for example, FSN secretaries normally would be responsible for
the entire secretarial workload.

These commissions do not in and of themselves confer either diplomatic or consular titles, which are granted separately for each assignment. They are, however, prerequisite to the granting of what are known in the Foreign Service as the "commissioned titles": minister, minister-counselor, counselor, and first, second, or third secretary of embassy on the diplomatic side; consul general, consul, and vice-consul for those at consular posts or likely to be engaged in consular operations. Personnel at missions abroad who should be formally included in the local diplomatic list but who are not commissioned members of the Foreign Service may be given the diplomatic titles of attaché or assistant attaché.

On our hypothetical staff, the deputy FAS representative's title, assistant agricultural attaché, is an interesting historical anomaly. Although fully entitled to use commissioned diplomatic titles since the FAS formally joined the Foreign Service family under the terms of the 1980 Act, the Department of Agriculture opted to continue using the attaché titles for all but its most senior field representatives—who have counselor titles—because its personnel were so well and favorably known around the world as agricultural attachés. For similar reasons, FCS representatives sometimes use commercial attaché as a working title.

The particular title granted an individual officer for an assignment depends on three factors: the size of the post and its staff, the position the officer will occupy, and his or her personal rank in the Service. At embassies, where diplomatic titles are used, the deputy chief of mission will have the title of minister or minister-counselor at a large post and counselor at a smaller one. At larger embassies, section chiefs with a personal rank of at least FSO-1 will be counselors; otherwise, they will be either first or second secretaries. In current practice, the title of first secretary is given to FSO-1s and FSO-2s (and to members of the Senior Foreign Service not holding a position that calls for a counselor title); that of second secretary to FSO-3s and FSO-4s; and that of third secretary to career candidates at the FSO-5 and FSO-6 levels. At consular posts, the title of vice-consul parallels that of third secretary in being accorded at the FSO-5 and FSO-6 levels, and consul is the normal title for all other commissioned officers except the single consul general, who is the boss at larger posts. As indicated in

Table 6.2, the title of consul general may also be given to the head of the consular section at an embassy—and the other officers on that staff will be consuls or vice-consuls in addition to holding diplomatic titles.

The offices of the ambassador and the deputy chief of mission, along with those of the defense attaché and the four embassy sections staffed by State Department personnel, will normally be housed in the chancery, which is the principal embassy office building (though some of the administrative or consular services occasionally spill over into an outbuilding). If the chancery is large enough, many of the other embassy elements will also have offices there, but it often proves necessary to house such components as AID, USIS, or a military assistance mission in separate quarters. This is a far cry from the situation at pre–World War II missions, when the small staff sometimes worked in a wing of the ambassador's house. Today, the ambassador's home is known formally as "the residence" to distinguish it clearly from the chancery (usually called simply "the embassy," though that term technically applies to the ambassador's dwelling place rather than to his or her office). Only in exceptional circumstances, such as during periods of heavy fighting in Beirut in the early 1980s, does the residence double as offices for the embassy staff.

At our hypothetical embassy, the personnel performing the traditional diplomatic and consular functions—basically, those in the consular, economic, and political sections of the mission— are in a distinct minority. This is often the case, especially in countries in which substantial staffs are required to design and implement military and economic assistance programs or where a number of U.S. government agencies are represented. This situation puts a premium on the leadership and coordination roles of the embassy's executive section, and it is here that we will begin our examination of the way the mission actually operates.

The Ambassador

The role of the ambassador, like that of all members of the Foreign Service, has changed substantially in the period since

World War II. Today's chief of mission may be called on to manage a large and complex organization in addition to performing more traditional diplomatic tasks. The changed role has fueled the internal debate within the Foreign Service regarding the proper balance in FSO training between functional specialization (i.e., in-depth area studies or advanced economics) and broad management experience (see Chapter 4). It has also rekindled the wider debate about the respective merits of career and noncareer ambassadors.

The early history of U.S. diplomatic representation is essentially a chronicle of amateurs, with true professionals making only rare appearances until the present century. Most eighteenth- and nineteenth-century U.S. ministers (the title of ambassador, thought to be too closely associated with monarchs and their courts, was not given to U.S. representatives abroad until 1893) were private citizens who served for a few years at a single post overseas, some with greater distinction than others. In many instances, particularly after the introduction of the spoils system in the 1830s, ambassadorial posts were rewards from the administration in power, and the qualifications that nominees brought to the office were distinctly secondary in importance to their political loyalty.

Noncareer ambassadorial nominations, whether of distinguished private citizens or of political supporters, are still made today, though the balance of the appointments has shifted in this century so that the majority are drawn from the ranks of the career Foreign Service. Since the early 1960s, through six administrations, ambassadors named from outside the career Service have constituted between 25 percent and 42 percent of the total at any given time, with the average slightly over 30 percent. Some, like Douglas Dillon, Ellsworth Bunker, and Mike Mansfield, have been in the tradition of the gifted amateur—individuals whose careers in other fields have brought them knowledge or skills that are especially appropriate to a particular ambassadorial assignment—and they have served with distinction. Others, chosen for political reasons rather than for their qualifications, either have muddled through or, in a few cases, have embarrassed the administration that named them.

The debate about the proper balance of career and noncareer chiefs of mission remains a Washington perennial.[1] Not surprisingly, career members of the Foreign Service contend strongly that professional experience gained during overseas diplomatic service should normally outweigh other considerations. The gifted amateur, in their view, should be the exception, chosen only when he or she brings to a post specific qualifications that members of the Service cannot match. Their cause has won a certain amount of sympathy in Congress, which incorporated into the 1980 Foreign Service Act requirements that chiefs of mission should possess a "clearly demonstrated competence" to perform their duties, "including, to the maximum extent practicable, a useful knowledge of the principal language or dialect of the country in which the individual is to serve, and knowledge and understanding of the history, the culture, the economic and political institutions, and the interests of that country and its people." In light of these requirements, the act continues, "positions as chief of mission should normally be accorded to career members of the Service," and "contributions to political campaigns should not be a factor" in such appointments.[2] Occasional attempts to go beyond this hortatory language by imposing a statutory limit on the percentage of noncareer chiefs of mission have thus far failed to muster a congressional majority.

On the other side of the argument, proponents of the judicious use of noncareer ambassadorial appointments point out that chiefs of mission are the president's personal representatives to other nations. In this role, they contend, what may be most important in a given situation is to have a representative the president knows and trusts, and who can cut through layers of bureaucracy when necessary to bring critical issues directly to the president's attention. Only appointees who are personally loyal to the president, they continue, can be counted on to give his foreign policy decisions the wholehearted support and vigorous execution he seeks. A complementary argument for noncareer chiefs of mission rests on a perception of the Foreign Service as an excessively cautious group of people who are too concerned with safeguarding their careers to be willing to take risks—and thus, who need shaking up from time to time by injecting new blood and new ideas at the ambassadorial level.

As this discussion suggests, the debate is not about whether there should be any noncareer chiefs of mission, which both sides seem to agree will remain a feature of the U.S. system. The discussion focuses instead on a possible limit on the number of noncareer appointees and, increasingly, on ensuring that all nominees—career as well as noncareer—are indeed qualified to serve as chiefs of mission. A Presidential Advisory Board on Ambassadorial Appointments was used during the Carter administration. It had only limited success, but it has inspired subsequent proposals for some form of professional screening body similar to the bodies that pass on prospective federal judges. The language of the 1980 Foreign Service Act further underscores the importance attached to finding an effective means of evaluating the qualifications of candidates for appointment as chief of mission.

Whether chosen from career ranks or from another profession, the new ambassador-designate has a great deal to learn in order to perform effectively at his or her new post. Even for career officers, the ambassadorial role is so different from what they have done before that the State Department includes FSO ambassadorial nominees in the three-day orientation it offers to first-time chiefs of mission—a series of lectures covering everything from dealing with intelligence activities to managing the official residence. Beyond this formal seminar, each new chief of mission, before leaving Washington, spends long hours mastering both the nature and extent of U.S. interests in the country to which he or she is being sent and the issues of principal concern in the bilateral relationship.

The learning phase does not end completely when the new chief of mission arrives at the post, but it does shift from full-time study to on-the-job training. An ambassador is in charge from the moment he or she steps off the plane to be met by the senior members of the embassy staff (at small posts, the entire staff may turn up at the airport for a look at the new boss). Although ambassadorial discretion in conducting diplomatic business has been circumscribed in this era of rapid telecommunications and special envoys, the authority of U.S.

chiefs of mission over U.S. government civilian employees abroad
has been significantly strengthened. In 1961, President Kennedy
sent a letter to all U.S. ambassadors affirming their authority
to "oversee and coordinate all the activities of the United States
Government" in the country to which they are accredited. "You
are in charge of the entire United States Diplomatic Mission,"
the presidential letter said, including not only State Department
personnel "but also the representatives of all other United States
agencies which have programs or activities" in the country.[3]
The only specific exclusion from this ambassadorial authority
was the U.S. military forces operating under a military area
command, but even here the chief of mission was instructed
to work closely with the area commander and to make his or
her views known.

The Kennedy letter, copies of which went to all executive-
branch agencies with personnel overseas, made it easier for
ambassadors to manage their sometimes fractious staffs. Its
statement of ambassadorial authority has been reaffirmed in a
similar message sent by every subsequent president and has
also been embodied in law. The first congressional pronounce-
ment along these lines came in a 1974 appropriations bill, the
language of which was picked up in the Foreign Service Act
of 1980. In the words of the latter statute, the chief of mission
has "full responsibility for the direction, coordination, and
supervision of all Government employees" in the country to
which he or she is accredited. The act requires that "any agency
having employees in a foreign country" keep the chief of mission
"fully and currently informed with respect to all activities and
operations of its employees in that country." Such agencies must
also ensure that their employees abroad "comply fully with all
applicable directives of the chief of mission."[4] The most recent
presidential letter, sent to all ambassadors by President Reagan
in 1981, refers to this "strong statutory mandate" in making
clear both to chiefs of mission and to the heads of executive
departments and agencies the president's expectation that it will
be enforced.

Although the ambassador is in charge of the mission from
the moment of arrival, the new chief of mission is in diplomatic
limbo on the local scene until he or she formally presents

credentials to the host chief of state. The delay may be anything from a few days to a month or more, depending on both local practice and the time of year (much of Europe, for example, vacations in the month of August). During this time in limbo, the ambassador may not pay formal calls either on government officials or on diplomatic colleagues, and a wise chief of mission will put the time to good use learning the strengths and weaknesses of the embassy staff.

The ceremonial presentation of credentials is one of the oldest traditions of diplomacy. As monarchies have dwindled in number around the world, the ceremony has lost some of the glamour that characterized it in days when envoys moved directly between two sovereigns, though some traces of this bygone era remain even in democratic societies. The process begins with a call by the ambassador on the country's foreign minister, to present copies of his or her letters of credence and the brief remarks he or she plans to make at the subsequent ceremony with the head of state. On the day of the formal presentation, the ambassador and senior colleagues are escorted by a Foreign Ministry protocol officer to the local equivalent of the White House. Although the traditional morning coat has given way in most capitals to a tailored dress or business suit, the defense attaché (if there is one at the mission) still adds a touch of color by appearing in uniform.

On arrival at the palace or presidential offices, the ambassador will normally be met by an honor guard, which is drawn up before the door for review. Once inside, the new chief of mission is greeted by the head of state, accompanied by anything from a handful of advisers to the entire government. The ambassador delivers prepared remarks (which the head of state has already read, thanks to the copy delivered in advance to the foreign minister), and the head of state responds with a few carefully chosen words of welcome. The two senior participants in the ceremony then retire to a more private setting, each usually with one or two aides, for fifteen or twenty minutes of conversation and refreshments, after which the ambassador is escorted back to the residence. The ceremony is over, and the ambassador is free to begin fulfilling all of his or her duties.

Ambassador Andrew Steigman and the Gabonese chief of protocol reviewing the Presidential Guard en route to present credentials—Libreville, Gabon, 1975.

From this point on, the full weight of the office descends on the ambassador's shoulders. The way each chief of mission spends the average workday varies enormously from one country to another. Are there pressing issues between the two governments that require constant high-level attention? Is there a large U.S. community placing demands on the ambassador's time? Are there many official visitors to whom the ambassador must devote time? Is there a heavy schedule of official entertainment impinging on the ambassador's time? Several former chiefs of mission and outside observers have written accounts of days in the life of a U.S. ambassador;[5] not surprisingly, they are alike only in the variety of tasks that confront a chief of mission on any given day and in the unpredictability of diplomatic life.

Whatever the nature of the workload, however, the basic responsibilities of the ambassador are essentially the same in every country of the world. Fundamentally, it is the ambassador's

Morning coat is still de rigueur at credentials ceremonies in some capitals—Ambassador and Mrs. John Condon with King Tupou IV of Tonga, 1980.

duty to preserve and advance the interests of the United States. Those interests may include such elements as security, trade, aid, access to resources, or protection of U.S. citizens. It is the ambassador's job to define for the entire mission staff the interests at stake in the country in which they serve and to mold their efforts into a concerted program for the preservation and advancement of those interests.

To do this job well, an ambassador must possess a unique blend of qualities and skills. To a considerable extent, a U.S.

The key moment of the ceremony: Ambassador Charles Dunbar delivers his credentials to the head of state in Qatar, 1983.

ambassador, wherever stationed, symbolizes the United States. The intelligence, sensitivity, and perception of the U.S. representative, and his or her ability to communicate American values and objectives, are critical to the way the United States will be viewed in the country to which that chief of mission is accredited—and to the ability of the embassy to accomplish its goals. In addition, the ambassador must be able to understand the political, economic, and social structures of the nation in which he or she serves, and to draw on this understanding in order to provide Washington with cogent analyses of current events and accurate forecasts of future developments.

In addition to this already formidable array of skills, keeping all elements of the embassy working together as a team requires considerable managerial talent. Although ambassadorial authority has been clearly spelled out, the representatives of most agencies still depend more on Washington than on the chief of mission for their career prospects, and thus, they may believe that compliance with the wishes of their home agencies is more important to their futures than responsiveness to ambassadorial directives. An ambassador with a good working knowledge of the Washington policy-making process can sometimes use personal contacts in the home agencies to help keep restless subordinates in harness, but diplomatic, managerial, and leadership skills are the basic tools in assuring a team effort by the entire mission staff.

To an increasing extent, ambassadors must also be skilled in the field of public relations. The ability to communicate effectively has long been an essential quality for successful diplomats, but this skill traditionally was used to convey information and to negotiate in private sessions. In today's world, however, the ambassador has become a public figure and must be able to deal with the media and with large audiences as well as with individual officials. As the foreign affairs positions of governments become more and more dependent on the broadly held views of their citizens, ambassadors are called on to help inform those citizens about the objectives and actions of the United States.

Finally, the ambassador must be sensitive to the needs of fellow citizens, from resident business people and embassy staff members to visiting members of Congress and tourists. An ambassador sets the tone not only for the embassy staff, toward whom the relationship is a mixture of in loco parentis and feudal overlord, but also for the entire U.S. community in the country. U.S. citizens abroad look to the chief of mission as a counselor and leader, particularly in areas of potential trouble where their security can become one of the ambassador's most delicate preoccupations.

In order to carry out his or her responsibilities, the ambassador—both personally and working through the embassy staff—must seek constantly to build and maintain effective working relationships in key sectors of the host government and society. Without a network that extends to all the potential players in the process of political, economic, and social change, the mission may be unable to anticipate future developments of critical importance to the United States—a lesson relearned most dramatically in Iran in the 1970s, when religious fundamentalists who were little known to U.S. officials emerged triumphant from a power struggle that toppled a U.S. ally. In addition, broad contacts serve to facilitate the task of fostering support for U.S. views and policies, one of the fundamental goals of every U.S. mission abroad.

The process of building and maintaining contacts can pose difficult choices for an ambassador. Ideally, embassy and consulate personnel should move freely throughout the society, talking not only with those currently in power but also with opponents of the regime who might someday occupy the seat of government. In some countries, however, governments are concerned that contacts with foreign diplomats will be claimed by members of an actual or a potential opposition as evidence that they enjoy external support, so the governments thus discourage, or even forbid, such contacts. (This was the case, for example, in Iran, where the government's hostility to embassy attempts to meet with opponents of the shah was a factor in limiting contacts and thus the range of information available to the embassy.) When this situation occurs, the ambassador must decide whether maintaining contacts with opposition elements is sufficiently important to risk incurring the displeasure of the government to which he or she is accredited. Sometimes a delicate balance can be struck by confining contacts with the opposition to the lower-level personnel of the embassy while the ambassador personally observes the wishes of the host government. If the government still objects, however, its wishes usually prevail, and the embassy is forced to operate at a severe disadvantage.

The restrictions can be applied subtly by "suggesting" a preferred pattern of behavior to a foreign diplomat. They can also be enforced by administrative fiat, as is done in a number of countries; for example, some require that all invitations to their citizens be transmitted through their Ministry of Foreign Affairs. Governments also use similar controls to limit the ability of diplomatic and consular personnel to observe personally what is going on outside the cities in which they are stationed and to develop contacts with citizens in the provincial centers. Travel throughout the country of assignment should be part of the job of every ambassador and of those staff members who have reporting responsibilities. Here again, however, nervous governments frequently impose restrictions—from requirements of lengthy advance notice ("so preparations can be made to receive you properly on your visit") to total prohibitions on travel to certain areas—which make an embassy's job more difficult.

The authority and responsibility of an ambassador can be very heady wine indeed. The deference paid to chiefs of mission by their own staffs, by host government officials, and by private citizens can be equally intoxicating, and it has diminished surprisingly little from the days when ambassadors represented sovereigns who considered themselves anointed by God. They are addressed as "Madam Ambassador" or "Mister Ambassador" by the embassy staff and other fellow citizens, as "The Honorable" John or Jane Doe in correspondence, and as "Excellency" by non-Americans, and they are normally the objects of considerable bowing and scraping. This kind of deference can erode perspective, and every ambassador needs to temper it regularly with touches of humility and a sense of humor. As one seasoned practitioner of diplomacy remarked, "The classic advice to take one's job seriously but never oneself is nowhere more applicable than to chiefs of diplomatic missions."[6]

The Deputy Chief of Mission

At all but the smallest embassies, the ambassador has an officer who is specifically designated to share the burdens of command—the deputy chief of mission, known familiarly as the DCM. The title is a coveted one for ambitious FSOs, who see it as a step on the career ladder toward eligibility for an ambassadorial post of their own (although serving as DCM has never been a formal prerequisite for becoming an ambassador, about two-thirds of career officer chiefs of mission have done so). The position of DCM is also considered one of the highest-risk jobs in the Foreign Service. Although there is no hard

Travel throughout the country is part of the job—Ambassador Hume Horan visits a pygmy tribe in the interior of Cameroon, 1983.

evidence to prove the contention, there is a widespread belief that half of all first-time DCMs "fail" at the job in some unspecified way.

What makes the position so difficult is the fact that there are no clear-cut guidelines regarding its content and responsibilities. In effect, each chief of mission defines the role of his or her own DCM. Some ambassadors want DCMs who are true alter egos, privy to all of the chief of mission's thoughts and able to make decisions in the boss's name. Others prefer that the DCM act as chief executive officer, ensuring coordination among mission elements and implementation of the ambassador's decisions but not taking independent action. Some want the DCM to be active in the local community; others want the DCM to handle "inside" chores while the ambassador handles contacts and ceremony. If the chief of mission makes his or her expectations clear to the DCM, there is every chance of an effective and harmonious relationship. All too often, however, the DCM is left to guess the ambassador's wishes with regard to his or her role. A wrong guess can provoke mistrust and unhappiness, and another "failed" DCM.

To be effective in the number-two role, the DCM must have many of the same qualities needed by a successful ambassador, especially the strong managerial skills that are required to coordinate the work of an embassy team. This need becomes particularly critical when an ambassador is away from the post or when there is a gap between chiefs of mission, at which time the DCM steps into the breach with the formal designation of chargé d'affaires ad interim. Until the chief of mission returns or a new ambassador arrives, the DCM shoulders the full responsibility for the embassy and its operations. The opportunity to run the show is welcomed by most DCMs as a chance to demonstrate their ability to command, but they are constrained in their actions by the knowledge that their moment of glory will be relatively short and that any steps they take will soon be subject to critical review by a returned or new ambassador. Indeed, most periods of service as chargé d'affaires are brief, covering ambassadorial consultations or holidays of a few weeks. Occasionally, however, a DCM will "strike it rich" by being left to preside for a year or more when there is a delay in naming a new ambassador.

One of the hardest things for a first-time DCM to avoid is a natural tendency to keep on doing whatever it is that he or she does best—the political or administrative or cultural work that previously has been the substance of the officer's career. The overall demands of the DCM's job, along with its reputedly high "failure rate," can lead DCMs to devote a disproportionate amount of time to the area in which they feel most comfortable and confident. This emphasis can mean both that the DCM neglects other critical areas of the embassy's operation and that there is a feeling of frustration on the part of the staff members of the particular section of the embassy that the DCM is doing what rightfully should be their work. Neither is a healthy situation, and the DCM must be careful to leave the professionals in each embassy section enough room to do their proper jobs.

The Country Team

At all but the smallest embassies, the task of keeping all the members of the team pulling in the same direction is a constant challenge. To achieve this purpose, the ambassador or DCM (especially the latter) will meet regularly with the heads of the mission's component elements and will monitor the cable traffic flowing between Washington and the various sections of the embassy. In addition, most chiefs of mission and DCMs, like their counterparts in Washington, utilize staff meetings of varying size and composition to bring members of their team together. Some ambassadors prefer to meet daily with a handful of key officers and weekly with a larger group; others, less fond of such sessions, may leave most of this chore to their DCMs and appear only irregularly.

The one meeting at which even the most reluctant ambassador usually can be counted on to appear in person is the gathering of the "country team." The country team concept was devised in 1951 as an initial response to the erosion of ambassadorial authority that had occurred during and after World War II when the number of government agencies operating abroad increased significantly. The heads of military and economic aid missions, who had considered themselves relatively independent of ambassadorial control, were to "constitute a team under the leadership of the Ambassador,"[7] and the team was to meet regularly to seek appropriate coordination of all U.S. activities in the country. Like many other management innovations, the country-team concept proved valuable to ambassadors strong enough to use it effectively and less helpful when the heads of the assistance programs were able to make their views prevail over a less confident chief of mission. As we have seen, ambassadorial authority was subsequently reinforced by both executive order and statute. In consequence, the country-team concept remains an important symbolic representation of the cooperative effort that ideally should emerge in each country, but it no longer carries the excessive burden of being the only device for keeping an embassy team in harness.

Because the concept of a team effort remains so important to the effectiveness of an embassy's operations, meetings of the country team—albeit simply another kind of staff meeting—tend to take on a special aura. Each ambassador is free to constitute and to use the country team as he or she finds most useful. If the ambassador at our hypothetical embassy wanted to use the country team as a sounding board for sensitive policy decisions, the membership might be restricted to the DCM; the heads of the political and economic sections; the USIS, AID, and MAAG chiefs; and the defense attaché. With this relatively limited group, the chief of mission might seek to stimulate an exchange of views and information on such issues as the likelihood of a coup, the desirability of an expanded aid program, the prospects for winning support from the host government for a U.S. initiative at the United Nations, or the political implications of persistent violations of human rights by local authorities.

As with any such meeting, limiting the membership can make dialogue easier and leakage less likely, but such limitation can also risk leaving out valuable sources of information. The agricultural attaché, for example, may know that drought conditions will soon lead to urban food shortages, which will have potentially serious consequences for the stability of the government; the consul general may have learned from recent visa applications that government leaders are sending their families out of the country; or the counselor for commercial affairs may be hearing new murmurs of discontent from a business community that has traditionally been loyal to the party in power. If these officers are not present at a country-team meeting in which political stability is being discussed, their views and information must be carefully gathered in advance, or the "regulars" run a serious risk of coming to very wrong conclusions.

Some chiefs of mission hold country-team sessions that are virtually indistinguishable in content from regular embassy staff meetings (and only slightly smaller in composition). Although such sessions may occasionally prompt a discussion of major policy issues, meetings of this kind are more likely to serve as an opportunity for the chief of mission to hear progress reports on the work of various embassy components, issue fresh instructions, and redefine basic policy goals for the entire staff. Even this limited use of the country team, however, acknowledges its importance as a symbol of the coordinated effort that the mission seeks to achieve and the endurance of the basic concept.

The Political Section

The political section has traditionally come second only to the executive section in any discussion of an embassy's constituent elements, in large measure because its core functions—reporting, negotiation, and representation—are at the heart of traditional diplomatic practice. In addition, the political section also owes its prominent place on every list to the fact that before 1924, its functions belonged to the perceived elite who then constituted the Diplomatic Service. The "political officers" from the old Diplomatic Service set the tone for the entire Foreign Service even after the Rogers Act merged the Diplomatic and Consular Services, and they tended to view with condescension all fields other than their own. This impression of political officers as a breed apart from, and somewhat above, the common herd has not entirely disappeared from the modern Foreign Service, but it is being vitiated by the current career structure, which brings candidates of comparable backgrounds into all four cones and encourages them to seek broad experience as they advance through the ranks (see Chapter 4).

Today's political officers are very different from their fore-bears, who tended to speak only to the Foreign Ministry, to other diplomats, and to a small elite of social leaders. The United States has learned and relearned since World War II that no element in a society may safely be overlooked in attempting to predict a country's future course, and much of the responsibility for guarding against fresh surprises rests with the political section. In consequence, political officers are expected to "cover the waterfront" in their range of contacts and acquaintances so that their reporting and analysis of political events of importance to the United States will reflect the broadest possible base of information. In the State Department's words, they "maintain close contact with political and labor leaders, third-country diplomats, and others of influence"[8]—the others may include anyone from military officers and clergymen to youth groups and university professors. The goal of this effort is a thorough understanding of the political forces, power structure, and per-sonalities of the country in which the officers are serving, as a foundation both for timely and accurate reporting and for effective performance of the political officers' other tasks.

This assessment is not meant to suggest that political officers do not spend a substantial part of their time talking to officials of the host government. If the government is one with which the United States maintains cordial relations, its officials may be among the political officer's most valuable sources of infor-mation. Even if the relationship is not especially friendly, the political officer (like his or her colleagues elsewhere in the mission) has the task of conveying the U.S. government's views to the host government and of soliciting its support for those views and for the policies that flow from them. When a key vote is pending in the United Nations, for example, it is the political officer who normally will be charged with explaining the U.S. position to the Foreign Ministry and asking that its representative be instructed to vote with the United States in New York. On a closely contested issue, the outcome may depend on the ability of political officers around the world to state the U.S. case with sufficient persuasiveness to win the necessary votes. Here again, the political officer who brings to the task a thorough understanding of the host country's own concerns as well as those of the United States is most likely to be able to find a thread of common interest to make his or her arguments more effective.

The qualities required for success as a political officer are, by and large, those that are needed in any of the Foreign Service's functional fields. The political officer, like officers in the other cones or agencies, must be an effective communicator, able to present ideas cogently in both oral and written form. He or she must be sensitive to both individual and group dynamics—able to sense when something is "not quite right" or when a host government official is saying "yes" out of courtesy, not with conviction. He or she must be able to think clearly and unemotionally in order to analyze the available facts and to draw logical conclusions. And, perhaps most critical, the political officer, like all members of the Service, must have the courage to report objectively and honestly even when the truth may be unpopular either at home or in the executive section of the embassy.

The importance—and sometimes the difficulty—of scrupulously honest reporting cannot be overstressed. If the ambassador or Washington officials insist that a policy is working, and the officer in the field uncovers evidence to the contrary, there may be considerable pressure to suppress the unwelcome news. Knowing full well that the messenger is sometimes held responsible for bad news, the officer may be sorely tempted to take the easy way out (and to protect his or her career) by letting the evidence go unreported. Members of the Service have more than once put their careers on the line to report the truth as they saw it, sometimes by using the dissent channel (see Chapter 5), and have still managed to attain senior positions. In the long run (and sometimes sooner than expected), the truth will out, and the individual with the courage to tell it sets the standard for other officers.

There is one respect in which some political officers *are* different from their colleagues in other fields, for it is among the political officers that the greatest concentration of language and area specialists is found—those officers who devote from one to three years of their careers to intensive study of a particular country or region and its principal language. Officers in other cones and agencies spend a great deal of time studying languages, including those requiring a year or more of effort to master, but their stock in trade is more likely to be functional skills, which are transferable from one part of the world to another, than an in-depth knowledge of a single area.

In addition to specializing in a particular area of the world, officers in the political cone can also opt to spend part of their careers in one of three subfunctions: labor, science, and politico-military affairs. The work of politico-military officers in Washington in the hypothetical policy process is described in Chapter 5. Officers serving overseas in this field will normally be assigned to posts in countries where the United States has either a military alliance relationship or military facilities, and they will be involved in reporting events in their field of responsibility, in negotiating military-related agreements, and in helping to resolve any difficulties that arise. Science officers, who may be drawn from any of the four State Department FSO cones and who need not have a background in "hard" science, represent one of the real "growth industries" of postwar diplomacy. Scientific issues have become increasingly prominent in a wide range of foreign policy questions, and the Foreign Service has introduced special training programs in an effort to develop the scientific literacy that is needed to deal effectively with them. At posts abroad, science officers have particular responsibility for coordinating programs for cooperation and exchange and for reporting developments in the scientific field. In countries that have a nuclear capability, science officers may also play a key role in efforts to enforce nonproliferation agreements.

Of the three political subfunctions, labor is the one with the longest history. The first labor attachés (or labor officers) were added to embassies in 1943. They grew in both number and importance after World War II, particularly in Europe where organized labor was a key target for both sides in the developing Cold War. Many of the earliest labor attachés came directly from the labor movement, initially on short-term appointments in what was then the Foreign Service Reserve category. A number of these officers converted to career Foreign Service status and stayed on, and their ranks were augmented by new recruits from organized labor and by regular FSOs who tried the new field and found it to their liking.

Although most of the veterans of organized labor did only labor work during their Foreign Service careers, the exam-entry FSOs have tended to spend only one or two tours in labor affairs before returning to the political mainstream. Since most new entrants into the labor field in recent years have come from within the FSO corps, this tendency has led to a lower level of in-depth knowledge and experience in the labor field and to expressions of concern from the Department of Labor that these less experienced officers may not be able to meet all of Labor's needs. On the other side of the coin, the change in composition of the body of labor officers has also brought the offsetting benefit that more and more political officers have had first-hand experience of labor affairs and thus are better able to take account of labor-related factors in reaching overall political judgments.

The debate between the State and Labor departments about the most appropriate way to staff the labor subfunction is lively. State is comfortable with the current situation, in which most labor duties are performed by regular FSOs, either as full-time labor attachés or on a part-time basis when the labor role does not justify the assignment of a full-time officer. For the present, State's view has basically prevailed, but with assurances to the Department of Labor that officers entering the labor field will be given adequate training and that special promotion consideration at the Senior Foreign Service level will be given to officers who have chosen to devote a substantial part of their careers to the labor field.

The work done by labor attachés (full-time) and labor officers (part-time) is essentially the same as the work done by all political officers, except that it is concentrated in a single sector of society. They report developments within the host country's labor movement and in the laws and policies that affect it. They join with their colleagues in seeking to predict the outcome of elections and extraparliamentary power struggles, in which labor often plays a key role. They work with the international affiliates of the U.S. labor movement to encourage free trade unions, and they may be involved in working with local labor groups on aid programs in such areas as the training of workers. And, of course, in order to perform these tasks effectively, they too seek out the widest possible circle of contacts in the labor field.

The Economic Section

The work of the embassy's economic officers largely parallels that of their colleagues in the political section (though they deal with a different subject matter) and also traces its origins back to the earliest days of U.S. representation abroad. Thomas Jefferson, as secretary of state, asked his sixteen consuls overseas to send him "such political and commercial intelligence as you may think interesting to the United States,"[9] and his successors turned economic reporting into a major activity—first for the separate Consular Service and then for the unified Foreign Service.

Today's economic officers, like their historic forebears, analyze and report on key economic trends and events that affect U.S. interests, gathering information both from published sources and from contacts with U.S. and foreign business people, bankers, economists, government officials, and political leaders. Like the political officers, they present the United States' views to the host government and seek support for U.S. policies in the economic field. Indeed, the interdependence of political and economic issues is so great that several embassies have simply combined their political and economic officers into a single section. Some who have done so report positive results, but the innovation has not been widely copied.

Since the work of the two sections is so similar, the qualities needed to do it well are also much the same: an ability to speak and write clearly, political and cultural sensitivity, skill at making cool and logical analyses, and the courage to report honestly even in the face of pressure to the contrary. The economic officer, however, must also have sufficient knowledge of economics to hold his or her own in professional company. For a number of years, the minimum requirement was an undergraduate degree in economics or equivalent training provided by a five-month intensive economics course offered by the Foreign Service Institute, supplemented for a few officers each year by additional graduate study at any of several leading universities. With the addition of FSI's mid-level course, all officers in the economic cone now receive a healthy amount of graduate-level instruction in economics immediately after receiving career status, an important first step toward the goal of ensuring a higher level of economic skills throughout the Service.

The range of topics for which the economic sections are responsible underlines the importance of a thorough grounding in economic skills. Depending on the post, an economic officer may be called on to analyze the economic situation of the host country or the status of its foreign debt; to assist in negotiating an agreement covering anything from U.S. investments to civil aviation; to report on developments in the local petroleum or textile industry; or to help a U.S. business person find an agent for his or her products or to cut through government red tape. In the over sixty countries in which the Foreign Commercial Service is represented, the last of these tasks would fall to the counselor for commercial affairs and his or her staff, but commercial affairs are still the responsibility of the economic section at all other posts around the world.

The economic field, like the political one, has several subspecialties to which officers may be attracted. Among these is science, which draws from both the economic and the political cones; transportation and communications; economic resources and commodities; and finance and economic development. The transportation and resources fields, as their names suggest, are highly specialized and offer only a handful of full-time positions in the State Department and at posts abroad. Financial economists, however, have a wider range of positions open to them, and they constitute the largest subspecialty within the economic cone. Officers who are qualified in this area, usually as a result of graduate study, can expect to focus their attention on such matters as monetary and banking problems, exchange rates, balance of payments, foreign loans, and international financial agreements.

The Consular Section

The consular section of an embassy or consulate has been aptly described as "the U.S. Government's human face to its own citizens and to the citizens of the host country."[10] Most U.S. citizens who visit overseas posts come in search of assistance, and it is the consular officer who furnishes them the services they require. For foreign nationals, the quest is usually for a U.S. visa in order to visit the United States, and once again it is the consular officer who will grant or deny their requests. Thus, it is not surprising that the consular officer is often perceived by both U.S. and foreign citizens as holding their future in his or her hands—what one experienced consular officer has described as "a heady but burdensome role in which to be cast."[11]

By the nature of their jobs, consular officers work more closely with the public than do any other members of the mission's staff. By far the largest number of consular officers worldwide (roughly two-thirds of the total) deal with visa applicants. Under U.S. law, both intending immigrants and prospective visitors must obtain visas before they may seek entry into the United States. (This is a fine but important point: A U.S. visa only allows *application* for entry, leaving the final decision to the Immigration and Naturalization Service; it does not guarantee admission to the United States.) Every potential traveler to the United States must therefore deal with a U.S. embassy or consulate and must persuade a consular officer that he or she is qualified under U.S. law to receive the desired visa. In countries like England or Japan, visas for tourists or business visitors are relatively routine, and most are issued on the basis of mail applications. Elsewhere in the world, however, where the pressure to emigrate to the United States is more severe, all requests must be carefully screened to weed out false applications and fraudulent documents, and there are countries in which the number of refusals exceeds the number of visas granted.

For U.S. travelers and residents abroad, the consular officer represents the United States away from home in time of need.

Consular sections provide a number of relatively routine services for U.S. citizens, from issuing passports and recording births to notarizing documents and forwarding Social Security checks. (When an individual's citizenship is in question, some of these services become anything but routine and may require both careful investigation and Solomonic judgment before a complex case can be decided.) In addition, the consular officer is there to help U.S. citizens who have been involved in a serious accident or have an emergency; to assist fellow citizens who run afoul of local law and assure them equal treatment in court or in jail with nationals of the host country; to deal with problems of U.S. vessels and seamen; to try to trace lost relatives; to arrange care and passage home for the sick or destitute; and to make necessary arrangements when U.S. citizens die overseas.

At a small post, a single consular officer may deal with the full range of consular affairs, issuing visas and passports and visiting jailed U.S. citizens in the course of a single day. At a larger post such as the one outlined in Table 6.2, the work of each officer in the consular section will tend to be more specialized, and there will be distinct subunits within the consular section for visas and for services to U.S. citizens. If the demand for visas is heavy, three of the four subordinate officers in our hypothetical section would probably spend their time on this function while the fourth officer would take care of U.S. citizens in need of assistance. Within the visa unit, two career candidate FSOs would do most of the actual visa issuance while a more seasoned consular officer would keep a watchful eye on the overall visa operation and provide advice and guidance to the more junior staff.

In addition to providing this array of services to the public on an individual basis, consular officers become involved in many of the same kinds of activities that occupy their colleagues elsewhere in the embassy. They too must develop and maintain a wide circle of contacts in the local government and society and contribute information and analysis to the post's reporting on developments of interest to the United States. When consular questions are at issue with the host government, it most often is the consular officer who will deal with local officials to resolve the issue or to expedite negotiation of an agreement. And, in the increasingly important areas of immigration and refugee policy, it is the consular officer who has been called on in recent years to play a leading role.

To be effective in performing this range of duties, a consular officer needs many of the same qualities as his or her colleagues in economic or political work. In addition, however, the consular officer must be comfortable with a job that involves working closely with large numbers of people and making rapid and firm decisions on issues that affect the lives of those people—the "burdensome" element of the consular role. Consular officers must also become expert in the intricacies of U.S. visa and nationality law and regulation and knowledgeable about the automated systems that have been developed to support consular operations. First-time consular officers receive basic instruction in the fundamentals of visa and citizenship law and of consular operations. All career consular officers explore these topics in greater depth during the mid-level course, and some of them go on to a year of university study in systems management or another consular-related topic.

For a number of years, consular operations were staffed in large part by a group of non-FSO specialists, and relatively few career FSOs opted to remain in consular work for more than one or two tours. The introduction of the cone system, under which FSOs are hired to work in one of four specific functional fields, has drastically changed the composition of the consular field. Today's consular officers are exam-entry FSOs with backgrounds and qualifications essentially identical to those of their colleagues in the other cones. They are encouraged to seek breadth of experience through work in other functional areas and to find opportunities in their own field to develop both management and policy skills. In consequence, the new breed of consular officers should prove fully qualified for a broad range of senior positions as they move up the career ladder.

The Administrative Section

In the early years of U.S. diplomacy, there was no such thing as an administrative section. More than one U.S. minister or consul spent his first months at a new post in a full-time search for a home and an office, unable to begin serious work until his lodging problems had been solved. Apart from a few buildings given to the United States by friendly governments, all premises were rented by the incumbent U.S. representatives, who had to make arrangements for plumbing repairs as well as conducting diplomatic or consular business. Not until 1911 did Congress appropriate money to buy property abroad for diplomatic and consular use, but prior to World War II, the authority was seldom used for anything beyond office buildings and ambassadorial residences. As a result, there was relatively little U.S. government property to be looked after, and administrative services at most posts tended to be the province of a single employee—full-time at the larger missions and part-time elsewhere.

The expansion in the number of U.S. civilian personnel overseas after World War II, and the proliferation of agencies involved, coincided with a time when goods and services were not readily available in many of the countries in which Americans were called upon to serve. Officers with other responsibilities could not spend the time required to arrange for such mundane but necessary matters as telephone service, furnace repairs, or travel arrangements and still get their work done. Nor were many of the new people working abroad as well equipped as the Foreign Service professionals to cope with the problems of obtaining goods and services in a difficult environment. The necessary response was that the U.S. government began providing civilian employees overseas with many of the same kinds of administrative support that routinely had been made available to the military—in some instances, even finding housing for most members of a staff.

The extension of the U.S. diplomatic presence to a number of newly independent nations during the 1950s and 1960s made government-supplied goods and facilities even more necessary. Many of the new capitals in the third world found it difficult to provide housing and services for the influx of foreign embassies, and even when they could cope, the sudden surge in demand often sent prices sky-high. To meet the immediate need and keep costs under control, the U.S. government resorted increasingly to building housing compounds as well as office buildings and ambassadorial residences, and in some areas regional supply centers were established to cut down on the delivery time of essential goods.

All of this increased activity required administrative personnel on a scale far beyond anything the Foreign Service had previously known. Initially, most of the administrative support was provided by specialists hired into the Foreign Service reserve or specialist categories to perform specific functions, and only a handful of exam-entry FSOs worked in the administrative field. Only with the introduction of the cone system did the pattern begin to change (as it also did in the consular field), so that today, most of the personnel doing general administrative work and a large number of those working in the administrative subspecialties are drawn from FSO ranks.

The administrative section at a post abroad may be anything from a single junior officer supervising a handful of Foreign Service national employees to a veritable empire, with several dozen U.S. employees and several hundred FSNs. Its size will tend to be directly proportionate to the total number of U.S. employees for whom the embassy provides services. The administrative section of an embassy furnishes logistic support to all the agencies attached to the mission, which reimburse the State Department annually for their share of the total expenses incurred. When there is a large AID contingent, the administrative section may be transformed into a Joint Administrative Organization (JAO), with staffing shared between AID and the State Department to ensure that the needs of both agencies can be met in full.

At our hypothetical embassy, the counselor for administration manages a section staffed entirely by State Department employees. Subordinates responsible for general services, budget and fiscal, and personnel operations may be either FSOs or Foreign Service specialists (FPs), and the balance of the section (except for the marine guards) will be staffed by FPs. Positions in each of the three principal administrative subspecialties are shared among FSOs in the administrative cone—for whom experience in all three fields is desirable in preparation for more senior responsibilities—and general services, budget and fiscal, and personnel specialists, who normally are expected to serve only within their particular field.

The general services officers, as the name suggests, have jobs with a great deal of variety. They are responsible for managing and maintaining the embassy's real estate, keeping it supplied with everything from typewriter ribbons to fuel oil, arranging for the receipt and shipment of household goods for members of the mission staff, keeping the embassy's cars on the road, and almost any other logistic problem that arises. General services officers get the complaints about blocked sinks and leaking roofs, and their ability and willingness to respond promptly and cheerfully can be a critical element in maintaining employee morale.

Both the budget and fiscal officer and the personnel officer perform functions that are more predictable. The former develops the embassy's operating budget and financial plan and then handles all the transactions involved in carrying them out, including preparing and certifying vouchers and making payments to suppliers and to employees. The personnel officer at a post overseas is involved primarily with the administration of programs for the embassy's FSN employees, since most personnel actions concerning U.S. employees are handled in Washington. Simply by being available as an adviser to individual employees and to the post's senior management, a good personnel officer nonetheless constitutes a valuable resource for the entire embassy staff.

In recent years, security officers have become increasingly important members of embassy complements. When the program was first established, the principal responsibility of security officers was the protection of sensitive material against loss or compromise. As the threat to diplomatic and consular personnel from terrorism has grown, however, the security of their embassy or consulate colleagues has become their number-one priority in many parts of the world. A number of security officers overseas have regional assignments, which means covering more than one country from a single base; this is especially the case for the still-more-specialized security engineering officers, who handle the installation and maintenance of the protective security systems that have become so much a feature of modern diplomatic life.

The security officer also serves as the supervisor of the embassy's marine guard detachment, which protects both the offices of the mission and the classified material they contain. The U.S. Marine Corps has been helping the Foreign Service and its predecessors since 1805, when the U.S. consul in Tunis enlisted the aid of a small marine detachment in an expedition to capture Tripoli. Marines have come to the rescue of diplomats and consuls under siege in Latin America and during the Boxer Rebellion in China, and have been providing guards for U.S. missions abroad since the first U.S. Embassy in Moscow opened for business in 1933.

Today, there are marine detachments at about half of the Foreign Service posts around the world. Each detachment is commanded by a noncommissioned officer known familiarly as "the gunny" (since most have the rank of gunnery sergeant) and is composed entirely of carefully chosen volunteers who have undergone a special training program. The number of "watchstanders" depends on the size of the mission and the number of buildings requiring guards; five is the minimum, and some larger embassies have as many as thirty-five marines. The marine corps prefers that "the gunny" be married, to provide stability for the detachment, but requires that the watchstanders remain single until the end of their two-year tours of duty.

The final major element of the administrative section is one of the most critical to embassy operations—the communications unit, which maintains and operates the umbilical cord linking the post to Washington. At the very smallest posts, a single employee will handle all the communications chores, from preparing the sacks of official mail (diplomatic pouches) to sending and receiving the cable traffic, and he or she may use local commercial facilities for the latter task. Most posts, however, have their own communications facilities, using state-of-the-art telecommunications equipment to provide prompt and secure links to the State Department and to other missions. Handling this sophisticated equipment requires a staff of highly trained specialists, backstopped by roving technicians in each region of the world who can perform any repairs necessary to keep the lines open. When the communicators at a post are not on duty twenty-four hours a day, one of them will always be on call to assure that the mission is never out of touch with the home office.

The Foreign Commercial Service

Before the FCS began operations in 1980, the work it now performs in over sixty countries around the world was the responsibility of a combined economic/commercial section at each post, staffed entirely by State Department employees. Some elements of the U.S. business community felt that commercial work came off second best under this arrangement and pressed for a separate service that would have the promotion of U.S. exports and the support of U.S. business as its number-one priority. Their efforts bore fruit in one part of the Trade Reorganization Act of 1979, which provided for creation of the FCS within the Department of Commerce as its new overseas arm.

Today, the FCS is represented in those countries that constitute the most important actual or potential markets for U.S. products. Its personnel act as brokers between U.S. and foreign businesses and between the U.S. government and foreign governments in a never-ending effort to maintain and expand U.S. exports. They identify agents and distributors for companies wishing to enter a new market, they help to locate sources of financing for businesses, and they conduct market research for U.S. firms. They introduce local business representatives who wish to import or represent U.S. products to U.S. firms, and they help resolve trade and investment disputes. In cooperation with other sections of the mission, they work with host government officials to reduce statutory or regulatory barriers to U.S. trade. They also organize trade promotion programs and exhibitions, and in some countries, they run an Export Development Office such as the one shown as a part of the hypothetical mission in Table 6.2.

Since the FCS, like Eve, was created by taking a rib from a living body, the process caused a certain amount of discomfort on both sides. The State Department resented having some of its functions stripped away, particularly since the action was accompanied by both implied and overt criticism of the adequacy of State's previous handling of commercial work. State was also unhappy about losing personnel resources to Commerce, since the overseas operations of FCS were staffed initially by transferring positions from the State Department complement to the Department of Commerce. On the FCS side, there was an early flexing of muscles as "the new kid on the block" sought to ensure that its turf would be fully recognized by other agencies, especially by ambassadors and counselors for economic affairs at posts abroad. In this situation, there could easily have been serious friction between State and Commerce in implementing the trade reorganization plan. Fortunately, however, senior officials on both sides made clear their firm intention of having a smooth transition and continuing cooperation, and their message was honored in both the letter and the spirit at all but a handful of posts. In consequence, the establishment of the FCS took place with only occasional squabbles, and there was no hiatus in the critical task of promoting U.S. exports.

The Foreign Agricultural Service

The FAS was reborn in 1954 for much the same reason that led to the creation of the FCS twenty-five years later: there was a job to be done promoting the sale of U.S. products abroad and a general feeling that the State Department personnel then serving overseas were not getting that job done. In this earlier case, however, there was a specific category of exports to be promoted—agricultural products—and a level of specialized skills was required for successful performance that the State Department contingent simply did not possess. In the thirty years since 1954, farm products have become the most valuable single category of U.S. exports, and this situation is due in large measure to the effectiveness of FAS efforts over the three decades and is graphic testimony to the continuing importance of its work abroad.

Today, there are FAS representatives in nearly sixty countries around the world. Most are attached as counselors for agricultural affairs or as agricultural attachés to U.S. embassies, but nearly a dozen head Agricultural Trade Offices, which they share with representatives of U.S. trade associations that cooperate with the Department of Agriculture in market development. The work of FAS personnel overseas in promoting agricultural exports substantially parallels that of their FCS colleagues with regard to other product categories. FAS personnel identify market opportunities, assist U.S. exporters, and work with host government officials to seek the reduction or elimination of barriers to U.S. trade. They also play a key role in administering the food aid and technical assistance programs of the Department of Agriculture. In addition, they report extensively on the agricultural output of the countries in which they serve, since the prospects for U.S. exporters are directly affected by the size of competing crops around the world. Crop forecasts by FAS representatives do not always agree with those of their host governments, which may be excessively optimistic for political reasons (or may be pessimistic to keep market prices high). Over the years, however, FAS projections have been so consistently correct that other governments have used them on occasion for planning purposes in preference to the figures produced by their own officials.

The Animal and Plant Health Inspection Service

APHIS, as its name implies, is concerned primarily with protecting U.S. agriculture from economically harmful pests and diseases. In that effort, the agency's Foreign Service component represents the first line of defense. Its international programs got their start in Mexico in the late 1940s, when the U.S. and Mexican governments joined forces in an attempt to control two major animal diseases, hog cholera and African swine fever, and to prevent their spread across the common border. During the 1970s, the veterinary programs were extended into Central and South America, and the APHIS plant protection and quarantine division bolstered its overseas operation to defend against threats from the Mediterranean fruit fly.

Some 70 percent of the APHIS Foreign Service positions are still located in Mexico in connection with cooperative programs (at nineteen locations in addition to Mexico City), but the service has since spread its operations to other countries and other activities. In all, APHIS now has personnel in about twenty nations around the world, from Peru to Australia. The range of activities includes joint programs on the Mexican model, some administered by special bilateral commissions, and pre-clearance of agricultural exports destined for the United States to certify them as free of pests and diseases.

The United States Information Service

USIS, the overseas arm of the United States Information Agency (USIA), is almost as widely dispersed abroad as the State Department element of the Foreign Service. USIS today has personnel at over two hundred locations abroad, most of them attached to embassies and consulates though a few serve in cities in which there is no regular Foreign Service post. These USIS establishments vary in size from one U.S. officer to as many as two dozen. The typical post will be located within an embassy. Most such posts are headed by a public affairs officer (PAO), who holds the title of counselor for public affairs if the size of the mission and his or her personal rank warrant it. The PAO has overall responsibility for the management and supervision of the public affairs activities of the embassy, and also advises the ambassador and other members of the mission staff on trends in local public opinion and their implications for U.S. foreign policy.

At the larger USIS posts, there may be a deputy public affairs officer to assist the PAO in much the same way a DCM backstops an ambassador in carrying out the work of the mission as a whole. The staff may also include an executive officer if the program budget and logistics are sufficiently complex to require an in-house expert to supplement the general support received from the embassy's administrative section.

The work of the USIS staff abroad is carried out through two principal operating arms, informational and cultural. The task of the former is to strengthen foreign understanding and support for U.S. policies and actions and to counter attempts to distort the objectives and policies of the United States; the cultural arm of the organization is charged with promoting and administering educational and cultural exchange programs designed to bring about a greater understanding between the people of the United States and the peoples of other nations.

In all but the smallest USIS outposts, the information officer (sometimes informally known as the press attaché) will be responsible for activities that directly concern the mass media— press, publications, radio, and television. He or she normally serves as the embassy press spokesman on U.S. government policies, provides background information, and publicizes embassy activities. The information officer handles arrangements for visiting U.S. journalists, provides a point of contact for resident correspondents, and usually is busiest when visits by congressional delegations or senior officials require special briefings, interviews, or press conferences. On a day-to-day basis, the information officer works closely with local media representatives and government officials in an unending effort to ensure that U.S. views are available to the people of the host country through their print and electronic media. One of the most valuable tools in this effort is the Wireless File, a compendium of news and features that is transmitted daily to posts around the world, where it is made available by information officers to the local media. At some posts, such as the one profiled in Table 6.2, there will be one or more assistant information officers to share what can at times become a very heavy burden indeed.

In carrying out the other part of USIS work, the cultural affairs officer (often known as the cultural attaché, though not formally titled as such) administers the embassy's educational and cultural exchange programs. This catchall heading encompasses such activities as managing the American library operated by USIS at most posts abroad; arranging for special exhibits or the visits of U.S. scholars, artists, or sports teams; assisting local publishers with reprints or translations of books published in the United States; and working with local organizations that are active in promoting an improved mutual understanding between the United States and the host country. To an increasing extent, the cultural affairs officer is expected to be able to speak

The USIS library in Madras.

knowledgeably about all aspects of American culture and society and thus personally to fulfill many of the functions that were once taken care of by visiting lecturers. The cultural affairs officer may be involved in checking local copyright laws one day and participating in a symposium on U.S. art the next; the job is one of the most varied in any mission. Again, when the magnitude of the program warrants it, one or more assistant cultural affairs officers will also be included on the USIS staff.

The Agency for International Development

AID personnel abroad serve in nearly seventy countries, in offices ranging in size from a single U.S. employee to over a hundred career employees and several hundred supporting contract personnel. Most common is the AID mission, a name that gives rise to some confusion because it is not an independent entity but a part of the overall U.S. diplomatic establishment— also known as the mission. The AID mission is, in effect, the AID section of the embassy. It is headed by a director who is normally supported by a deputy director and several staff officers. For example, most missions have a controller who is responsible not only for the mission's own operating and program funds but also for the financial analysis of proposed projects and of local institutions that are proposed as aid recipients.

The core of an AID mission's work lies in its programs and projects. In recent years, the emphasis in AID activities overseas has been placed on private sector development, institution building, technology transfer, and dialogue with host governments on policies that appear either to stimulate or to discourage economic growth. Our hypothetical mission is one in which the major effort is being directed toward the agricultural sector, but other missions might well include support for industrial development, urban planning, or the energy sector. The sample staffing pattern includes two officers who plan programs and three who implement them.

The mission planners are the program officer and the project development officer. The former is charged with planning the medium- and long-term strategy of the assistance effort in the host country. He or she works closely with the mission director in shaping the budget requests that are submitted annually to AID headquarters, a process that requires hard decisions about which sectors will receive emphasis in future years. The program officer may also handle mission responsibilities in connection with the Food for Peace program.

The other half of the planning team is the project development officer, who tends to operate in a shorter-term perspective. He or she has the task of translating a program proposal into a specific project for implementation, usually as the head of a design team comprising appropriate specialists from within the mission, from regional offices, or even from AID headquarters in Washington. A project involving agricultural credit, for example, might involve experts in loans, agricultural economics, cooperatives, agronomy, and finance; it is the job of the project development officer to draw a finished project proposal from their collective deliberations and then to work with the mission director in obtaining the host government's concurrence in its terms.

Once projects are designed, approved, and funded, it is the task of specialized personnel within the mission to ensure their execution. Working with local officials and citizens, these personnel oversee the implementation phase of the projects. In

Ambassador Samuel Hart (in striped shirt) visits an AID project in Ecuador, 1984.

some cases, the work will be done entirely by the people of the host country; on larger projects, the supervising mission officer may have the support of additional U.S. personnel brought in on a contract basis for the particular project.

In several countries that do not have full-fledged AID missions, the agency does its business either through an AID Office headed by an AID representative (still a separate AID section of the embassy, but on a smaller scale) or through an AID affairs officer, normally assigned as a member of the embassy's economic section. In addition, AID has regional offices in both Central America and the Caribbean, handling programs for several countries, and Regional Economic Development Services Offices (REDSOs) in East and West Africa. The latter are essentially support offices for the more than thirty AID missions and offices on the African continent and are staffed by technical specialists in a variety of fields. Each of the missions or offices in Africa is likely to need expert assistance from time to time, but none could by itself justify having one or several of these specialists assigned on a full-time basis. Thanks to the REDSOs, however, help is close at hand when needed, and the combined requirements of the African AID missions and offices provide more than enough work to justify keeping the experts in the field.

Support Staffs

No discussion of embassy staffing would be complete without mention of the support personnel who are so essential an element of the mission's total workforce. Not all of them appear on the list of our hypothetical embassy, but that list does include the U.S. secretaries in the Foreign Service who form part of nearly every Foreign Service component of the embassy from the executive section on down. As was noted earlier (see Chapter 4), secretaries at the more senior levels perform duties that range far beyond the minimum requirements for the entry level. Particularly at a small or medium-sized embassy, such as the one in Table 6.2, which does not have a junior officer as a full-time staff assistant to the ambassador, the secretaries in the front office will be called on to handle many of the responsibilities associated with such a position—everything from following up on instructions from the ambassador and the DCM to arranging their travel and handling the protocol details for official entertainment.

Throughout an embassy, the wise supervisor will take full advantage of the education and experience that most Foreign Service secretaries bring with them (many are college graduates, and nearly all have worked in private business before joining the Service). Morale among Foreign Service secretaries is highest when they are challenged to use all of their skills, and those skills often mean they can match their bosses' ability to draft documents ranging from letters and administrative memoranda to basic biographic reports. When a section includes Foreign Service secretaries (which is generally the case wherever classified material is handled on a regular basis), a supervisor can make his or her own performance look far better by utilizing the secretaries' talents to the full.

Since Table 6.2 includes only U.S. staffing, it omits the largest single group of Foreign Service employees at posts abroad—

the eighteen thousand Foreign Service nationals, whose occupations range from professional to janitorial and whose work is critical to the ability of the U.S. missions to meet their responsibilities. As noted earlier (see Chapter 3), the FSNs bring to each post unique skills and knowledge that no U.S. employee could match, and in many instances, they provide a degree of continuity that is otherwise unobtainable because of the rotational personnel system utilized by the foreign affairs agencies.

Constituent Posts

Although their total number has diminished in recent decades, the 106 consulates general and consulates—known as constituent posts because they are nearly always subordinate to an embassy—are still an important part of the official U.S. presence overseas. In many nations, the interests of the United States simply cannot be represented effectively by the embassy in the capital alone. Some governments, for example, have built administrative capitals far from their commercial or industrial centers (such as Brasília or Canberra); in other cases, the sheer size of a country or the diversity of its regions makes it impossible to respond to demands for consular services or to keep up with developments from any single vantage point. When any of these factors obtains, the common practice is to seek permission from the host government to open one or more constituent posts, to be designated as consulates general or consulates depending on the size of their staffs and the range of the functions to be performed.

Historically, consular posts mainly confined their work to consular duties: passport and citizenship services to U.S. citizens and assistance to U.S. businesses. Most of today's consular posts still offer basic consular services, which, since World War I, have included the issuance of visas to foreign nationals, but they are now expected to carry on a wide range of other duties as well. Some constituent posts exist primarily to provide economic and political reporting on developments in their outlying districts, and may in fact have almost no call for the consular services that were once the bread and butter of all such establishments. Posts of this type are likely to be among the smaller consulates, with consular work as such handled on a part-time basis by one of the two or three officers on the roster.

At all but the smallest consular posts, however, the staff is likely to replicate in miniature the staff of the embassy, with sections (or individual officers) responsible for all the functions that the foreign affairs agencies perform in the capital. At major consulates general, the staffs will often be larger than those of most U.S. embassies, and they may include representatives of a number of non–foreign affairs agencies in their total workforce.

The principal officer of a consular post, whether at a two-officer consulate or a fifty-officer consulate general, is in effect the ambassador's proconsul for the consular district. Cables and other official correspondence from the post are sent over the name of the consul or consul general, rather than that of the ambassador, and the principal officer has the right to fly a U.S. flag and a consular flag on his or her official car for ceremonial occasions. Whether the consul or consul general has any real authority behind this impressive facade depends, however, on the wishes of the ambassador, who remains the ultimate boss over all U.S. representatives in the country. Some chiefs of mission exercise very close control over their constituent posts, permitting them no independent decision-making authority and requiring that all their reports on events in the consular district be sent to the embassy rather than directly to Washington. Other ambassadors simply set the basic policy, and their subordinate principal officers are allowed considerable leeway in running their posts and in reporting developments to Washington agencies. When this latter practice prevails, ambassadors usually encourage embassy and consulate personnel to exchange views and visits on a regular basis, and they may also hold regular meetings in the capital with principal officers from all the embassy's constituent posts.

The Non–Foreign Service Agencies

As we have seen, the core staffing of embassies and their constituent posts comes from personnel of the career foreign affairs agencies. At most Foreign Service posts, however, they are not alone. At any given time, representatives of forty or more U.S. government agencies may be attached to diplomatic and consular establishments around the world—one or two agencies, like the Peace Corps or the Defense Department, at smaller posts and as many as twenty or thirty at some of the larger embassies or consulates general.

The hypothetical embassy in Table 6.2 includes personnel from only two non–Foreign Service agencies. Like many developing nations, this embassy's host country has a Peace Corps program, and thus there is a small resident staff to support the group of volunteers working outside the capital. For some of its smallest programs, the Peace Corps sends only a single resident representative, but this sparse staffing severely limits the ability of that representative to pay regular visits to volunteers in the field. In consequence, a minimum staff of two is preferable to permit simultaneous travel and coverage of the office in the capital. When the size of the volunteer contingent is sufficiently large to justify it (and local medical facilities are limited), a Peace Corps physician is a welcome addition to the office complement.

Peace Corps staff members, who serve on thirty-month limited Foreign Service appointments (renewable once, for a maximum total service of five years), normally work out of an office that is physically apart from the embassy. Although they are part of the embassy staff and, like all other U.S. officials in the country, are under the authority of the ambassador, their ability to gain acceptance often depends on their success in keeping a certain distance between themselves and the more formal diplomatic establishment. The balance is delicate, but when there has been good will on both sides, it has worked effectively since the Peace Corps came into existence in 1961.

The only other agency in our hypothetical embassy is the Department of Defense, which in this instance is present in two distinct capacities. The defense attaché and his or her colleagues represent the more traditional military role in U.S. overseas representation, one that dates back to the nineteenth century. Once called military attachés, these officers perform functions in the military sphere that are identical with those of the embassy's political or economic sections—observing, reporting, and analyzing developments relative to the military forces of their host country and advising the ambassador on issues in their field of specialized knowledge.[12]

Prior to World War II, attaché service was not much sought after by ambitious military officers, who correctly viewed command and senior staff positions as the more promising routes to rapid advancement. Not until after the war, when military intelligence received increasing emphasis within the armed services, was serious attention focused on the selection of officers for attaché duty. Today's attachés are selected and trained with care. The senior service representative normally will be a graduate of the National Defense University or one of its service equivalents, and all attachés will have received both necessary language training and special instruction at the Defense Intelligence School. To the extent possible, they also will have had recent command experience in order to assure them readier professional acceptance by their host country counterparts.

Since the unified Defense Intelligence Agency (DIA) was established in 1961, the ranking officer among the attachés at each embassy has been designated as defense attaché and made the clear boss. The defense attaché also serves as the representative of his or her particular branch of service, and other officers on the staff serve as attachés for one or more of the remaining services. In our hypothetical embassy, the defense attaché is from the air force, and only the army has an additional attaché on the staff; when the navy also has an interest in local developments, it too would include an officer on the embassy roster. Each of the attachés may have one or more deputies, and the office will normally include such support personnel as an administrative officer and several enlisted clerks.

The second component of the Department of Defense presence at our hypothetical embassy is the Military Assistance Advisory Group (MAAG), a relative newcomer to the diplomatic scene. The United States only got into the military aid business after World War II, and the MAAGs (or their equivalents under various other names) were developed as the administrative components of these assistance programs. In many respects, they parallel on the military side the work of the AID missions in economic assistance: they analyze needs, recommend programs, and ensure that the training and equipment provided the recipient country are utilized in accordance with the terms of the aid agreements. Although much of the training that necessarily accompanies new equipment is furnished either in the United States (such as pilot instruction) or by visiting teams of specialists, some of it may be provided by personnel assigned to the MAAG, as is the case with the group shown in Table 6.2.

In early 1985, there were MAAGs or their equivalent in over fifty countries around the world. Since most of these also have defense attachés in residence, it has been suggested that the attachés might in some cases be superfluous. This seeming duplication is more apparent than real, however, because officers assigned to a MAAG are entitled to ask only for information that is needed to evaluate requests for military assistance and to judge whether equipment is being put to good use. MAAG personnel who pry into other matters would risk compromising their basic task of making a military aid program work effectively. In consequence, they tread cautiously in this area, which means there is ample work for defense attachés even when MAAGs are present.

In addition to the Peace Corps and the military, embassies and consulates also play host to a remarkable variety of U.S. government agencies, some of which are found in only one or two countries while others operate around the world. The non–Foreign Service agency with the longest history of overseas representation is the Treasury Department, which initially sent customs officials abroad in the 1930s and began assigning financial experts to major capitals shortly before World War II. Since that time, Treasury representatives have observed and reported on financial and monetary developments in the world's more complex economies, providing a highly specialized capability that few members of the more generalist Foreign Service can match. Treasury officials performing these duties are normally incorporated in embassy economic sections and hold the diplomatic title of attaché. In addition, there are still customs officials at a number of posts, as well as representatives from the Treasury Department's Internal Revenue Service on the lookout for unmet tax liabilities.

The Justice Department's contribution to the U.S. overseas presence comes from the Federal Bureau of Investigation, which stations officers in a number of key countries to maintain a liaison with major law-enforcement agencies, and from the Immigration and Naturalization Service. Representatives of the latter were first assigned abroad in 1924, and since 1957, they have regularly staffed regional offices in key centers that have heavy immigrant-visa workloads in order to ensure close coordination with consular officers in reaching decisions on potential immigrants.

Other agencies with overseas representation include, for example, the Federal Aviation Administration, which performs inspections abroad on aircraft and facilities used by U.S. flag carriers; the General Accounting Office, which has personnel at several key posts to carry out tasks set by Congress; the National Institutes of Health, whose personnel are engaged in medical research in a number of countries; and the American Battle Monuments Commission, which is responsible for maintaining U.S. military cemeteries and monuments in Europe. These agencies, and several dozen others, are all formally part of the ambassador's domain and depend on the embassy or consulate for logistic support. They perform such disparate functions, however, that a busy ambassador and DCM are often hard put to keep track of their activities, and in practice, most organizations that are not directly involved in an embassy's priority policy issues will be allowed to operate under fairly loose control.

The Intelligence Community

The role of the intelligence community in relation to the Foreign Service warrants at least passing mention, if only because it has been the subject in recent years of a great deal of sensational treatment. The defense attachés are an overt part of the intelligence apparatus, as their Washington organizational base is the Defense Intelligence Agency and their acknowledged mission is the collection and reporting of military-related information. Many members of the Foreign Service are contributors to the intelligence effort in the same way as the defense attachés, since they also perform reporting and analysis tasks. (Indeed, overt reporting by Foreign Service personnel, which is routinely shared with intelligence agencies in Washington, regularly provides over half the items included in the daily intelligence summaries prepared for the president and other senior officials.) Unlike the defense attachés, however, members of the Foreign Service abroad are not part of the intelligence community—nor, except for the State Department's Bureau of Intelligence and Research, are the foreign affairs agencies for which they work. As a result, the contribution to intelligence made by Foreign Service reporting, though substantial, is considered incidental to its basic purpose of helping to inform and shape policy decisions.

DIA, which is represented abroad by defense attachés, is only one element of the U.S. government's intelligence community, which also includes such major organizations as the National Security Agency (NSA), the Central Intelligence Agency (CIA), and the intelligence arms of the individual military services. Among them, it is the CIA that is most widely known, in large part because of revelations during the 1960s and 1970s about covert activities, some of which stretched the agency's authority while others outraged U.S. moral sensibilities. The attendant publicity called attention to the presence of CIA personnel around the world and raised serious questions about what they were doing.

Doubts about intelligence activities are not new, and can in fact be traced back to the sixteenth century and the first resident diplomatic missions to be exchanged between nation states. When such exchanges occurred between sovereigns who were not allies, one commentator wondered, "what could a resident be but an official liar or a licensed spy, unless . . . he was the instigator of a treasonable conspiracy?"[13]—and a number of early diplomats did indeed engage in just such undiplomatic practices. In modern times, however, governments have recognized the desirability of keeping diplomacy and intelligence as separate and distinct professions, with the result that career members of the Foreign Service at posts abroad stand completely outside the U.S. intelligence community.

In a world in which the spread of terrorism abroad is seemingly paralleled by growing paranoia at home, the overseas operations of U.S. intelligence agencies and their relationship with the foreign affairs agencies—though widely discussed in the media—are technically classified and thus not open to further coverage here. Readers seeking additional information on this topic should be able to satisfy their curiosity in the extensive literature produced in recent years by authors not subject to prepublication clearance agreements.

Life Outside the Office

Thus far, this chapter has examined in some detail the kind of work that is done from day to day by members of the Foreign Service (and by their non–Foreign Service colleagues) serving at embassies and consulates overseas. When these same individuals are stationed in the United States, the workday ends for most of them when they leave the office. Outside their agencies, they are simply private citizens and free to spend the evening in perfect anonymity, bowling or watching television or going to dinner with old friends.

U.S. officials abroad seldom enjoy the same sort of anonymity, or the freedom that goes with it. Whether in the office or outside it, they are representatives of the United States, and their behavior reflects for good or ill on the government that employs them. At large posts in friendly countries, all but the most senior personnel may be able to disappear in a crowd from time to time—but even then, neighbors and local shopkeepers will usually know their identities and keep a judgmental eye on their activities. In the smaller capitals, every action of all personnel is a public one, and the slightest misstep can result in embarrassment, not only for the individual concerned, but also for the post and the U.S. government.

This life in a goldfish bowl can put great pressure on members of the Foreign Service during their tours abroad— and on their families as well. It can make life particularly difficult in countries behind the Iron Curtain, where hostile intelligence services are constantly seeking incidents that can be exploited to their advantage and where electronic surveillance is an accepted fact of life. Being constantly "on show" and on the alert can be wearing, and more than one member of the Foreign Service has sighed with relief on arriving for a tour in Washington because he or she can once again spend a few years as a private person when the workday is at an end.

Another element of overseas Foreign Service life outside the office involves official entertaining—"representation" in the sense of offering hospitality to local officials and other selected guests with the goal of winning friends and influencing people. (The term "representation" is also used in a very different sense to describe the process by which U.S. views are conveyed to the host government.) Among the major tasks of the entire mission staff, from the ambassador down, is the cultivation of the widest possible range of working relationships in key sectors of the local government and society. Some of this contact can be accomplished through formal calls and visits, but experience has shown that close and confident relationships are sometimes easier to forge in an informal social setting.

In recognition of this truth, Congress annually makes available to each of the foreign affairs agencies a fixed sum of money to be used for representation. Each agency then allocates the available representation funds to its senior representative at each post (the ambassador for the State Department contingent), who in turn provides specific amounts to members of his or her staff whose work might be eased by judicious entertaining of key contacts. At most missions, the ambassador retains a substantial share of the available funds for his or her use, since the largest functions (such as a Fourth of July reception) will be held at the residence and charged to the ambassador's account. Although the amounts appropriated for representation have increased substantially in recent years, they still fall short of what is needed at most posts, and many conscientious FSOs dig into their own pockets every year in order to do the job as they feel it should be done.

At first, the opportunity to entertain at U.S. government expense may seem appealing, but Foreign Service practitioners quickly learn that representation involves far more hard work than glamour. The guests at official dinners and receptions are not the personal friends who would be invited by private citizens at home in the United States but people who have been chosen for their actual or potential importance to the attainment of the mission's overall goals. Some among them may turn out to be fascinating conversationalists and ultimately become good friends, but the average guest list will include its share of unattractive invitees who are there only for professional reasons. And, in most instances, representational entertaining is added on to an already full workday and calls for considerable extra effort by the employee and his or her family in order to assure appropriate hospitality.

Both in representational entertaining and in other efforts to expand the embassy's circle of acquaintances, the primary emphasis is placed on the nationals of the host country. The extent of access to local citizens varies considerably from one capital to another, with both Iron Curtain countries and some third-world nations imposing restrictions on contacts between their nationals and foreign diplomats. Whenever conditions permit, however, all members of a well-run mission, from top to bottom, will be encouraged to seek out opportunities to meet members of the local community. The occasions for such encounters may be professional or social, ranging from diplomatic receptions to sporting events, and may be found both in the capital and during visits to outlying areas. In working to expand their range of contacts, members of the mission must never lose sight of the reasons for doing so—not for its own sake, but as a means of enhancing their own understanding of the local scene and of building support for the United States and its policies.

A second layer of useful acquaintances for Foreign Service personnel comprises the local diplomatic or consular corps. The relationships among the diplomats of various countries accredited to a given capital can take many forms. When contact with host country nationals is restricted in any way, the representatives of other states can be a source of otherwise unavailable information and insights. For the most part, relationships among career diplomatic or consular personnel tend to be those of professionals in the same field who exchange views with greater or lesser frankness depending on the extent to which they as individuals, and their countries behind them, trust one another. The U.S. ambassador, backed up by a solidly professional staff, is often one of the best informed members of the diplomatic corps. In this situation, he or she must always be on guard against the tendency of other chiefs of mission to treat their U.S. colleague as a convenient source of current news, engaging in one-sided exchanges of views that demand a great deal of time but frequently produce little or nothing in return.

A further professional diplomatic hazard lies in the tendency at some posts for reciprocal entertaining within the diplomatic corps to become almost incestuous. Especially in a closed society, where there is little or no opportunity to mix with the local citizens, diplomatic and consular personnel sometimes seek distraction by hosting events for each other. Even when such restrictions do not apply, the national-day receptions offered in major capitals by a hundred or more countries can be a major burden for a chief of mission who attempts to make a personal appearance at every one. In these circumstances, members of the Service may have to remind themselves from time to time that the local citizens are still their number-one priority.

Finally, valuable contacts will often be found in the resident foreign community. As already noted earlier in this chapter, the ambassador has responsibilities in regard to the private U.S. citizens who live in the country to which he or she is accredited, whether they be business people, missionaries, educators, or retirees. The relationship with either these U.S. citizens or the nationals of other countries can be a two-way street. Many long-term foreign residents have a knowledge of the country that transient U.S. officials are unlikely to acquire during relatively brief tours of duty, and they often are eager to share their experience. They represent a unique resource, which a wise chief of mission will make every effort to develop both personally and through the efforts of the mission staff.

Notes

1. The role of the ambassador was the subject of a 1983 symposium at Georgetown University and of a corollary book, *The Modern*

Ambassador: The Challenge and the Search, ed. Martin F. Herz (Washington, D.C.: Institute for the Study of Diplomacy, Georgetown University, 1983), on which this section is largely based.

2. PL 96-465 (22 USC 3927), sec. 304(a).

3. Quoted in Herz, ed., *The Modern Ambassador*, p. 183.

4. PL 96-465, sec. 207.

5. Ellis O. Briggs, "A Day with the Ambassador," and Langston Craig, "Leisure, Gentility and Decorum," in Herz, ed., *The Modern Ambassador*, pp. 37–45 and 50–59; and Martin F. Herz, *215 Days in the Life of an American Ambassador* (Washington, D.C.: School of Foreign Service, Georgetown University, 1981).

6. William Macomber, *The Angels' Game: A Handbook of Modern Diplomacy* (New York: Stein and Day, 1975), p. 147.

7. W. Wendell Blancke, *The Foreign Service of the United States* (New York: Frederick A. Praeger, 1969), p. 137.

8. U.S. Department of State, *Foreign Service Careers*, Department of State Publication 9202 (Washington, D.C.: U.S. Department of State, 1984), p. 7.

9. William Barnes and John Heath Morgan, *The Foreign Service of the United States* (Washington, D.C.: Historical Office, Bureau of Public Affairs, U.S. Department of State, 1961), p. 57.

10. Brooke C. Holmes, "The Consular Career," in Martin F. Herz, ed., *The Consular Dimension of Diplomacy* (Washington, D.C.: Institute for the Study of Diplomacy, Georgetown University, 1983), p. 75.

11. Ibid.

12. This section draws in part on Paul C. Davis and William Fox, "American Military Representation Abroad," in Vincent M. Barnett, Jr., *The Representation of the United States Abroad* (New York: Frederick A. Praeger, 1965), pp. 129–183.

13. Garrett Mattingly, *Renaissance Diplomacy* (Boston: Houghton Mifflin, 1955), p. 239.

7

IN SEARCH OF
A CONSTITUENCY: CONGRESS,
PRESS, AND PUBLIC

> . . . *Foreign Service Officers are the eyes, ears, fingers and tongues of the U.S. government abroad.*
>
> —*Life*, editorial, 1945

For many years, two overlapping truisms have been widely accepted whenever pundits or practitioners have gathered to discuss foreign policy. The first holds broadly that there is no constituency for foreign affairs; the second, closely related, affirms specifically that the Foreign Service has no constituency. Like most truisms, each contains a kernel of truth, but insofar as they are taken at face value, they discourage any serious effort to analyze the problem.

The truism about the Foreign Service tends to be secondary to the more general assumption about the place of foreign affairs in the U.S. consciousness. As this broader truism is usually put, there are two main reasons why the foreign affairs agencies are political orphans. First, they are unable to provide voters and their representatives in Congress with any specific "goodies" like those which pour from the cornucopias of most federal agencies with a basically domestic orientation. Agriculture provides farm subsidies, Housing and Urban Development offers money for housing programs, Commerce comes to the aid of the business community, Defense operates bases with large payrolls and awards major contracts, Transportation helps to finance urban mass transit systems; the list goes on and on. The foreign affairs agencies, on the other hand, are perceived as bringing no direct benefit to the U.S. people—and even, in some cases, as giving money away to foreigners.

Equally important, these agencies and their problems are sometimes not considered to be a part of what really matters to Americans. For most of its history, the United States has looked inward, first to its western frontier and then to its industrial development. When the secretary of state and his minions insisted that Americans turn their eyes outward to focus on foreign policy concerns, it usually meant trouble. Sometimes that trouble was war or an imminent crisis; at other times, "those diplomats" performed the unpleasant task of telling the president and the Congress—and, through them, the people of the United States—that a preferred course of action would have undesirable consequences abroad and thus should not be pursued. As a general rule, dramatic foreign policy initiatives are the province of the president, and successes redound to his credit; the professionals tend to come into public view only when things go wrong. Even today, domestic issues rather than events abroad preoccupy most U.S. citizens, and there remains a strong nostalgia for an era when the rest of the world seemed largely irrelevant to the country's future. In this context, foreign policy issues are all too easily perceived as unwelcome intrusions.

Along the way, the Foreign Service and the State Department (and later, the other foreign affairs agencies) have tended to become muddled together in people's minds—and "those diplomats" in the Foreign Service were already objects of suspicion. Part of this confusion is rooted in the history of the profession. "Unlike the military," French diplomatist Jules Cambon once wrote, "the diplomat is not the spoilt child of history."[1] Diplomats have traditionally been plagued by what one observer has called "an image of sharp practice, secrecy, and deceit" and an "aroma of snobbery, cookie pushing, and striped pants"[2]—not a reputation calculated to win either the respect or the confidence of fellow citizens. Another part of the problem lies in the inevitable clash between diplomacy, with its protracted processes, and the U.S. preference for quick solutions. U.S. diplomats who engage in lengthy negotiations find themselves at odds with the national style and are perceived as having become infected with "foreign ways."

There are some other specific reasons why the Foreign Service is sometimes considered to be a little too "foreign" for the popular taste. To begin with, prior to World War II, its members were drawn predominantly from the nation's social elite and were, in many cases, independently wealthy. Although most were serious professionals, there was just enough truth to the striped-pants-and-white-spats image to make it hard for the average U.S. citizen to understand the Foreign Service, let alone love it. Beyond this point, however, a good part of the problem was of the Foreign Service's own making. Few members of the Service, particularly in the years before World War II, had any interest in seeking a constituency either for themselves or for foreign policy generally. Writing about the Service of the 1930s, one observer noted wryly that its members agreed that "foreign policy should be run from the foreign office, not from the White House or Congress" and that "diplomacy should in no way depend upon public opinion."[3] Thus, any attempt to develop a constituency would have been tantamount to acknowledging that foreign policy should in some way depend on public and congressional views, a concept that was anathema to the tra-ditionalists who dominated the prewar Service.

The world changed drastically after 1945, and, as we have seen, so did the way the U.S. government organized itself to deal with foreign policy issues. The primacy of the State De-partment and of the Foreign Service in the field of foreign policy was eroded as new agencies took to the field, and the executive branch as a whole found itself being challenged by a newly assertive Congress. In consequence, foreign policy decision-making began more and more to require the devel-opment of a consensus involving at least Congress and the executive, and sometimes the American people as a whole. Successive administrations and their foreign affairs agencies learned the dynamics of consensus building, and in the process, they educated those members of the Foreign Service whose duties involved them in these efforts.

Despite this experience, however, the Foreign Service as a body was slow to recognize that it was in its own interest to develop a distinct constituency, both for the foreign policy its members were charged with executing and for the Foreign Service itself. Many members of the Service still felt either diffident or disdainful about constituency building. To some extent, they simply failed to understand the new power relationships in postwar Washington and the consequent importance of developing constituencies that would support them when they ran up against other agencies in the policy-making process. Thus, for a number of years after the war, neither they nor the foreign affairs agencies made much effort to enlist active support— either in the policy process or for the Foreign Service as an institution—from any of its three natural constituencies: Congress, the press, and the public. Each, in its own way, impinges on the day-to-day operations of the Foreign Service; each is also an important potential constituency for the Service and its members.

Congress

For more than a century after the United States had gained its independence, Congress and the Foreign Service had little occasion to get acquainted. Although the Constitution gave Congress considerable potential power in the foreign affairs field, the legislators paid only sporadic attention to foreign policy. The Senate took seriously its charge to advise and consent to treaties (but was often bypassed once presidents learned that executive agreements and exchanges of letters served almost as well), and both houses occasionally balked at expenditures in the foreign affairs area. By and large, however, decisions on foreign policy were left to the executive, and liaison between the State Department and Capitol Hill was not a major concern of either party.

Within the State Department, congressional relations were handled for many years on a part-time basis by one of the secretary's senior assistants. (Jefferson, as secretary of state, had personally conducted all relations with Congress in addition to his other duties, which clearly indicates that the liaison function was not then an onerous one.) The low priority attached to this function backfired most seriously just after World War I, when congressional opposition blocked U.S. membership in the League of Nations. Even after that fiasco, however, congressional relations in the State Department remained a part-time job for another decade.

It was Cordell Hull, himself a former member of Congress, who first established a separate office in the State Department to deal with Congress. Its first boss was, like Hull, an ex-congressman with wide contacts among his former colleagues on Capitol Hill; among later heads of that office was Dean Acheson, who put the experience to good use when he served as secretary of state. The office performed well during the Roosevelt administration, but there were still lingering doubts about the importance of the congressional liaison function until the Hoover Commission finally put them to rest in 1949. Its foreign affairs task force called congressional relations the number-one foreign policy issue confronting the United States and urged the administration to commit whatever resources were necessary to do the job properly. Responding to the commission's recommendations, Secretary of State George Marshall elevated the congressional relations office to full bureau status within the department and substantially augmented its staff.

It was this development that, for the first time, brought a significant number of Foreign Service personnel into the Washington end of the congressional relations process—though the Foreign Service had already been getting acquainted with representatives and senators abroad. Beginning right after World War II, members of Congress became world travelers on a grand scale. There were new overseas programs to be evaluated, and the availability of air transportation made it easy for members of Congress to fit a trip abroad into their busy schedules. The result was an unprecedented boom in congressional travel, and scarcely an embassy or consulate escaped the attention of one or another party of visitors from Capitol Hill.

The combination of increased status for the congressional relations function at home and an exponential growth in contacts between Congress and the Foreign Service abroad wrought a profound change in the role of the Service with regard to the legislative branch. Since the late 1940s, members of the Foreign

Service have been called on to play an important part in the efforts of successive administrations to deal effectively with congressional concerns in the foreign policy arena.

The relationship was relatively trouble free through the late 1950s as strong secretaries of state (George Marshall, Dean Acheson, and John Foster Dulles) dealt one-on-one with strong chairmen of the Senate Foreign Relations Committee (Tom Connally, Arthur H. Vandenberg, and Walter George). Thereafter, however, difficulties mounted as the number of players in the foreign policy game proliferated on both ends of Pennsylvania Avenue, and the process became impossible for even a strong leader to control. The Vietnam conflict unraveled what little remained of the cooperative relationship of the postwar years. In its wake, the foreign affairs agencies confront a Congress in which foreign affairs responsibilities are dispersed among a number of committees, suspicion of the executive is still prevalent, and nearly every member pays close attention to foreign policy issues. It is also a Congress that is greatly strengthened in its ability to deal with policy issues, largely through the expansion both of professional staffs and of the support available to committees and to individual members from such sources as the Congressional Research Service and the Congressional Budget Office. In summary, the situation presents a real challenge to those officials who bear the daunting responsibility for congressional liaison.

The number of Foreign Service personnel directly involved in the congressional relations function varies from agency to agency. It tends to be greatest in the State Department, where one of the deputy assistant secretaries in the responsible bureau (originally called the Bureau of Congressional Relations and now called the Bureau for Legislative and Intergovernmental Affairs and known within the department by the initial "H") and most of the line officers are drawn from Foreign Service ranks. Foreign Service involvement is least in the Departments of Agriculture and Commerce, which are essentially domestic agencies with a relatively small Foreign Service component, and in USIA, where the congressional relations function is handled from the general counsel's office. AID, which includes some Foreign Service personnel in its congressional relations office, falls between these two poles.

The bureaus or offices directly responsible for congressional relations play an important part in helping develop the necessary consensus on foreign policy issues. They are the principal interpreters between Congress and the foreign affairs agencies in this area, helping to bridge the gap between the sometimes conflicting cultures of the legislative and executive branches.[4] It is a process of two-way communication. As one FSO engaged in congressional relations for the State Department described his work, "Congress tells the Department what's on the mind of the people, and we at State communicate to the Congressmen something about the international environment in which we're living."[5] The success the congressional relations staffs have in smoothing the sometimes rocky relationship depends in large measure on the willingness of any given administration to consult with Congress before policies are locked in concrete. "Congress resents being told too little and too late," Secretary of State Henry Stimson once said,[6] and liaison officers find their work easiest when they have something more to discuss than faits accomplis.

Although the congressional relations personnel bear the heaviest responsibility for dealing with Capitol Hill, they are by no means alone in the effort. In all five foreign affairs agencies, including those with no Foreign Service personnel assigned to liaison duties, members of the Service are often involved in preparing testimony and briefing materials for senior officials who are scheduled to appear at congressional hearings (and sometimes in briefing senators and representatives themselves); in responding to congressional mail; and (particularly at more senior levels) in testifying before congressional committees. On occasion, members of the Service will be sent as escort officers with congressional delegations traveling overseas. In addition, part of the liaison function at the State Department is handled outside the "H" bureau and involves still more FSOs. The department's operating budget, for example, is handled on Capitol Hill by the office of the under secretary for management (primarily with the appropriations committees in both houses) while several other bureaus have their own full-time coordinators for congressional relations.

This active involvement of Foreign Service personnel in the congressional relations operation has been furthered by the assignment each year of up to ten mid-level FSOs from the State Department to congressional offices and committees. These employees, like their colleagues handling congressional relations for the foreign affairs agencies, emerge from the experience far more sensitive to congressional concerns and better able to take them into account when they themselves become policy-makers in years to come.

Even with this expanded role in congressional relations, relatively few members of the Foreign Service deal directly with senators and representatives in Washington. Overseas, however, the opportunities for personal contact between members of the Service and members of Congress are far more abundant. When members of Congress travel abroad, either alone or in a group, they become a CODEL—short for congressional delegation— and the responsibility of the Foreign Service posts along their line of march. (If congressional staffers travel without their bosses, they use a different label—STAFFDEL—in the cable announcing their plans.) Each post will be asked to arrange accommodations and transportation, as well as such events as briefings, formal calls, appropriate hospitality, and sometimes ceremonial occasions. Large embassies may host dozens of CODELS a year, in the course of which most members of the mission's staff are likely to become involved at one time or another in prior arrangements, escort duties, or both. At smaller missions, where CODELS are less frequent, a visit is likely to be a major event for all hands, with personnel from each of the agencies at the post being involved in one or more events on the schedule.

To members of the Service abroad, the imminent arrival of members of Congress does not always spark great enthusiasm. In the first rush of congressional travel immediately after World War II, a number of the members treated their trips abroad as a perquisite of office rather than as an opportunity to expand their knowledge and horizons. They were difficult and demanding guests at posts around the world and made the derogatory term "junket" synonymous in many minds with congressional travel. Fortunately, however, such travelers have grown rare over the ensuing years, and today's congressional visitors, almost without exception, are genuinely interested in learning what is at stake for the United States in the countries on their itinerary. Their presence, particularly in smaller capitals, can offer an excellent opportunity to demonstrate U.S. interest in the host country's welfare and to reinforce U.S. views on key policy issues.

In addition to paying visits, members of Congress also write letters both to the foreign affairs agencies at home and to posts abroad. Most letters are straightforward requests for information that a congressional office needs in order to reply to a constituent—anything from how to join the Foreign Service to the status of a visa application. Some letters to posts abroad include a request for services, usually in the form of courtesies to be extended to a traveling friend or constituent. As a general rule, neither members of Congress nor their staffs expect letters of this kind to produce miracles; what they seek is a prompt reply with enough solid facts so that they can be responsive to the original inquirer. The foreign affairs agencies, like nearly all executive-branch departments, try to send at least an interim answer to all congressional correspondence within three working days, a courtesy that does much to keep relations smooth even when the substance of the reply is unlikely to give complete satisfaction.

Whether at home or overseas, most contacts between members of the Service and members of Congress involve foreign policy issues rather than the concerns of the Foreign Service as a distinct institution. Even so, these contacts tend to be highly beneficial to the Service. Not surprisingly, many new members of Congress arrive in Washington with the cookie-pusher stereotype of Foreign Service employees in mind. When they see the Foreign Service in action, however, whether in their own offices or under the difficult conditions that often prevail abroad, the stereotype becomes hard to sustain. The Service has won many friends on Capitol Hill among senators and representatives who have come to know personally its members and their work.

Only when legislation directly affecting the Foreign Service is under consideration does the Service as an institution become the subject of the congressional relations effort of the foreign affairs agencies—as, for example, during discussions of the Foreign Service Act of 1980 or of amendments to that statute. When this situation does occur, members of the Service sometimes find themselves in difficulty, since the views of the foreign affairs agencies (or of the Office of Management and Budget, which has the final word on each department's legislative proposals) and the views of career Foreign Service personnel on the future shape of the Service do not always coincide. In such a situation, some FSOs may be found speaking officially for their agencies while others make contrary personal views known on Capitol Hill either directly or, most often, through their union representatives.

The American Foreign Service Association and the American Federation of Government Employees, which represent Foreign Service personnel at State, AID, and USIA (see Chapter 3), are regularly engaged in presenting the views of their members to both houses of Congress. Not surprisingly, their pace of activity picks up when major legislation is under consideration (such as the 1980 Act or subsequent administration proposals for changes in federal retirement systems). Their ongoing lobbying and information efforts on Capitol Hill play an important continuing role in helping to build congressional understanding of the Foreign Service as a distinct institution.

Press

Relationships with the Fourth Estate present a challenge to any profession that depends in large part for its success on being able to work things out quietly behind the scenes. In his classic book on diplomacy, Sir Harold Nicolson commented wryly that "a satisfactory adjustment between the needs and rights of a popular Press and the requirements of discretion has yet to be found" and added that on occasion, "publicity has proved the enemy rather than the friend of sensible diplomacy."[7] He nevertheless concluded that this phenomenon simply had to be accepted as part of the price of a democratic system. "The advantages of a free Press are so immeasurably greater than its disadvantages that this particular problem of democratic diplomacy need not cause anxiety. It is little more than a minor inconvenience."[8]

Despite Nicolson's comforting words, Foreign Service personnel dealing with media representatives do not always find the task an easy one. In Washington, resident correspondents for the print and electronic media prowl the corridors of the foreign affairs agencies as well as other government departments, constantly seeking current information on events around the world and on evolving U.S. policies. At the State Department, there is a formal daily briefing for journalists (who are provided office space in the building), and personnel throughout the foreign affairs community receive press queries relating to their areas of responsibility. Each of the foreign affairs agencies has an office specifically charged with press relations (usually in combination with public affairs and general public information activities), and a number of bureaus and offices within the agencies have their own full-time public affairs officers.

Overseas, Foreign Service posts deal both with the resident press corps and with visiting journalists. At larger posts, one officer—usually from the USIS contingent—will have the primary responsibility for responding to press inquiries, but as in Washington, most members of the mission will be regarded by journalists as potential sources of information. On the occasion of a presidential visit or another major event, the post may face the added burden of a traveling press corps (on presidential trips abroad, often upward of three hundred strong) for which it will have the task of arranging briefings, accommodations, transportation, and communications facilities.

In summary, dealing with the press is an important item of business for the Foreign Service, both at home and abroad. And, in doing so, its members face the problem so aptly noted by Nicolson: balancing the need of the Service for discretion in the conduct of its business with the press requirement of disclosure.

Fortunately for both sides, there is far more collaboration than conflict between these divergent professions. Both seek accurate information on events and insight into what is likely to happen next, and they sometimes find it profitable to col-

laborate in the effort. When journalists have confidence in the
Foreign Service personnel at a post, they often will stop by to
share (and to cross-check) the latest information and rumors as
they acquire them. Especially in fast-breaking situations, journalists who are willing to do so can greatly enhance a post's
ability to keep abreast of new developments by adding what
are, in effect, extra reporting officers to the mission's staff.

The key to making this collaboration work is mutual trust.
The journalists must know that they are getting straight answers
to their questions (not necessarily complete answers, if part of
the information they seek is classified, but answers that do not
mislead); the Foreign Service personnel must be able to depend
on their media contacts to respect the rules under which information is made available. The counselor of an embassy who
finds his or her name on page one during a delicate negotiation
is unlikely ever again to trust the reporter who put it there
after being told the story was off the record—nor will the
counselor's colleagues. On the other hand, the journalist who
uses not-for-attribution information merely to ensure the ac-
curacy of his or her reporting, and in the process of exchanging
views contributes to the embassy's understanding of a situation,
will be more than welcome on the next call.

On occasion, the press plays yet another role that warrants
special mention—that of floating "trial balloons" for an administration or of bringing dissenting views to public attention
by disseminating material "leaked" outside official channels. As
previously noted (see Chapter 5), the propriety of "leaks" has
been hotly debated within the Foreign Service (as in other
branches of government), and the emerging consensus is that
the Service as a whole pays a disproportionately high price for
the personal satisfaction that a single member may gain by
venting his or her policy dissent through press leaks. Trial
balloons, on the other hand, are in an entirely different category,
since they are officially sanctioned attempts to test the reaction
of the public (or of Congress, or even other governments) to a
possible policy in a way that does not involve the prestige of
the administration. Since trial balloons are customarily launched
at senior levels, few Foreign Service employees are likely to be

engaged directly in the process until the later stages of their careers.

Both leaks and trial balloons are part of a broader process that increasingly has made the media an arena in which struggles over the future direction of U.S. foreign policy take place in full public view. In this situation, it is all too easy for members of the Service (and particularly those at policy-making levels) to get sucked into a debate, but this is a temptation to be resisted if they wish to succeed in maintaining the confidence of the administration to which they owe their loyalty.

With the press, as with Congress, the Foreign Service itself is seldom the primary topic of discussion. Nonetheless, here too, the Foreign Service is dealing with individuals who influence the way the Service is perceived by the people of the United States. The image of the Foreign Service in the minds of the journalists who work with its members is likely, consciously or unconsciously, to color their references to the Service and its responsibilities, and thus in turn to affect the media audiences' image of the Service. Here again, the Foreign Service has a natural constituency, to be won over by establishing a relationship of trust and respect.

Public

Relatively few U.S. citizens have ever come face to face with a member of the Foreign Service; even fewer have any clear idea of what the Service is or what it does. The Iranian hostage crisis and other attacks on diplomatic personnel have helped to erode the striped-pants image of previous years and to make the U.S. public more aware of the modern Foreign Service, but the Foreign Service still has a long way to go before it becomes a household word. The three original foreign affairs agencies (State, AID, and USIA) are only minimally involved at home in any kind of service to the public that attracts favorable notice. (Indeed, State's principal public service, passport issuance, only makes the news when delays occur during the peak season.) The other elements of the foreign affairs community—FAS, APHIS, and FCS—do have a much larger "service" component in their mission, but they have become a part of the Foreign Service too recently to have made much impact in terms of constituency building for the Service per se. It has been suggested that the addition of these elements of Commerce and Agriculture, two departments with domestic political clout, may eventually strengthen the base of political support for the Service as a whole,[9] but time is needed before that hypothesis is proved true or not.

Most direct contacts between the Foreign Service and U.S. citizens take place overseas, where service to the public is a major concern of every Foreign Service post. Service under this rubric falls principally into two traditional categories, consular and commercial, both of which have been discussed in the previous chapter. Many consular services are routine (passports, notarial services, reports of birth) and are often performed for U.S. citizens who live abroad, for whom the consulate or consular section of the embassy substitutes for all levels of government from the township to the federal establishment. Resident U.S. citizens may also be on the receiving end of emergency assistance, but this aid is more frequently provided to travelers. The tourist or visiting business representative who falls ill, is robbed, or runs afoul of the local constabulary looks to the consular officers for help, and a duty officer is on call around the clock at every post to provide it. With rare exceptions, U.S. citizens with a genuine need for assistance are helped promptly and courteously, and most recipients of consular services under these circumstances return home as new recruits to the Foreign Service constituency.

The Foreign Service has received more mixed reviews on its commercial work, the other traditional area of public service to U.S. citizens abroad, though the overall balance is strongly positive. As noted earlier (see Chapter 6), the creation of the Foreign Commercial Service was in part a reflection of dissatisfaction on the part of U.S. business with the performance of commercial duties when they were primarily the responsibility of the State Department, and some of the specific complaints have already been addressed by the FCS. To a far greater extent than in the past, personnel performing commercial functions today have themselves had experience in the private sector, and they spend longer tours at each post in order to become fully effective. Most important, they come from the Department of Commerce, an agency perceived by business as being committed to the advancement of U.S. interests, rather than from the Department of State, which many regard as being excessively preoccupied with the views of other nations.

The transfer of most overseas commercial work to the FCS and the resources subsequently committed by that agency have helped to improve the image of commercial officers in the eyes of most business people, but dissatisfaction has not completely disappeared. Grumbling persists in the U.S. business community as many of its members still feel they are not getting the kind of support they seek and expect. In part, the problem lies in unrealistic expectations about what the Foreign Service can deliver, which is limited to what U.S. statutes authorize. Business people whose foreign competitors get assistance from their governments that the United States fails to match find it all too easy to blame the commercial officers (whether from FCS or State) who have the thankless job of trying to explain why their hands are legally tied.

Beyond this aspect, many experienced commercial officers feel that U.S. business sometimes holds the Foreign Service responsible for business's own shortcomings. Nearly every officer who has done commercial work abroad has his or her own litany of complaints about U.S. companies. Most such lists would include, for example, the reluctance of firms to bid on opportunities developed by posts abroad, a lack of offers when new markets open, a failure to meet local specifications in bidding or to respond in the local language, an erratic delivery of spare parts and after-sale service, and delays in responding to inquiries from foreign companies. As these commercial officers see the situation, too many U.S. companies treat foreign markets as a simple extension of their domestic market and are unwilling to make the extra effort that is required for success in other countries. When ill-prepared attempts to sell abroad result in failure, commercial officers are a convenient scapegoat.

Despite these difficulties, the work of the Foreign Service in support of U.S. business, whether performed at home or overseas, offers yet another opportunity for the Foreign Service to build support among an influential segment of the U.S. public. Members of the Service who provide cogent briefings to visiting business representatives on the economic or political situation of the host country (a service that many business travelers consider more important than purely commercial assistance), or who exchange views with business leaders in the United States through the programs of such groups as the Business Council for International Understanding, enhance the image of the Service as a whole. Similarly, when a commercial officer finds an effective representative for a U.S. exporter, settles a trade dispute on terms favorable to the U.S. complainant, or negotiates an end to tariff barriers that are harmful to U.S. trade, he or she may also have won another constituent for the Foreign Service.

Some U.S. citizens meet members of the Foreign Service in the course of seeking assistance, whether consular or commercial. Others have their first direct contact when one of the foreign affairs agencies accepts an invitation from a university or a Rotary Club and sends a member of the Service to speak on some current foreign policy issue. Participants in the public-speaking programs organized by each agency's public affairs office include noncareer appointees and civil servants as well as Foreign Service personnel, but the last generally do the lion's share of the work. When Foreign Service speakers make a favorable impression on such occasions, they help to create a positive image from which all their colleagues benefit.

In addition, members of the Service participate from time to time on their own in meetings of professional organizations, world affairs seminars, and the like. They sometimes do so with financial assistance from a private foundation established by the late Mrs. Una Chapman Cox, an unusual member of the Foreign Service constituency. Mrs. Cox, owner of an extensive ranch and other properties in Texas, was favorably impressed by members of the Foreign Service who came to her assistance while she was on a trip overseas and subsequently grew concerned that the Service was so poorly understood in its own country. In 1980, she set up a foundation bearing her name to underwrite activities designed to make the Foreign Service better known to the U.S. people and to further the professional development of its members. Since that time, the Una Chapman Cox Foundation has funded study and travel grants for members of the Service as well as programs undertaken by the American Foreign Service Association (AFSA) and the Association of American Foreign Service Women (AAFSW).

AFSA has already been mentioned several times in this book as the union that represents Foreign Service employees in State and AID. In its relationship with the Cox Foundation, however, AFSA wears its other hat, for AFSA predates the right of federal employees to union representation, having come into existence in its present form in 1924 as the professional organization of the career Foreign Service. Even though it subsequently took on the additional job of formally representing Foreign Service personnel, AFSA still has a dual role, and thus it continues to serve as the professional voice of the Service. Both in this latter capacity and as a union, AFSA has been directly engaged in efforts to enhance the professional status of the members of the Foreign Service and to develop a greater public understanding of their work. Among its programs to this end, AFSA provides information to members of Congress and their staffs; makes itself readily available to the media as a spokesman for the career Service; meets with groups of educators visiting Washington; and encourages Foreign Service retirees around the country to engage in public relations efforts on behalf of their still-active colleagues.

As a final note, there may be more potential support for the Foreign Service among the U.S. public than this history of constituency-building efforts might otherwise suggest. U.S. citizens may not know much about the Foreign Service, and they may harbor an instinctive distrust of people who deal with "those foreigners," but they have consistently ranked "diplomat in the U.S. foreign service" high on their list of prestigious occupations. In 1947, diplomats tied with cabinet members for fourth place in a National Opinion Research Center survey (behind U.S. Supreme Court justices, physicians, and state governors), and in 1963, the diplomatic profession still ranked eleventh among the ninety occupations surveyed.[10]

Notes

1. Quoted in William Macomber, *The Angels' Game: A Handbook of Modern Diplomacy* (New York: Stein and Day, 1975), p. 19.

2. Ibid.

3. Martin Weil, *A Pretty Good Club: The Founding Fathers of the U.S. Foreign Service* (New York: W. W. Norton, 1978), p. 61.

4. For a discussion of the problems inherent in executive-legislative relations, see Stanley J. Heginbotham, "Dateline Washington: The Rules of the Game," *Foreign Policy*, no. 53 (Winter 1983-1984), pp. 157–172; and Macomber, *The Angels' Game*, pp. 181–190.

5. Robert A. Flaten, "Congressional Relations," Department of State *Newsletter*, no. 200 (April 1978), pp. 7–8, quoted in Thomas M. Franck and Edward Weisband, *Foreign Policy by Congress* (New York: Oxford University Press, 1979), p. 265.

6. Quoted in Franck and Weisband, *Foreign Policy by Congress*, p. 265.

7. Harold Nicolson, *Diplomacy*, 2d ed. (London: Oxford University Press, 1952), p. 98.

8. Ibid., pp. 99–100.

9. William I. Bacchus, *Staffing for Foreign Affairs* (Princeton, N.J.: Princeton University Press, 1983), p. 227.

10. John Ensor Harr, *The Professional Diplomat* (Princeton, N.J.: Princeton University Press, 1969), pp. 202–203.

8

OPEN QUESTIONS

The environment for international relations is changing at an accelerating rate, confronting the foreign policy maker with new challenges and complexities.

—Murphy Commission, 1975

When the society at large changes, institutions within it sometimes have to scramble to keep up. The process is particularly difficult for the Foreign Service, because it must adjust to changes both in the United States and in the world environment. Today, the Foreign Service is trying to cope with the changed nature of diplomacy and the foreign policy process in the wake of World War II as well as with three major phenomena of the 1960s and 1970s: the women's movement, a shift in American attitudes in the post-Vietnam era, and the spread of international terrorism. All four changes already have had an impact on the shape and functioning of the Service. Equally important, they pose continuing questions for the future to which the answers are by no means clear.

The New Foreign Policy Environment

The years since the end of World War II have been a period of radical change in a diplomatic profession that had remained relatively set in its ways since the Congress of Vienna first codified the rules in 1815. The number of independent nations in the world community has tripled since 1945, and the number and variety of international organizations have grown with equal speed. In this new setting, three key changes have had a special impact on U.S. diplomatic practice, and thus on the Foreign Service: involvement in the foreign policy process of a host of government departments beyond the foreign affairs agencies, the increasingly operational nature of diplomacy, and a shift in diplomatic style required by the "democratization" of foreign policy.

The last of these has been easiest to deal with. Although some U.S. diplomats of the 1930s were comfortable only when consorting with society's elite, the national style of the United States tends to the open and the informal. Nevertheless, the change has required some adjustment in both attitude and modus operandi. As one ambassador ruefully observed: "Once all you had to do was walk with kings. Now you have to be acceptable to the president, local importers, television viewers, and the trade unions."[1] In large part because of the increased influence of the mass media, foreign policy has become public business to a greater extent than ever before, and success in diplomacy (and in the Foreign Service) has come to require skill in reaching out effectively to the new constituencies.

More difficult for the Foreign Service was the increased emphasis on operations. As we have seen, there was a great deal of thrashing about at the end of World War II when it became clear that the United States would have to maintain its active role in world affairs (see Chapter 2). Foreign aid and information activities were going to be big business for some time to come, and new staffs were needed to carry them out. The only existing body of personnel available for overseas service was the traditional Foreign Service, an element of the Department of State. Was this the right group to assume these new responsibilities, so different from what its members had been doing in past years? The prewar Service, one member said, had as its basic responsibility "to observe, report to the Department, and await instructions which rarely came."[2] State did in fact take on the information function for a few years, but its senior officers, in the words of one later report, "had little appetite for the more activist role the nation's radically changed position in the world demanded of the United States."[3] The members of the Foreign Service, as one observer commented tartly, "protected their exclusiveness, but in the process they lost control of much of the action."[4]

As the Hoover Commission had recommended, the State Department and the Foreign Service deliberately chose coordination rather than operations. They made the choice, however, at a time when the number of players in the foreign policy process was growing geometrically. With the United States deeply involved in postwar reconstruction, trade expansion, and the security policies necessitated by the Cold War, it seemed that everybody in Washington had a legitimate claim for getting in on the foreign policy act. Thus, coordination turned out to be far more difficult than had perhaps been anticipated at the time the choice was made. Whereas the State Department (and thus, to a large extent, the Foreign Service) had previously been virtually unchallenged in foreign affairs, it now found itself struggling for acceptance even as primus inter pares in the policy process.

Although the primacy of the ambassador abroad has been strengthened and reaffirmed regularly since 1961 (see Chapter 6), there has not been an equally effective clarification of the lines of authority in Washington. The authority and responsibility of the secretary of state were formally affirmed in 1966 in a National Security Action Memorandum,[5] which also created new mechanisms through which the secretary and the State Department were to play their leading roles. In practice, however, power has flowed back and forth between the State Department and the National Security Council (NSC), between State and Defense, and among the myriad other agencies with an interest in foreign policy, reflecting to a considerable extent the personal and political strength of the individuals heading each organization. When an Acheson, a Marshall, or a Dulles has served as secretary of state, for example, with the full confidence of the president, State has had the lead role in the foreign policy apparatus. When presidents have placed their trust in their immediate staffs at NSC or diffused authority among several agencies, State has been just one of the players in a decision-making process they once all but owned.

For a number of years after World War II, both the State Department and the Foreign Service struggled to redefine their roles, and some members of the Service found the new ways hard to swallow. For years, they had regarded themselves as part of an elite corps, their primacy in foreign policy acknowledged by nearly all elements of the bureaucracy. Suddenly, there were a lot of upstarts horning into their act, treating them like ordinary mortals and challenging them successfully on their own turf. Strong secretaries of state partially concealed the malaise by infusing their own influence into the department and the Foreign Service, but the department's periodic "dry spells" in the Washington power competition increasingly led the Foreign Service to question its own relevance. Thus, the new social and political shocks of the 1960s and 1970s burst upon a Service that was less sure of itself than it had ever been since it had gained career status a half-century before.

Spouses and Families

Serious reexamination of the role of women in U.S. society began in the 1960s, but the process took awhile to catch up with the Foreign Service. It was not until 1971, under pressure from increasingly militant women employees and in anticipation of a forthcoming statutory ban against all forms of discrimination based on sex, that the Department of State dropped a long-standing Foreign Service requirement that a woman employee resign when she married while imposing no comparable requirement on her male colleagues. The following year, the department took a parallel step with regard to Foreign Service spouses by declaring that they were henceforth to be recognized as essentially "private persons" and could no longer be rated in an employee's performance evaluation.[6]

From the perspective of the 1980s, as one observer aptly noted, "both of these old ways of doing business seem archaic in the extreme."[7] The women's movement has been so successful in raising the consciousness of most people in the United States that the situation which existed prior to 1971 becomes harder to imagine with each passing year. Nonetheless, the pre-1970 Foreign Service was, in many respects, a bastion of male chauvinism. In 1950, for example, a standard work on U.S.

diplomatic practice included this description of Foreign Service attitudes toward women FSOs:

> There is a certain amount of reluctance to admit women to the career Foreign Service. They must be granted special considerations of various sorts and often are prone to take advantage of their privileged position. Rightly or wrongly, male candidates for, and junior members of, the Foreign Service are particularly opposed to the woman career officers, in part because competent potential male officers are thereby deprived of the positions the women occupy.[8]

The few women who successfully ran the gauntlet and gained appointments as FSOs often faced further handicaps in the form of the attitudes of those male colleagues and supervisors who found professional women hard to accept. As the same author observed, "there appears to be little opposition to the employment of women in the Staff corps"[9]—i.e., in secretarial or other support positions, which is where many male FSOs clearly felt women belonged. And, of course, a woman FSO who had the bad luck to fall in love had to choose between marriage and career, since the former called automatically for her resignation from the Service.

The women whose Foreign Service connection came about through marriage to a male member of the Service received even less official attention. Family members were virtually unacknowledged until 1919, when Congress, for the first time, authorized payment of their travel expenses to and from a post. Standard works on the Foreign Service written in 1925 and 1948 make no mention whatever of spouses or families,[10] and in 1961, the State Department's own official history simply described the accepted role of wives overseas as that of setting up and running their households and helping to represent the United States. "Besides being a housekeeper," the book noted, "she must be a gracious hostess and enter into many social and community activities required by her position. In addition she must be ready at all times to assist the wife of the principal officer in carrying on the representational activities of the post."[11] All of these duties, of course, were to be performed without salary, but the wives were subject to favorable (or unfavorable) mentions on their husbands' performance evaluations.

Although the women's movement began to make impressive headway all across the United States, the Foreign Service seemed blissfully unaware of its potential impact on the world of diplomacy. As late as 1968 and 1970, working groups on the future of the Service, established by AFSA and by the Department of State, produced reams of studies and recommendations,[12] but only after protests by women employees did the department give initial consideration to problems that affected their careers. (Neither report accorded even a passing mention to Foreign Service families.) Indeed, the fact that the State Department maintained its policy that a woman member of the Foreign Service had to resign upon marriage as late as 1971 suggests the extent to which the Foreign Service was misreading the society from which it sprang.

After this policy was abandoned, several women who had been forced to resign simply because they had married sought and obtained reappointment in the Foreign Service. It was not until 1974, however, that the State Department issued a general invitation to all former women employees in this category to apply for reappointment, a step that led to the return of approximately forty women to the payroll over the next two years. More important, however, was the impetus the decision gave to the recruitment of women into the Service. As noted earlier (see Chapter 4), efforts to attract more women to Foreign Service careers were substantially augmented during the 1970s, and removal of what was, in effect, a bar to marriage undoubtedly made the Service appear more promising to potential female applicants.

For spouses, the expectations quoted earlier from the 1961 history of the Foreign Service had long prevailed throughout the international diplomatic community. "Two for the price of one" neatly summarized the situation. The husband was on the payroll, and the services of the wife were regarded by the Foreign Service (as by comparable services in other countries) as a no-cost extra benefit to the government that sent the couple abroad. Wives at Foreign Service posts found themselves in a hierarchical structure paralleling that of the official establishment, with the wife of the ambassador, or of the principal officer at a consular post, very much in command. One British writer commented that "the ambassadress is a figure to be regarded and treated with wariness by other wives. Sometimes she is hated; she is usually feared."[13] Most senior wives in the U.S. Foreign Service treated other wives with courtesy and consideration. However, there were just enough examples of "dragon ladies" issuing petty and peremptory orders—including one ambassador's wife who insisted on having her personal laundry hand washed by the wife of the most junior officer at the post—to make the system difficult for even the most hidebound conservatives to defend. (It should be noted that not all young officers or their wives let themselves be abused by the "dragon ladies," and those with the moral courage to refuse outrageous demands usually found their careers none the worse for the experience.)

The real problem with the two-for-one system was that the status and role of wives caught in the system were not theirs as individuals but derived solely from their husbands' positions. Thus, not surprisingly, they found it increasingly difficult to arrive at a satisfactory definition of their roles in light of the changing values of U.S. society. The way of life of women in the United States was being radically altered by "increased mobility, longevity, education" as well as by "economic necessity, brought about by inflation and soaring divorce rates."[14] At the same time, a fundamental reexamination of the appropriate roles for both men and women was under way, with a resultant movement toward "independent, individual, employment-related prime identities for men and women whether or not they are married."[15] With their derivative identities, Foreign Service wives—like the wives of such other public figures as members of Congress, ministers, and military officers—felt themselves left behind as the overall status of women began to shift.

Responding to pressure for change in the traditional two-for-one approach, the Department of State swept away the old system in 1972. Under the terms of the new directive, spouses were thenceforth to be regarded as "private persons," free to participate or not in the official activities of posts abroad as they themselves saw fit. To protect them against pressure to play an official part in community activities, all mention of spouses in an employee's performance evaluation was expressly forbidden. The 1972 directive was viewed by many spouses as tantamount to "liberation" for Foreign Service wives; others saw it as "an important first step in eliminating many of the injustices of the past,"[16] but they recognized that the full impact on the Foreign Service of the broader issues raised by the women's movement still remained to be addressed.

The continuing problem for Foreign Service spouses has several aspects. In a society that tends increasingly to define individual identities in terms of employment, Foreign Service life is not conducive to spouses' pursuing most careers. The Service itself is perfectly candid about this part of the problem and accords the subject relatively lengthy treatment in its recruitment brochure.

> Married applicants whose spouses seek their own careers should weigh carefully the implications of joining a highly mobile service in which worldwide availability is required. Both in Washington and overseas, the Foreign Service spouse is at a career disadvantage. Prospective employers often are reluctant to hire a spouse for a limited period of time. It is difficult to maintain professional contacts and to keep up-to-date in a given field. Abroad, where about 60% of a person's career may be spent, some spouses are able to work, but local regulations and circumstances typically limit opportunities severely.[17]

In effect, only highly portable or transferable careers will fit the pattern of Foreign Service life. Writers, artists, and teachers can follow a Foreign Service employee spouse around the world with some hope of working at their professions wherever they go, but few others can anticipate equal success. Even such seemingly mobile careers as medicine, nursing, and law frequently run afoul of local licensing laws and employment prohibitions that bar highly skilled professionals from working in their fields during tours of duty abroad.

To its credit, the Foreign Service has taken a number of steps aimed at improving overseas employment opportunities for spouses. The Family Liaison Office (FLO), established in

1978 (in response to a recommendation from the Association of American Foreign Service Women) as a two-way communications channel between Foreign Service spouses and senior management in the foreign affairs agencies, has been especially active in this area. FLO provides counseling and assistance to spouses seeking to reenter the labor force when they return to Washington, and it has represented the State Department in negotiating bilateral agreements with over a dozen countries under which diplomatic spouses are permitted to work abroad without requiring individual work permits. Although these programs are aimed primarily at opening professional career opportunities outside government service, the foreign affairs agencies have also made available to spouses an increasing number of part-time and full-time positions at posts overseas (along with training courses at the Foreign Service Institute that are prerequisites for certain jobs in the consular and administrative fields). Inevitably, in a Service that depends primarily on career staffing, few of these positions are at the professional level sought by many spouses, but they do at least make it possible for over half of today's Foreign Service spouses to hold salaried jobs while overseas.

None of these remedies addresses the second aspect of the dilemma that confronts many Foreign Service spouses, and especially those married to personnel at senior levels. For regardless of their personal wishes to "do their own thing," diplomatic and consular spouses are still implicitly expected to participate in aspects of their employee spouse's job. As one trained observer noted, "in most of the communities where we serve, and less overtly in our own society, wives of public persons are also *by definition* public persons with their positions defined as extensions of their husbands'."[18] For Foreign Service spouses, this means that the 1972 directive is a double-edged sword. Although it frees them from the *obligation* to participate in official activities, it cannot remove the community's *expectation* that they will do so—nor their own sense that their employee spouses need their help in order to operate at full effectiveness. Thus, most Foreign Service spouses, and particularly those at senior levels, have continued to fill something akin to the traditional "spouse role," but in the wake of the 1972 directive, they do so without any formal acknowledgment of their contributions.

This sense of having been cut adrift and of being less a part of a team is evident in the replies to a questionnaire circulated by AAFSW to Foreign Service spouses in 1984. More than half of the thirty-seven hundred respondents said they would feel a greater commitment to the Foreign Service if there were official recognition of their contributions, and half said they felt themselves to be unappreciated by the Service. These attitudes are part of a broader spectrum of views which reveal that the feelings of spouses toward the Foreign Service are generally less positive today than they remember them to have been ten years prior to the survey. In addition to the lack of recognition of their contributions and the disruption of career plans, spouses cite a number of other factors that they believe discourage overseas service—among them, difficulties in providing for children's education, health hazards and inadequate health care, the cost and disruption of frequent moves, and the threat of terrorism. Yet despite all these negatives, 79 percent of all respondents still "enjoy" Foreign Service life, and nearly two-thirds are still willing to make "the sacrifices demanded by life in the Foreign Service."[19]

The Foreign Service is indeed fortunate that most spouses do continue to participate in the life and work of posts abroad, for the Service would be far poorer without them. Most spouses who accompany members of the Service overseas actively support their employee spouses in representational activities, whether entertaining at home or participating in outside events. Some are active in local volunteer organizations that work with schools or hospitals or lend their talents to fund raising for charitable purposes. In all of these activities, they add an extra dimension beyond that provided by U.S. officialdom. As one veteran Foreign Service spouse has described the role:

> Wives extend American understanding of another country by moving beyond official circles into the daily life of schools, neighborhoods, social institutions. They serve as ears, eyes and hearts for husbands who are chancery-bound. They serve, too, by balancing the foreign image of America. A caring, active

American family counteracts Hollywood-fed stereotypes of America as a land of gangsters or bunny-girls.[20]

Although spouses fulfilling this more traditional role make a major contribution to the success of U.S. diplomacy abroad, not all spouses find it personally rewarding. Roughly four hundred of the respondents to the AAFSW survey (and nearly six hundred Foreign Service employees in all) have opted to become part of the team in the fullest possible sense by becoming career members of the Foreign Service along with their spouses. The "dual-career couple" has become increasingly familiar throughout U.S. society, and the Foreign Service has not remained immune. As of mid-1984, "tandem couples"—the official Foreign Service name for couples when both spouses are career employees of any of the five foreign affairs agencies—made up 8.5 percent of the Department of State's Foreign Service workforce[21] and a significant (though somewhat smaller) percentage in the other agencies. And, as in the society at large, the tendency is growing in Foreign Service ranks. Nearly half the nontandem spouses in the AAFSW survey indicated some interest in acquiring career status, and one in six has already taken the Foreign Service examination.

The foreign affairs agencies have been very supportive of tandems, and thus far have been generally successful in accommodating their needs within the overall personnel assignment system. Figures from the State Department are illustrative of the situation. As of mid-1984, the Foreign Service component of the State Department included 582 registered tandem employees (each member of the Service is assigned as an individual unless he or she formally asks to be considered as part of a tandem couple). Of these, 524 were married to other State Department employees while the spouses of the other 58 worked for USIA (45), AID (12), and FCS (1). Thus, there were 262 State-State tandems; 210 of them had assignments together, 29 were separated by assignment to different posts, and 23 couples had one spouse on leave without pay. USIA on the same date had nearly 80 tandems, including the 45 whose spouses worked for the State Department; AID had 64, of which 48 had both spouses within that agency; FCS had 4; and the Department of Agriculture elements of the Foreign Service had 2.

Except for career candidates, whose limited appointments are too short to permit both leave without pay and a fair test of their suitability for career status, the choice is left to the couple whenever assignments together are not possible. They may pursue their separate careers by taking assignments at different posts, or one spouse can drop off the payroll for two or three years and accompany the working member of the couple as a dependent. Like all members of the Service, tandems may also request leave without pay to meet other personal needs—whether to further their education or to spend more time with their children. Such requests, however, need not be granted unless there will be some benefit to the Foreign Service; leave without pay for tandems unable to find assignments at the same post is granted as a matter of right.

Finding assignments together poses a major problem for tandem couples that their nontandem colleagues do not face: the prohibitions on nepotism embedded in federal statute and regulations. In essence, no member of a family may be in a position that has any supervisory relationship to another member of the same family—or that gives the appearance of such a relationship. One spouse may not give orders to the other or evaluate the performance of or in any way influence the career of his or her mate. In Washington, where spouses can be dispersed within the large bureaucracies of the foreign affairs community, the problem is relatively manageable. Overseas, however, it often proves difficult to fit both members of a tandem couple into a small post without running afoul of the nepotism statute. Except at the most junior levels, spouses usually may not work in the same section of an embassy or a consulate; at senior levels, the spouse of an ambassador cannot work at all within the mission, and the spouses of other senior officers find themselves severely limited in the range of available jobs.

This latter problem is well on its way to becoming more acute as the promotion process moves more and more members of tandem couples toward the upper ranks of the Service. Only about 6 percent of today's tandems are in the Senior Foreign Service, but nearly half are in the middle grades from FS-3 to

Carleton Coon and Jane Coon, the first married couple in the career Foreign Service to serve simultaneously as ambassadors.

FS-1. As the latter advance up the ladder, joint assignments inevitably will become more difficult to arrange. The Foreign Service has already had husband-and-wife ambassadors from the career ranks serving in neighboring countries (Nepal and Bangladesh), and other couples choosing to serve apart when one member became a chief of mission. Success in Foreign Service terms has a bittersweet aspect for tandems.

A related problem for tandems is that they must decide, at each reassignment, how high a price they are prepared to pay for togetherness. As the current statistics suggest, joint assignments are possible more often than not, but these figures almost certainly conceal several cases of employees in jobs outside their fields of interest or beneath their abilities. In order to remain together, one or both members of a tandem couple will on occasion agree to take a position that is less than ideal in career terms—in effect, place marriage above career. A number of

Foreign Service tandem couples follow an informal rule that the lead role in assignments will alternate from tour to tour. One time the wife picks a career-enhancing job, and the husband takes whatever he can get (including leave without pay, if necessary); the next time, the husband chooses first, and the wife follows along. Whatever the course followed by a particular couple, their tandem status almost inevitably handicaps their careers and may, in consequence, breed the kind of resentments that can strain their marriage. For many couples, tandem assignments offer a welcome opportunity to pursue mutually fulfilling careers, but they are not without their drawbacks.

As the foregoing discussion suggests, both tandem couples and nontandem spouses are more likely to find professionally rewarding jobs in Washington than at most overseas posts, a fact of life that complicates the pursuit of career satisfaction within the Foreign Service context. One immediate consequence has been a reluctance on the part of some members of the Service to leave Washington at the end of a normal domestic tour of duty. In some cases involving nontandems, families come to depend on two incomes, one of which is likely to be lost when they return abroad. For tandems, the problem may be simply the difficulty of finding two career-enhancing jobs at the same post or, as both members of the couple become more senior in rank, of finding any post overseas where they can serve together. To cope with this growing reluctance to leave home, all of the foreign affairs agencies in recent years have established a maximum tour length for most categories of domestic assignment that is shorter than the eight-year limit specified in the Foreign Service Acts of 1946 and 1980, with the State Department's five-year limit being the most generous.

Another factor that sometimes causes Foreign Service personnel to seek extended domestic assignments is a desire to provide a degree of continuity in their children's education. "The problem of educating their children," the department's official history noted in 1961, "is probably the most difficult one which Foreign Service parents have to face."[22] Most children who grow up in the Service attend a variety of schools for relatively short periods of time as their parents transfer every few years from post to post. And, of course, the schools come in all shapes and sizes. Some posts offer excellent American or international schools (many of which receive modest grants from the U.S. government though they are basically self-financed through tuition payments); a few have schools run by missionaries or (where there are U.S. military commands) by the Department of Defense; some have good public or parochial schools; and some have no adequate schools at all. Even when the quality of the schools is high, the curriculum or the language of instruction may not be the same as in the United States; in the Southern Hemisphere, the summer vacation falls in December and January so that a transfer to South America or Australia can cost children an entire school year.

Parents adopt a wide range of strategies to cope with these difficulties. When schools are adequate, most U.S. personnel tend to keep their children with them, at least through the primary grades. Even in the absence of good schools, Foreign Service parents generally resort to home teaching using correspondence courses rather than send primary-age children away to boarding schools. At the secondary level, however, when concern with qualifying for entrance to a college or a university comes to the fore, parents serving abroad are more likely to opt for good boarding schools unless the local facilities are of top quality. As a general rule, the education allowances payable under the Foreign Service Act are intended to assure all children an education equivalent to what they would receive from the public school system if they were living in the United States. To this end, the allowances cover tuition for schools at a post when these have been certified as satisfactory by the Department of State's Office of Overseas Schools. In the absence of such schools, the allowances are designed to meet full tuition and travel costs to allow children to attend appropriate schools away from post.

In addition to discontinuity in their formal education, children of Foreign Service parents also pay an emotional price for having to give up friends every few years and make new ones. On the positive side, they acquire first-hand knowledge and experience of different peoples and cultures, and they often acquire early language skills. On balance, most parents think their children come out ahead in the process. In the 1984 AAFSW survey of spouse attitudes, a clear majority (53 percent) said that "my children have gained more than they have lost through life in the Foreign Service," and only 16 percent of respondents felt that "living overseas has created difficult problems for my children."[23]

For some parents, the simplest answer to educational problems as well as to career concerns is to remain for extended periods in the United States. Since this option quickly runs up against the maximum tour-of-duty policies of the foreign affairs agencies, however, it has only limited utility for Foreign Service employees. Under the 1980 Foreign Service Act, an additional option is now available to families willing to accept separation in order to pursue educational or career goals—the separate maintenance allowance (SMA). An allowance to meet the expenses of families separated from the employee member was first introduced during World War I, when families were evacuated from potentially dangerous posts that were within reach of the contending armies. Over the next sixty years, the allowance was available at government option whenever it became necessary to remove families from beleaguered posts.

In 1980, the SMA was made available to families on a voluntary basis for the first time. A spouse who wishes to remain in the United States for whatever reason (most commonly, to pursue a career or to permit a child to complete his or her education) may now be granted an SMA simply on the basis of the employee spouse's request. (Since the government is spared both transportation and allowance costs associated with sending family members abroad, an SMA on this basis is virtually a no-cost option for the taxpayer.) Thus far, the total number of families receiving a voluntary SMA has been small—only about three hundred as of mid-1984, compared with a total Foreign Service population overseas of nearly seven thousand. However, the stated willingness of 39 percent of the respondents to the AAFSW survey to accept separation from their spouses if necessary for career, education, or other reasons suggests that voluntary SMAs may be more widely utilized in the future.[24]

Shifting Attitudes

The women's movement of the 1960s was only part of a broader rethinking of values that was taking place across a wide spectrum of U.S. society. The same decade saw equally dramatic changes in other areas of life in the United States: the growing activism of the civil rights movement, highlighted by a massive march on Washington in the late summer of 1963; the parallel growth of two distinct strains in a new youth culture, "hippies" who rejected organized society and student radicals seeking its transformation; and, perhaps most important, the emergence as the decade progressed of a broad movement in opposition to U.S. involvement in Vietnam. These various strains of protest sometimes flowed together and sometimes apart, but they shared an important common characteristic. Each of them challenged established authority and the established way of doing things; each refused to accept the values and institutions of the generations that had gone before.

The changes in attitude occasioned by the social turbulence of the 1960s affected all elements of U.S. society, and once again, the Foreign Service could not remain apart. In 1970, the Department of State took formal note of what it called "a fundamental estrangement between youth and our political, social and economic institutions"[25] and went on to note "the disposition of young people today to challenge established traditions, to assert their individuality in a world increasingly big and impersonal, to demand greater freedom of expression and greater participation in the decisions of the organization than bureaucracies have traditionally allowed."[26]

One highly visible result for the Foreign Service was a drop in the number of applicants for the Foreign Service examination as potential candidates who were hostile to the U.S. role in Vietnam rejected any form of government service as a career option. Another result was an increased willingness on the part of many younger members of the Service to challenge their own establishment—the management of the foreign affairs agencies. Although the American Foreign Service Association was not to become a union until 1973 (see Chapter 3), it adopted a stance of greater activism on behalf of its members during the late 1960s following the election of a slate of officers who soon came to be known as "the Young Turks." In the early 1970s, the extension to federal workers (including those of the Foreign Service) of the right to negotiate collectively with their agencies was a further manifestation of this broad phenomenon of social change, and both AFSA and the American Federation of Government Employees proved willing to bargain tenaciously with agency managements.

With the final U.S. withdrawal from Vietnam, much of the steam went out of the protest movement in the United States. Its legacy, however, remained and combined with the continuing pressure of the women's movement to produce an impact on the Foreign Service characterized in these terms in a 1977 memorandum from the director general of the Foreign Service to the secretary of state: "The changing social mood of the nation over the past decade has created a population far less inclined to accept arguments of 'service needs' or 'national interest' as overriding individual or family preferences and needs."[27]

What had emerged in the society at large quickly gained the nickname of the "me generation," a sobriquet that, in suggesting its members were motivated purely by selfishness, took insufficient account of the complex events by which that generation had been formed. Indeed, members of the "me generation" came back to the Foreign Service in record numbers, with the number of applicants for the annual examination rising steadily through the late 1970s and early 1980s. Nor has the quality of the new appointees suffered in any way; in both their educational attainments and their prior experience, they are of uniformly high caliber. Where they—men and women alike—differ from their predecessors is in their greater readiness to question established authority and conventional wisdom and in their willingness to fight "the system" if they feel they have been treated unfairly rather than simply to accept management decisions.

They also differ in having what appears to be less of a lifetime career commitment than was once the rule. Today's recruits belong to a more mobile generation than their predecessors, and they are prepared to switch careers if an initial choice does not measure up to expectations. Indeed, the average age of entering FSOs is about thirty and that of Foreign Service secretaries about thirty-five; in most cases, they have already tried another career before joining the Service, and many indicate a readiness to make yet another change if the Service proves incompatible with their own or their spouses' career expectations.

Thus far, resignations from the Foreign Service remain relatively rare (below 5 percent of the total Service per year). Nonetheless, as tandem couples rise in seniority and encounter the inevitably more difficult problem of finding assignments not tainted by the reality or appearance of nepotism, and as non-tandem spouses become increasingly insistent on having access to their own career opportunities, the shape of the Service may well change. One perceptive commentator has suggested the possibility "that fewer individuals will be willing to serve full Foreign Service careers and that, instead, a larger number of individuals and family members will spend a part but not all of their working lives in the Service."[28] The Service has not yet reached that point, but existing trends may well influence its employees in that direction.

Meanwhile, the Foreign Service structure and career patterns described earlier (see Chapters 3 and 4) reflect to a considerable extent the needs and concerns of this new generation of Foreign Service employees, whose formative years coincided in many cases with the challenges to society mounted in the 1960s by women, students, and other groups. The flexibility of the assignment process, which seeks to take account of personal and family considerations as well as the needs of the Service; the readiness of the foreign affairs agencies to accommodate the growing number of tandem couples; the existence of employee representative organizations in several agencies, which are prepared to bargain with management and to lobby Congress on traditional pocketbook issues as well as on broader questions concerning the future of the Service; and the availability to all personnel of an impartial grievance mechanism to investigate and redress individual complaints of alleged management wrong-doing—these and other features of the system are simply institutionalized mechanisms to accommodate an employee population that is no longer prepared to leave decisions about its own future entirely in the hands of others.

The attitudes of the new generation in the Foreign Service have been much bemoaned by some (but by no means all) of their elders, just as the attitudes of some younger spouses have dismayed the more senior spouses who are themselves products of the traditional system in which an ambassador's wife once ruled supreme. Their expressed concern is not entirely without justification. Some Foreign Service employees have proved reluctant to return abroad, particularly to hardship posts, often pleading such legitimate reasons as spouse careers, children's education, and dangerous or difficult conditions at the proposed post of assignment. Others have taken advantage of the "open assignments" system to avoid a fair share of duty at less attractive posts; a few have abused the grievance mechanism to frustrate otherwise appropriate management actions by alleging minor procedural flaws. Fortunately, however, such individuals are a distinct minority within the Service (indeed, in the State Department component, AFSA has joined with management in reemphasizing the vital importance of discipline to the Service as an institution). Beyond this relative handful of problem cases, there remains above all a sense of discomfort on the part of managers accustomed to an era of unquestioning obedience, and there is the likelihood of a period of further uncertainty as both sides continue the process of adjusting to the new relationships derived from the society at large.

Terrorism and Other Dangers

For all its seeming glamour, diplomacy as a profession has never been entirely free of risk. Although the right of ambassadors to personal security and to immunity from civil and criminal jurisdiction has been an accepted legal principle since Roman times, there have always been risks against which legal principles provide scant protection. In the lobby of the State Department, there are two marble tablets bearing the names of U.S. diplomatic and consular officers "who while on active duty lost their lives under heroic or tragic circumstances." The first

A once-rare sight becomes all too familiar as workmen chisel new names into the memorial tablets at the State Department.

tablet, with eighty names, took the Service from its origins through the mid-1960s; the second, of comparable size, has been nearly filled in less than two decades.

As the tablets in the lobby make clear, members of the Foreign Service have faced a variety of risks over the past two hundred years. Travel, so much a part of Foreign Service life, has brought its share of danger for U.S. representatives abroad.

Indeed, the first U.S. consular official formally named by Congress, William Palfrey, was lost at sea in 1780 en route to his post in Paris. (Between 1827 and 1918, six other U.S. officials suffered a similar fate.) A successor at the Paris embassy, Joel Barlow, died of exposure in 1812 when he got caught up in Napoleon's retreat from Russia while attempting to maintain contact with the peripatetic emperor. Even under the greatly improved conditions of the twentieth century, there have been travel-related deaths, not all of which are recorded on the memorial tablets: one FSO died while attempting to cross the Sahara on his way to a new post, couriers have perished in plane crashes, and several members of the Service have been killed in automobile accidents around the world.

For many years, disease was the greatest killer of U.S. officials abroad. Yellow fever, cholera, smallpox, and a variety of undiagnosed "epidemics" and "fevers" carried off diplomats and consuls from Mexico City to Monrovia and from Baghdad to Venice. (The list of victims includes famed political cartoonist Thomas Nast, scourge of New York's infamous Boss Tweed, who died of yellow fever in Guayaquil, Ecuador, in 1902, less than a year after accepting a consular appointment from his friend and admirer Theodore Roosevelt.) Only in the last half-century have deaths from disease finally been brought under control, thanks to advances in medical knowledge and in the medical support provided by the foreign affairs agencies to their personnel and families overseas. At many posts that lack adequate local medical facilities, a doctor or nurse (usually from the State Department, but sometimes from the Peace Corps) forms part of the embassy complement and provides diagnosis and initial treatment on the spot. In cases of serious illness, patients are evacuated to a neighboring country with good hospitals, to a U.S. military installation, or even to the United States. Although these improvements in available medical care have sharply reduced the fatality rate from disease, the threat of major or minor illness remains a constant worry for Foreign Service employees and their families at many posts around the world.

In recent years, as the risks to life from travel and disease have diminished, the new threat from international terrorism has made all the earlier dangers pale by comparison. In the past, diplomatic and consular personnel who died in the nation's service were for the most part unintended victims. When a ship sank or a plane crashed, when disease struck, or when an earthquake or a volcanic eruption ravaged a city, U.S. officials who died lost their lives simply because their duties had put them in a situation of risk. U.S. representatives abroad rarely were the targets of violence directed specifically at them. Only twice during the nineteenth century did U.S. consuls lose their lives as the result of individual attacks—one was murdered in Colombia in 1825 and one in Madagascar in 1888. Even in the present century, there were only two such episodes prior to World War II—one member of the embassy staff was killed by an angry mob in Teheran in 1924 when he inadvertently intruded into a religious procession, and another officer was murdered in Beirut in 1937.

In the years following World War II, however, a new pattern emerged. Diplomatic and consular offices and personnel came to be viewed as legitimate targets by groups protesting policies they disliked or merely seeking to attract media attention. Equally important, diplomats and consuls tend to be relatively "soft" targets. To do their work effectively, they must be available to a variety of visitors in their offices, and they also must reach out actively to all segments of the society. In doing so, they expose themselves to potential attacks. As they improve their security by bolting the doors and traveling only under escort, they limit their own ability to do the jobs for which they have been sent abroad in the first place.

Since the early 1970s, diplomatic and consular officials have become the major targets of international terrorism. In 1975, 30 percent of all international terrorist attacks were directed against diplomats; by 1980, that figure had increased to 54 percent, and has remained at or near the same level ever since. Diplomats of many nations have been victims of terrorist attacks. U.S. diplomats have led the list of targets, followed by official representatives of Israel, the Soviet Union, the United Kingdom, and Cuba. They have not been alone. Among others, a French ambassador was assassinated in Beirut; Saudi and Iraqi embassies have been destroyed by bomb attacks; and a number of Turkish diplomats (including five ambassadors) have been gunned down by Armenian "nationalists." In all, the embassies of forty countries have been seized by international terrorists, and diplomats from nearly fifty countries have been kidnapped and held hostage by terrorist groups.[29]

U.S. personnel occupy a discouragingly prominent place among the victims. A sniper in Jerusalem in 1945, a grenade in Nicosia in 1956, an embassy bombing in Saigon in 1965 all claimed victims. Since then, the intervals between attacks have grown shorter. The first U.S. ambassador killed in the line of duty fell to terrorists in Guatemala in 1968, the second in Khartoum in 1973; they have since been joined by three others, as well as by a growing number of colleagues of lesser rank who are memorialized on the tablets in the State Department lobby.

There is no way to provide total security to diplomatic and consular personnel and still leave them with enough freedom of movement to get their jobs done. ("If diplomacy is to go forward," one ambassador has observed, "there must be a compromise.")[30] While recognizing this inherent dilemma, the foreign affairs agencies have made a major effort to augment the security of Foreign Service personnel and establishments abroad. With strong support from Congress, the agencies have launched a security enhancement program, which includes, for example, a variety of measures to improve the physical security of diplomatic and consular premises; armor plating for official vehicles; stepped-up guard services both for high-risk individuals and for homes and offices; and a special training course for employees and family members that focuses on ways of coping with the terrorist threat.

Although these and other improvements offer somewhat greater protection for Foreign Service personnel abroad, the risks clearly remain. In 1972, when a number of Israeli Olympic athletes were murdered by Palestinians in Munich, the *Economist* magazine featured on its cover a grainy photograph of one of the assassins—a shadowy figure in a stocking mask. Its caption was grimly prophetic: "He and his kind will be among us for the rest of our lives."[31] The years since that statement was made have done nothing to dim its force.

A number of embassies have been terrorist targets. In 1983, it was the one in Beirut (top, as Ambassador Robert Dillon, flanked by guards, leaves the shattered chancery); in 1984, the targets included the embassy in Kuwait (bottom) and a replacement embassy building in Beirut.

Notes

1. Eric Clark, *Corps Diplomatique* (London: Allen Lane, 1973), p. 9.

2. American Foreign Service Association, *Toward a Modern Diplomacy* (Washington, D.C.: American Foreign Service Association, 1968), p. 4.

3. Ibid., p. 22.

4. William Macomber, *The Angels' Game: A Handbook of Modern Diplomacy* (New York: Stein and Day, 1975), p. 88.

5. National Security Action Memorandum (NSAM) 341, March 4, 1966. The text of this document is reproduced in John Ensor Harr, *The Professional Diplomat* (Princeton, N.J.: Princeton University Press, 1969), pp. 361–366.

6. The story of this "revolution" is told in Homer L. Calkin, *Women in the Department of State: Their Role in American Foreign Affairs*, Department of State Publication 8951 (Washington, D.C.: U.S. Department of State, 1978), pp. 131–149.

7. William I. Bacchus, *Staffing for Foreign Affairs* (Princeton, N.J.: Princeton University Press, 1983), p. 154.

8. Elmer Plischke, *Conduct of American Diplomacy* (Princeton, N.J.: D. Van Nostrand Company, 1950), p. 188.

9. Ibid.

10. Tracy Hollingsworth Lay, *The Foreign Service of the United States* (New York: Prentice-Hall, 1925); J. Rives Childs, *American Foreign Service* (New York: Henry Holt and Company, 1948).

11. William Barnes and John Heath Morgan, *The Foreign Service of the United States* (Washington, D.C.: Historical Office, Bureau of Public Affairs, U.S. Department of State, 1961), p. 325.

12. American Foreign Service Association, *Toward a Modern Diplomacy*; U.S. Department of State, *Diplomacy for the 70's: A Program of Management Reform for the Department of State*, Department of State Publication 8551 (Washington, D.C.: U.S. Department of State, 1970).

13. Clark, *Corps Diplomatique*, p. 93.

14. Lesley Dorman and Patricia Ryan, in Martin F. Herz, ed., *Diplomacy: The Role of the Wife* (Washington, D.C.: Institute for the Study of Diplomacy, Georgetown University, 1981), p. 1.

15. Margaret W. Sullivan, in ibid., p. 61.

16. Dorman and Ryan, p. 1.

17. U.S. Department of State, *Foreign Service Careers*, Department of State Publication 9202 (Washington, D.C.: U.S. Department of State, 1984), p. 19.

18. Sullivan, pp. 62–63.

19. Association of American Foreign Service Women, *The Foreign Service Spouse Overseas* (Washington, D.C.: Association of American Foreign Service Women, 1984), sec. 7, p. 8, and the balance of sec. 7.

20. Joan R. Wilson, in Herz, *Diplomacy*, pp. 19–20.

21. Janet G. Buechel, "Tandem Employees," *State*, no. 269 (July 1984), pp. 20–21.

22. Barnes and Morgan, *The Foreign Service of the United States*, p. 326.

23. Association of American Foreign Service Women, *The Foreign Service Spouse Overseas*, sec. 8, p. 3.

24. Ibid., sec. 5, p. 4.

25. American Foreign Service Association, *Toward A Modern Diplomacy*, p. 401.

26. Ibid., p. 303.

27. Quoted in Bacchus, *Staffing for Foreign Affairs*, p. 98.

28. Ibid., p. 159.

29. All statistics in this section are drawn from U.S. Department of State, *Terrorist Incidents Involving Diplomats* (Washington, D.C.: Office for Combatting Terrorism, U.S. Department of State, August 1983).

30. David D. Newsom, "The Diplomat's Task Versus Security," in Martin F. Herz, ed., *Diplomats and Terrorists: What Works, What Doesn't* (Washington, D.C.: Institute for the Study of Diplomacy, Georgetown University, 1982), p. 10.

31. *Economist* 224:6733 (September 9–15, 1972).

9

CONCLUSION—A LOOK AHEAD

. . . the issues of diplomacy are of ever greater importance, since a stupid move could destroy us all in a few minutes.
—Lord Humphrey Trevelyan, 1973

The Foreign Service is still trying to come to terms with the post–World War II world and with the triple whammy of recent years: the impact of the women's movement, the parallel shift in American attitudes, and the spread of terrorism. This has been a period of radical changes in the international environment, the agenda of foreign policy, the domestic decision-making structure, and U.S. society. For a tradition-bound institution like the Foreign Service, the process of adjustment has not been easy.

The task has been further complicated by a recurrent debate about whether the Service is still relevant in the foreign policy process—or, if it is relevant, whether it is appreciated by the elected officials who are the ultimate decision-makers in foreign affairs. Part of the problem stems from a growing politicization of foreign policy. The bipartisan character of policy-making in the immediate postwar years, when it was commonly said that "politics stops at the water's edge," gave way to the situation prevailing today in which domestic political considerations impinge on nearly every foreign policy decision. Slow to recognize and to accept this change, the Foreign Service too often interpreted its role narrowly and failed to include domestic political factors in its recommendations. Under those circumstances, administration officials sometimes viewed the Service as naive,

225

unhelpful, or obstructionist (if not all three) and turned elsewhere (to the NSC, to other government departments, and even to experts outside the government) for advice and counsel.

The Foreign Service contributed in another way to bringing its own relevance into question. Earlier in this book I have discussed the attempts made by the Service (and the State Department) to adjust to the postwar loss of their virtual monopoly over foreign affairs and the arrival on the scene of new claimants to power in the decision-making process. As one former ambassador noted, "We declined to press upon ourselves and the Department of State the urgent need for facing these new areas of international policy,"[1] with the result that much of the new foreign affairs agenda was put in the hands of agencies outside the Foreign Service structure.

Fortunately, the Service has largely overcome the problems that gave rise to these particular challenges to its relevance in the foreign policy process. Members of today's Service have grown increasingly knowledgeable about the interplay between domestic politics and foreign affairs, and thus they can be more responsive to the concerns of administrations for which they work. The Foreign Service has also come to terms with the new Washington power structure and is learning to operate effectively in the multi-agency bureaucracy that is now concerned with foreign affairs. Training courses (and especially State's new program for recently tenured FSOs) teach the techniques that lead to influence in the decision-making process, and officers are detailed to other agencies and to Capitol Hill to learn at first-hand the concerns and the modus operandi of the other players in the game.

As this discussion suggests, most of the soul-searching about relevance has focused on the Foreign Service role at home. Members of the Service have seldom had serious doubts about the relevance of their work overseas, even though debate on the topic has been common since the invention of the telegraph in the nineteenth century. Prior to that time, an envoy normally was sent abroad "with written instructions indicating to him the general line which he should follow and the main purpose which he should strive to achieve. Once he reached his post he became almost cut off from his own government and had to steer his course by his own compass and under alien stars."[2] In this marvelously mechanical age, however, when an ambassador is never more than a few minutes away by phone or cable from his or her home office (and often only a few hours away from having senior officials from home drop in for a working visit), some have argued that chiefs of mission and their staffs are little more than messengers, running telegrams between governments, and that their work could be done equally well (and more economically) by envoys sent from home as the need arises.

Members of the Foreign Service, however, and people who have watched them at work, harbor no such illusions. They recognize that the role of the man or woman on the spot has become more, rather than less, critical in a world in which the business of diplomacy is increasingly complex and the price of failure is infinitely greater. Foreign Service personnel today deal with issues that were unknown in "traditional diplomacy," running the gamut from economic assistance and information activities to science, narcotics, and human rights. If they are doing their job right, the ambassador in the field, in the words of one of their number, "ought to have a better feel for the local situation, the local feelings, the local intentions, and the local responses than even the most exalted habitué of the periphery of the Oval Office or the State Department's sacred seventh floor."[3] With that knowledge in hand, the chief of mission and the embassy staff can make sure that neither the host government nor the U.S. government is caught off guard, can provide information and recommendations to guide U.S. decision-making, and can ensure that the policy emerging from the Washington process is faithfully and effectively carried out.

Thus, the Foreign Service—both at home and abroad— retains an essential role in the execution of U.S. foreign policy and remains a major contributor to its formulation. Despite the problems outlined in the preceding chapter, the Service continues to attract and retain the personnel it needs to do the job effectively. The number of applicants taking the annual Foreign Service examination has stayed at near-record levels, vacancy announcements in the nonexamination functions continue to attract well-qualified candidates, and resignations from the Service remain few and far between. Although some potential candidates are lost to higher-paying jobs in the private sector, there are still more than enough capable men and women to meet the need—including those like one recruit who took a 50 percent salary cut when he switched to the Foreign Service and explained his decision with the simple statement, "I figured that I would find more adventure in the Service than in any bank."[4]

One final question warrants further exploration. The opening chapter of this book notes that the Foreign Service of the United States is, by statute, a single service, yet in practice, it operates almost as though it were six separate services belonging to five different agencies. The clear intention of the framers of the Foreign Service Act of 1980 was to move toward a single service in fact as well as in law. However, that goal thus far has been stymied, largely by the caveats regarding the residual authority of agency heads that were written into the act as part of the compromises that brought it into being.

For now, there is little prospect of any significant change in this situation. Unless the functions performed by the various agencies operating under the Foreign Service Act are brought under a single roof, it is hard to see how their personnel can be consolidated into a single corps. The comments of a State Department task force that examined the issue in 1970 remain equally valid today: ". . . many students of foreign affairs have been intrigued by the idea of creating a single foreign affairs agency bringing together all the activities and personnel of the executive agencies presently engaged in foreign affairs. The task forces do not believe this goal can be realized in the foreseeable future."[5]

Nonetheless, the Foreign Service Act of 1980 has made a start in this direction simply by bringing the six foreign affairs services under a single Foreign Service umbrella for the first time. Whether the Foreign Service likes it or not, those "operational" aspects of the new diplomacy which the Foreign Service spurned after World War II are now part of its responsibilities, albeit in the hands of agencies other than the State Department. In addition, several of the agencies that State was charged with coordinating now find themselves inside the Foreign Service family, even though they remain essentially autonomous in both programs and internal management. Members of the Foreign Service increasingly share a sense of common purpose that extends across their parent agencies, especially at many missions abroad. In time, they may themselves prove to be the catalysts of the necessary changes that could someday give more than statutory unity to the Service of which they are all a part.

Today's Foreign Service, spanning five agencies and including roughly thirteen thousand U.S. citizens (plus another eighteen thousand foreign nationals), represents, in a very real sense, the United States' first line of defense. War and diplomacy, as Karl von Clausewitz aptly noted, are basically two aspects of a single process through which nations seek to achieve their aims. When diplomacy (broadly defined to include the formulation of policy as well as its execution) fails in its task of defending national interests, governments sometimes feel impelled to resort to war. That option has always been costly for the nations and peoples affected by the conflict; in the nuclear age, it could prove catastrophic for all mankind. Thus, the wisdom and common sense of those who make policy, and the skills of those who implement it, are of greater importance today than ever before. In the process, there is no substitute for a corps of skilled professionals who are ready and willing to meet the United States' foreign policy responsibilities at home and abroad. The Foreign Service of the United States has met that need for over two hundred years; it stands ready to carry on in the same tradition as it moves into its third and most challenging century.

Notes

1. Ambassador Lucius Battle, speaking to the American Foreign Service Association in 1963, as quoted in John Ensor Harr, *The Professional Diplomat* (Princeton, N.J.: Princeton University Press, 1969), p. 281.

2. Harold Nicolson, *Diplomacy*, 2d ed. (London: Oxford University Press, 1952), p. 74.

3. Kingman Brewster, "Advice to a New Ambassador," in Martin F. Herz, ed., *The Modern Ambassador: The Challenge and the Search*

(Washington, D.C.: Institute for the Study of Diplomacy, Georgetown University, 1983), p. 28.

4. Eduardo Lachica, "Lost Luster: A Foreign Service Post Isn't the Prize It Was for Best and Brightest," *Wall Street Journal* 204:42 (August 29, 1984), p. 14.

5. U.S. Department of State, *Diplomacy for the 70's: A Program of Management Reform for the Department of State*, Department of State Publication 8551 (Washington, D.C.: U.S. Department of State, 1970), p. 29.

Appendixes

FOREIGN SERVICE PERSONNEL

This table includes all full-time U.S. personnel holding career or career-conditional (that is, candidates for career status) appointments in the Foreign Service as of September 30, 1984. They are listed by grade in three categories: SFS (Senior Foreign Service) and FSO (Foreign Service Officer) appointments, made by the President by and with the advice and consent of the Senate; and FP (Foreign Service Personnel) appointments, made by the heads of the individual foreign affairs agencies. The grade structure comprises the four SFS ranks of Career Ambassador (CA), Career Minister (CM), Minister-Counselor (MC), and Counselor (OC), and the Foreign Service scale from FS-1 down to FS-9. (Career candidate FSOs, who hold FP appointments until they receive tenure, are included in the FSO totals to provide a clearer picture of the functional distribution of personnel within each agency.)

	State	AID	USIA	FCS	FAS	APHIS
SFS-CA	3					
SFS-CM	43	6	5	1	2	
SFS-MC	329	62	44	1	8	1
SFS-OC	362	192	134	11	10	1
Subtotal	737	260	183	13	20	2

	State		AID		USIA		FCS		FAS		APHIS	
	FSO	FP	FSO	FP	FSO	FP	FSO	FP	FSO	FP	FSO	FP
FS-1	717	270	321	276	249	83	32		39			6
FS-2	859	482	309	331	239	97	41		57			20
FS-3	774	697	125	128	121	42	29		33			23
FS-4	850	823	69	27	73	59	9		9			20
FS-5	338	734	76	30	70	27			1			23
FS-6	90	632	10	49	25	11				8		1
FS-7		710		13		17				7		2
FS-8		387		4		7				6		
FS-9		53		1						1		
Sub-total	3,628	4,788	910	859	777	343	111		139	22		95
Agency total	9,153		2,029		1,303		124		181		97	

Source: Data furnished by the personnel offices of the foreign affairs agencies.

FOREIGN SERVICE POSTS, SEPTEMBER 30, 1984

The following list includes all posts staffed by career Foreign Service employees from one or more of the five foreign affairs agencies and indicates which of the agencies is represented at each of the posts. Diplomatic and consular posts are identified by the symbols (E) for an embassy, (M) for a mission, (USINT) for a U.S. Interests Section in a country with which the United States does not maintain diplomatic relations, (CG) for a consulate general, and (C) for a consulate. (Posts for which no symbols are shown do not have diplomatic or consular status.) In each case, the country is listed first, followed by the city or cities in which a post is located.

Post	State	USIS	AID	FCS	FAS	APHIS
Afghanistan -- Kabul (E)	x					
Algeria --						
Algiers (E)	x	x		x		
Oran (C)	x					
Antigua and Barbuda --						
St. Johns (E)	x					
Argentina -- Buenos Aires (E)	x	x		x	x	
Australia --						
Canberra (E)	x	x		x	x	x
Brisbane (C)	x					
Melbourne (CG)	x			x		
Perth (CG)	x			x		
Sydney (CG)	x	x		x		
Austria --						
Vienna (E)	x	x		x	x	
Salzburg (C)	x					
Bahamas --						
Nassau (E)	x	x				x
Freeport						x
Bahrain -- Manama (E)	x	x		x		
Bangladesh -- Dhaka (E)	x	x	x	x		
Barbados -- Bridgetown (E)	x	x	x	x		

Post	State	USIS	AID	FCS	FAS	APHIS
Belgium --						
Brussels (E)	x	x		x	x	
Antwerp (CG)	x					
Belize -- Belize City (E)	x		x			
Benin -- Cotonou (E)	x	x				
Bermuda -- Hamilton (CG)	x					x
Bolivia -- La Paz (E)	x	x	x			
Botswana --						
Gaborone (E)	x	x	x			
Selebi Phikwi		x				
Brazil --						
Brasília (E)	x	x		x	x	
Belo Horizonte		x				
Pôrto Alegre (C)	x	x				
Recife (C)	x	x				
Rio de Janeiro (CG)	x	x		x		
Salvador de Bahia (C)	x	x				
São Paulo (CG)	x	x		x		
Brunei -- Bandar Seri Begawan (E)	x					
Bulgaria -- Sofia (E)	x	x				
Burkina Faso -- Ouagadougou (E)	x	x	x			
Burma -- Rangoon (E)	x	x	x			
Burundi -- Bujumbura (E)	x	x	x			
Cameroon --						
Yaoundé (E)	x	x	x	x		
Douala (CG)	x	x		x		
Canada --						
Ottawa (E)	x	x		x	x	
Calgary (CG)	x			x		
Halifax (CG)	x					
Montreal (CG)	x	x		x		
Quebec (CG)	x					
Toronto (CG)	x	x		x		
Vancouver (CG)	x	x		x		
Winnipeg (CG)	x					
Cape Verde -- Praia (E)	x		x			
Central African Republic --						
Bangui (E)	x	x				
Chad -- N'Djamena (E)	x	x	x			
Chile -- Santiago (E)	x	x		x	x	x
China --						
Beijing (E)	x	x		x	x	
Guangzhou (CG)	x	x		x		
Shanghai (CG)	x	x		x		
Shenyang (CG)	x					

Post	State	USIS	AID	FCS	FAS	APHIS
Colombia --						
Bogotá (E)	x	x		x	x	x
Cali		x				
Medellin		x				
Congo, People's Republic of --						
Brazzaville (E)	x	x				
Costa Rica -- San José (E)	x	x	x	x	x	x
Cuba -- Havana (USINT)	x	x				
Cyprus -- Nicosia (E)	x	x				
Czechoslovakia -- Prague (E)	x	x				
Denmark -- Copenhagen (E)	x	x		x	x	
Djibouti -- Djibouti (E)	x		x			
Dominican Republic --						
Santo Domingo (E)	x	x	x	x	x	x
Ecuador --						
Quito (E)	x	x	x	x	x	
Guayaquil (CG)	x	x				
Egypt --						
Cairo (E)	x	x	x	x	x	
Alexandria (CG)	x	x		x		
El Salvador -- San Salvador (E)	x	x				
Equatorial Guinea -- Malabo (E)	x					
Ethiopia -- Addis Ababa (E)	x					
Fiji -- Suva (E)	x	x	x			
Finland -- Helsinki (E)	x	x		x		
France --						
Paris (E)	x	x		x	x	
Bordeaux (CG)	x					
Lyon (CG)	x					
Marseille (CG)	x					
Nice (CG)	x					
Strasbourg (CG)	x					
French Caribbean Department --						
Martinique (C)	x					
Gabon -- Libreville (E)	x	x				
Gambia, The -- Banjul (E)	x		x			
German Democratic Republic --						
Berlin (E)	x	x			x	

Post	State	USIA	AID	FCS	FAS	APHIS
Germany, Federal Republic of --						
Bonn (E)	x	x		x	x	
Berlin (M)	x	x				
Bremen (C)	x					
Cologne		x				
Dusseldorf (CG)	x	x		x		
Frankfurt am Main (CG)	x	x		x		
Hamburg (CG)	x	x		x	x	
Hanover		x				
Heidelberg		x				
Mannheim						x
Munich (CG)	x	x		x		
Nürnberg		x				
Stuttgart (CG)	x	x		x		
Ghana -- Accra (E)	x	x	x			
Greece --						
Athens (E)	x	x		x	x	
Kaválla		x				
Rhodes		x				
Thessaloníki (CG)	x					
Grenada -- St. George's (E)	x					
Guatemala -- Guatemala (E)	x	x	x	x	x	x
Guinea -- Conakry (E)	x	x	x			
Guinea-Bissau -- Bissau (E)	x		x			
Guyana -- Georgetown (E)	x	x	x			
Haiti -- Port-au-Prince (E)	x	x	x			x
Holy See -- Vatican City (E)	x					
Honduras -- Tegucigalpa (E)	x	x	x	x		x
Hong Kong -- Hong Kong (CG)	x	x		x	x	
Hungary -- Budapest (E)	x	x		x		
Iceland -- Reykjavik (E)	x	x				
India --						
New Delhi (E)	x	x	x	x	x	x
Bombay (CG)	x	x		x		
Calcutta (CG)	x	x				
Madras (CG)	x	x				
Indonesia --						
Jakarta (E)	x	x	x	x	x	
Medan (C)	x	x				
Surabaya (C)	x	x				
Iraq -- Baghdad (E)	x	x		x		
Ireland -- Dublin (E)	x	x			x	
Israel -- Tel Aviv (E)	x	x		x	x	

Post	State	USIS	AID	FCS	FAS	APHIS
Italy --						
Rome (E)	x	x		x	x	x
Florence (CG)	x	x				
Genoa (CG)	x	x				
Milan (CG)	x	x		x		
Naples (CG)	x	x	x			
Palermo (CG)	x	x				
Trieste (C)	x	x				
Turin (C)	x	x				
Ivory Coast -- Abidjan (E)	x	x	x	x	x	
Jamaica -- Kingston (E)	x	x	x	x		
Japan --						
Tokyo (E)	x	x		x	x	x
Fukuoka (C)	x	x				
Kyoto		x				
Nagoya		x				
Naha (CG)	x					
Osaka-Kobe (CG)	x	x		x		
Sapporo (C)	x	x				
Jerusalem -- Jerusalem (CG)	x	x				
Jordan -- Amman (E)	x	x	x			
Kenya --						
Nairobi (E)	x	x	x	x	x	
Mombasa (C)	x					
Korea --						
Seoul (E)	x	x		x	x	
Kwangju		x				
Pusan (C)	x					
Taegu		x				
Kuwait -- Kuwait (E)	x	x		x		
Laos -- Vientiane (E)	x					
Lebanon -- Beirut (E)	x	x	x			
Lesotho -- Maseru (E)	x	x	x			
Liberia -- Monrovia (E)	x	x	x			
Luxembourg -- Luxembourg (E)	x					
Madagascar -- Antananarivo (E)	x	x				
Malawi -- Lilongwe (E)	x	x	x			
Malaysia -- Kuala Lumpur (E)	x	x		x	x	
Mali -- Bamako (E)	x	x	x			

Post	State	USIS	AID	FCS	FAS	APHIS
Malta -- Valletta (E)	x	x				
Mauritania -- Nouakchott (E)	x	x	x			
Mauritius -- Port Louis (E)	x	x				
Mexico --						
Mexico, D.F. (E)	x	x		x	x	x
Ciudad Altamirano						x
Ciudad Chihuahua						x
Ciudad Guzmán						x
Ciudad Juárez (CG)	x					
Ciudad Victoria						x
Guadalajara (CG)	x	x		x		x
Hermosillo (C)	x					x
Matamoros (C)	x					x
Mazatlán (C)	x					x
Mérida (C)	x					x
Monterrey (CG)	x	x		x		x
Morelia						x
Nuevo Laredo (C)	x					
Puebla						x
San Luis Potosi						x
Satillo						x
Tampico						x
Tapachula-Metapa						x
Tepic						x
Tijuana (CG)	x					
Tuxtla Gutiérrez						x
Vera Cruz						x
Morocco --						
Rabat (E)	x	x	x		x	
Casablanca (CG)	x	x		x		
Marrakech		x				
Tangier (CG)	x	x				
Mozambique -- Maputo (E)	x	x				
Nepal -- Kathmandu (E)	x	x	x			
Netherlands --						
The Hague (E)	x	x		x	x	x
Amsterdam (CG)	x			x		
Lisse						x
Rotterdam (CG)	x			x		
Netherlands Antilles --						
Curaçao (CG)	x					
New Zealand --						
Wellington (E)	x	x		x	x	
Auckland (CG)	x					
Nicaragua -- Managua (E)	x	x	x			
Niger -- Niamey (E)	x	x	x			
Nigeria --						
Lagos (E)	x	x		x	x	
Ibadan		x				
Kaduna (CG)	x	x		x		
Kano		x				

Post	State	USIS	AID	FCS	FAS	APHIS
Norway -- Oslo (E)	x	x		x		
Oman -- Muscat (E)	x	x	x			
Pakistan --						
Islamabad (E)	x	x	x		x	
Karachi (CG)	x	x		x		
Lahore (CG)	x	x				
Peshawar (C)	x	x				
Panama -- Panama City (E)	x	x	x	x		x
Papua New Guinea --						
Port Moresby (E)	x	x				
Paraguay -- Asunción (E)	x	x	x			
Peru -- Lima (E)	x	x	x	x	x	x
Philippines --						
Manila (E)	x	x	x	x	x	x
Baguio		x				
Cebu (C)	x	x				
Davao		x				
Poro		x				
Tinang		x				
Poland --						
Warsaw (E)	x	x		x	x	
Krakow (C)	x	x				
Poznan (C)	x	x				
Portugal --						
Lisbon (E)	x	x	x	x	x	
Oporto (C)	x					
Ponta Delgada, Azores (C)	x					
Qatar -- Doha (E)	x	x				
Romania -- Bucharest (E)	x	x		x	x	
Rwanda -- Kigali (E)	x	x	x			
Saudi Arabia --						
Riyadh (E)	x	x		x		
Dhahran (CG)	x	x		x		
Jidda (CG)	x	x		x	x	
Senegal -- Dakar (E)	x	x	x			
Seychelles -- Victoria (E)	x					
Sierra Leone -- Freetown (E)	x	x	x			
Singapore -- Singapore (E)	x	x		x	x	

Post	State	USIS	AID	FCS	FAS	APHIS
Somalia -- Mogadishu (E)	x	x	x			
South Africa --						
Pretoria (E)	x	x			x	
Cape Town (CG)	x	x				
Durban (CG)	x	x				
Johannesburg (CG)	x	x		x		
Spain --						
Madrid (E)	x	x		x	x	
Barcelona (CG)	x	x		x		
Bilbao (C)	x					
Seville (CG)	x					
Sri Lanka -- Colombo (E)	x	x	x			
Sudan -- Khartoum (E)	x	x	x			
Suriname -- Paramaribo (E)	x	x				
Swaziland -- Mbabane (E)	x	x	x			
Sweden --						
Stockholm (E)	x	x		x	x	
Göteborg (CG)	x					
Switzerland --						
Bern (E)	x	x		x	x	
Geneva (Emb. Office)	x					
Zurich (CG)	x					
Syria -- Damascus (E)	x	x	x		x	
Tanzania -- Dar es Salaam (E)	x	x	x			
Thailand --						
Bangkok (E)	x	x	x	x	x	
Chiang Mai (C)	x	x				
Songkhla (C)	x					
Udorn (C)	x					
Togo -- Lomé (E)	x	x	x			
Trinidad and Tobago --						
Port of Spain (E)	x	x		x		
Tunisia -- Tunis (E)	x	x	x		x	
Turkey --						
Ankara (E)	x	x		x		
Adana (C)	x					
Istanbul (CG)	x	x		x		
Izmir (CG)	x	x				
Uganda -- Kampala (E)	x	x	x			
U.S.S.R. --						
Moscow (E)	x	x		x	x	
Leningrad (CG)	x					

Post	State	USIS	AID	FCS	FAS	APHIS
United Arab Emirates --						
Abu Dhabi (E)	x	x		x		
Dubai (Emb. Office)	x			x		
United Kingdom --						
London (E)	x	x		x	x	
Belfast (CG)	x					
Edinburgh (CG)	x					
Uruguay -- Montevideo (E)	x	x				
Venezuela --						
Caracas (E)	x	x		x	x	
Maracaibo (C)	x	x				
Yemen Arab Republic -- Sanaa (E)	x	x	x			
Yugoslavia --						
Belgrade (E)	x	x		x	x	
Ljubljana		x				
Sarajevo		x				
Skopje		x				
Titograd		x				
Zagreb (CG)	x	x				
Zaire --						
Kinshasa (E)	x	x	x		x	
Bukavu (C)	x					
Lubumbashi (CG)	x	x				
Zambia -- Lusaka (E)	x	x	x			
Zimbabwe -- Harare (E)	x	x	x			

U.S. Missions to International Organizations

Post	State	USIS	AID	FCS	FAS	APHIS
Brussels --						
European Communities	x	x		x		
North Atlantic Treaty Organization	x	x				
Geneva --						
United Nations European Office and other organizations	x	x		x		
Montreal --						
International Civil Aviation Organization	x					
New York --						
United Nations	x	x				

Post	State	USIS	AID	FCS	FAS	APHIS

Paris --
      United Nations Educational,
        Scientific, and Cultural

Post	State	USIS	AID	FCS	FAS	APHIS
Organization	x					
Organization for Economic Cooperation and Development	x	x	x		x	
Food and Agriculture Organization	x		x		x	
United Nations Office, International Atomic Energy Agency, and United Nations International Development Organization	x					
Organization of American States	x					

Rome --
      Food and Agriculture

Vienna --
      United Nations Office,
        International Atomic
        Energy Agency, and
        United Nations Inter-
        national Development

Washington, D.C. --
      Organization of American

GUIDE TO FOREIGN SERVICE RECRUITMENT

Five separate agencies employ career personnel under the Foreign Service system in a wide range of fields. To make it easier for anyone seeking a Foreign Service career, this appendix will summarize, by agency, the categories of personnel normally hired and the procedure for applying. It should be noted that three of the agencies (State, USIA, and the Department of Commerce) recruit junior Foreign Service Officers through a common examination. Thus, anyone taking that examination automatically becomes a candidate for an FSO appointment with all three of the agencies that use this shared examination process.

The Department of State

Potential candidates for Foreign Service positions with the Department of State should start by consulting the latest edition of the department's publication, *Foreign Service Careers* (which is revised annually to ensure that its contents are always current). The booklet describes the career fields in which openings exist and can be obtained from the Recruitment Division, Department of State, Box 9317, Rosslyn Station, Arlington, Virginia 22209.

Foreign Service Officers

Between 1975 and 1984, the State Department has hired an average of 200 junior FSOs each year, with the actual number ranging from 135 to a high of 275. This hiring level is likely to be maintained in coming years, with candidates continuing to be chosen through the examination process that State administers jointly with USIA and Commerce. The Foreign Service written examination is administered once each year, in early December, by the Educational Testing Service, and the deadline for applications is normally about six weeks before the test date. The test is offered throughout the United States and may also be taken on request at any U.S. diplomatic or consular post abroad. Sample questions from the examination will be found in the *Foreign Service Careers* booklet; application forms are available from the Department of State's Recruitment Division, from federal personnel offices in most large cities, and from many college and university placement offices. Candidates must be U.S. citizens, at least twenty years old on the date of the examination (there is no maximum age), and available for worldwide assignment; there is no specific educational requirement. There is no charge for taking the exam, and it may be taken more than once without penalty of any kind.

Candidates who pass the written examination will be invited to an oral assessment, an all-day evaluation given either in Washington or by panels of traveling examiners in a number of cities around the country. The oral assessment includes a written essay and a written summary exercise; an oral interview with a panel of two or three examiners; an in-basket exercise designed to test managerial and problem-solving skills; and a group exercise that measures oral communication skills, interpersonal awareness, and the candidate's ability to work effectively with others.

Candidates who pass both the written examination and the oral assessment process are subject to both suitability and medical clearances before they can be appointed to the Foreign Service. The background investigation for a suitability/security clearance normally requires from three to nine months after the necessary forms have been submitted by the candidate.

Once this entire process has been completed successfully, a candidate is assigned a final score based both on examination results and on such other relevant information as education and employment history. Each candidate's name is then placed on one or more rank-order registers for which he or she has qualified through the examination process and from which offers of appointment will be made. These registers represent the six fields in which FSOs work within the three agencies that share the examination process: political, economic, consular, and administrative registers for the State Department; an information/cultural register for USIA; and a commercial register for Commerce. As the State Department forms classes of FSO candidates, appointment offers are made to persons on its registers in strict rank order until the desired class size has been reached.

As noted in Chapter 4, being included on a rank-order register does not guarantee an offer of employment. A candidate's name remains on the registers for a maximum of eighteen months. Any candidate who is not offered an appointment within that time, or who is unable or unwilling to accept such offers as may be made, will be dropped from the registers. Candidates may again become eligible for appointment only by beginning the entire process again from step one.

Foreign Service Specialists

The Department of State also offers career opportunities to professionals in specialist functions that are needed to meet Foreign Service responsibilities around the world. Applicants must be U.S. citizens, at least twenty-one years of age, and high school graduates or the equivalent. Like the FSO candidates, they must be available for worldwide assignment and able to pass both a rigorous medical examination and a thorough background investigation.

The State Department has a continuous need for Foreign Service secretaries and Foreign Service support communications officers, and it conducts an ongoing recruitment program for these positions. Applicants for secretarial positions must offer three to five years of progressively responsible experience in general office clerical, secretarial, or administrative work (or may substitute education beyond the high school level for part of the experience required). In addition, they must pass a written clerical examination, a shorthand test at eighty words per minute, and a typing test at forty words per minute. Candidates for positions as support communications officer must have a minimum of eighteen months of progressively responsible experience in the communications field within the last five years and must be able to pass qualifying tests in typing, clerical, and verbal abilities.

From time to time, the State Department also recruits candidates in a number of other specialist fields. As the need arises, the department issues calls for applicants who are qualified to serve as budget and fiscal officers, personnel officers, general services officers, security and security engineering officers, building and maintenance specialists, construction engineers, communications electronic officers, physicians, nurses, and medical technologists. Brief descriptions of the qualifications for several of these fields appear in the booklet *Foreign Service Careers*, but interested candidates should write for full information to the Recruitment Division, Department of State, Box 9317, Rosslyn Station, Arlington, Virginia 22209.

The United States Information Agency

Foreign Service Officers

FSO candidates seeking a career with USIA should follow the guidelines set forth for State Department candidates, since the application and examination procedures are conducted jointly by the two agencies. As previously noted, all applicants who take the annual Foreign Service written examination automatically are considered as candidates for State, USIA, and Commerce, and those who qualify in the information/cultural field will have their names placed on the functional register from which USIA appointments are made. Thus, anyone interested in an FSO career with USIA should also request the current edition of *Foreign Service Careers* from the Recruitment Division, Department of State, Box 9317, Rosslyn Station, Arlington, Virginia 22209, and should get an application for the written examination from that office or from one of the other locations suggested in the State Department FSO section above. USIA currently expects to hire approximately fifty junior FSOs per year through the examination process.

Foreign Service Specialists

Like the State Department, USIA also from time to time seeks candidates for Foreign Service specialist positions. The agency offers secretarial positions, for which the qualifications are essentially similar to those already described for State Department candidates in this field, and also recruits qualified applicants in the fields of English teaching, library science, and radio engineering. Information on possible openings and qualifications may be obtained by writing to the Employment Branch, USIA, 301 Fourth Street S.W., Washington, D.C. 20547.

The Department of Commerce

The Foreign Commercial Service of the Department of Commerce, like State and USIA, recruits junior Foreign Service Officers through the joint examination process previously described. The five or six FSOs to be hired each year will be selected in rank order from the list of candidates who qualify for inclusion on the functional register in the commercial field at the end of the examination process. Applicants interested in FSO careers with the FCS should request a copy of the *Foreign Service Careers* booklet from the Recruitment Division, Department of State, Box 9317, Rosslyn Station, Arlington, Virginia 22209, as well as an application form for the annual written examination.

The Agency for International Development

AID differs in its hiring practices from the three agencies already described. Whereas State, USIA, and Commerce hire nearly all new employees at the junior level, AID in recent years has offered roughly two-thirds of its initial appointments at the mid-level (defined by AID as spanning pay grades FS-4 through FS-2) and expects to continue this pattern.

The list of functional specialties for which AID hires is a varied one. It includes experts in such fields as accounting, contracting, computers, economics, engineering, family planning, and nutrition; specialists in agriculture, energy, public health, regional planning, and urban/rural development; and qualified secretaries and project development officers. For most of these fields, the agency seeks candidates with at least a master's degree in a related area and a minimum of three years of work experience; new recruits for mid-level positions normally will have worked at least five years in their fields before joining AID.

In many of these fields, positions are available both at the mid-level and, for junior officer candidates, in AID's International Development Intern (IDI) program. Mid-level appointments are made throughout the year as needs arise. IDI candidates are appointed to two classes each year, which normally begin in February and September. The agency's functional requirements will vary from year to year, but the annual total of appointments is expected to remain constant at about a hundred for the foreseeable future.

Interested candidates should send a completed Personal Qualifications Statement (SF-171, available from federal personnel offices) or a résumé with salary history to the Recruitment Staff, Office of Personnel, Agency for International Development, Washington, D.C. 20523. This same office can also provide current information on actual and prospective vacancies in each of AID's functional fields. Candidates wishing to apply specifically for appointment into the IDI program should address their Personal Qualifications Statement or résumé to International Development Intern Recruitment, M/PM/R, Agency for International Development, Washington, D.C. 20523.

The Department of Agriculture

Unlike the other foreign affairs agencies, the Foreign Agricultural Service and the Animal and Plant Health Inspection Service do not hire people directly into the Foreign Service. Instead, they select their Foreign Service personnel from employees already serving with the agency in a Civil Service capacity. Thus, candidates for Foreign Service positions with either FAS or APHIS must first apply for and obtain a Civil Service appointment, following the standard procedures established by the Office of Personnel Management for all Civil Service applicants. Information on these procedures is available from the Office of Personnel Management, 1900 E Street N.W., Washington, D.C. 20415, or from any Federal Job Information Center.

In FAS, positions are normally available for secretaries and for agronomists and agricultural economists; APHIS seeks doctors of veterinary medicine, entomologists, plant protection and quarantine officers (usually qualified in biology, entomology, or animal husbandry), biological and animal health technicians, and specialists in general administration and in personnel, budget and fiscal, and procurement and supply work.

Both FAS and APHIS require a minimum of two years of Civil Service experience before an individual may apply for a Foreign Service appointment. APHIS announces potential openings on an individual basis, and FAS solicits applications once a year and offers appointments to the best qualified candidates in numbers sufficient to meet anticipated needs.

Additional information on FAS career opportunities may be obtained from the Recruitment Officer, FAS Personnel Division, Room 5627 South Building, 14th and Independence Avenue N.W., Washington, D.C. 20250. For APHIS, inquiries should be sent to the International Programs Management and Liaison Staff, Human Resources Division, Room 225, Federal Building, 6505 Belcrest Road, Hyattsville, Maryland 20782.

BIBLIOGRAPHY

American Assembly. *The Secretary of State*. Englewood Cliffs, N.J.: Prentice-Hall, 1960.

American Foreign Service Association. *Toward a Modern Diplomacy*. Washington, D.C.: American Foreign Service Association, 1968.

Association of American Foreign Service Women. *The Foreign Service Spouse Overseas*. Washington, D.C.: Association of American Foreign Service Women, 1984.

Bacchus, William I. *Staffing for Foreign Affairs*. Princeton, N.J.: Princeton University Press, 1983.

Bailey, Thomas A. *The Art of Diplomacy: The American Experience*. New York: Appleton-Century-Crofts, 1968.

Barnes, William, and John Heath Morgan. *The Foreign Service of the United States*. Washington, D.C.: Historical Office, Bureau of Public Affairs, U.S. Department of State, 1961.

Barnett, Vincent M., Jr. *The Representation of the United States Abroad*. New York: Frederick A. Praeger, 1965.

Blancke, W. Wendell. *The Foreign Service of the United States*. New York: Frederick A. Praeger, 1969.

Buechel, Janet G. "Tandem Employees." *State*, no. 269 (July 1984), pp. 20–21.

Calkin, Homer L. *Women in the Department of State: Their Role in American Foreign Affairs*. Department of State Publication 8951. Washington, D.C.: U.S. Department of State, 1978.

Callieres, Francois de. *The Art of Diplomacy*. Edited by H.M.A. Keens-Soper and Karl W. Schweizer. New York: Leicester University Press, 1983.

Campbell, John Franklin. *The Foreign Affairs Fudge Factory*. New York: Basic Books, 1971.

Childs, J. Rives. *American Foreign Service*. New York: Henry Holt and Company, 1948.

Clark, Eric. *Corps Diplomatique*. London: Allen Lane, 1973.

Commission on the Organization of the Government for the Conduct of Foreign Policy (Murphy Commission). *Commission on the Organization of the Government for the Conduct of Foreign Policy*. Washington, D.C.: U.S. Department of State, August 1983.

Committee on Foreign Affairs Personnel (Herter Committee). *Personnel for the New Diplomacy*. Washington, D.C.: Carnegie Endowment for International Peace, 1962.

Esterline, John H., and Robert B. Black. *Inside Foreign Policy*. Palo Alto, Calif.: Mayfield Publishing Company, 1975.

Estes, Thomas S. and E. Allan Lightner, Jr. *The Department of State*. New York: Frederick A. Praeger, 1976.

Franck, Thomas M., and Edward Weisband. *Foreign Policy by Congress*. New York: Oxford University Press, 1979.

Gigliotti, Donna. "Foreign Service Families: 'Tandem' Teams Complicate the Assignment Process." *State*, no. 223 (May 1980), pp. 19–22.

Harr, John Ensor. *The Professional Diplomat*. Princeton, N.J.: Princeton University Press, 1969.

Heginbotham, Stanley J. "Dateline Washington: The Rules of the Game." *Foreign Policy*, no. 53 (Winter 1983-1984), pp. 157–172.

Henderson, John W. *The United States Information Agency*. New York: Frederick A. Praeger, 1969.

Herz, Martin F. *215 Days in the Life of an American Ambassador*. Washington, D.C.: School of Foreign Service, Georgetown University, 1981.

———. "View from the Top." *Foreign Service Journal* 60:6 (June 1983), pp. 26–27 and 32–33.

Herz, Martin F., ed. *The Consular Dimension of Diplomacy*. Washington, D.C.: Institute for the Study of Diplomacy, Georgetown University, 1983.

———. *Diplomacy: The Role of the Wife*. Washington, D.C.: Institute for the Study of Diplomacy, Georgetown University, 1981.

———. *Diplomats and Terrorists: What Works, What Doesn't*. Washington, D.C.: Institute for the Study of Diplomacy, Georgetown University, 1982.

———. *The Modern Ambassador: The Challenge and the Search*. Washington, D.C.: Institute for the Study of Diplomacy, Georgetown University, 1983.

Hilton, Ralph H. *Worldwide Mission: The Story of the United States Foreign Service.* New York: World Publishing Company, 1970.

Hilton, Ralph H., ed. *Tales of the Foreign Service.* Columbia: University of South Carolina Press, 1978.

Ilchman, Warren Frederick. *Professional Diplomacy in the United States, 1779–1939.* Chicago: University of Chicago Press, 1961.

Lachica, Eduardo. "Lost Luster: A Foreign Service Post Isn't the Prize It Was for Best and Brightest." *Wall Street Journal* 204:42 (August 29, 1984), pp. 1 and 14.

Lay, Tracy Hollingsworth. *The Foreign Service of the United States.* New York: Prentice-Hall, 1925.

Macomber, William. *The Angels' Game: A Handbook of Modern Diplomacy.* New York: Stein and Day, 1975.

Mattingly, Garrett. *Renaissance Diplomacy.* Boston: Houghton Mifflin, 1955.

Mayer, Martin. *The Diplomats.* New York: Doubleday and Company, 1983.

Newsom, David D. "The Executive Branch in Foreign Policy." In *The President, the Congress, and Foreign Policy.* Washington, D.C.: Atlantic Council, forthcoming.

Nicolson, Harold. *Diplomacy.* 2d ed. London: Oxford University Press, 1952.

_____. *The Evolution of Diplomatic Method.* London: Constable and Company, 1954.

Plischke, Elmer. *Conduct of American Diplomacy.* Princeton, N.J.: D. Van Nostrand Company, 1950.

Plischke, Elmer, ed. *Modern Diplomacy: The Art and the Artisans.* Washington, D.C.: American Enterprise Institute, 1979.

Secretary of State's Public Committee on Personnel (Wriston Committee). *Toward a Stronger Foreign Service.* Department of State Publication 5458. Washington, D.C.: U.S. Department of State, 1954.

Teixeira, Bernardo. *Diplomatic Immunity.* Washington, D.C. and New York: Robert B. Lucey, 1971.

Thayer, Charles W. *Diplomat.* New York: Harper and Brothers, 1959.

Trevelyan, Lord Humphrey. *Diplomatic Channels.* Boston: Gambit, 1973.

U.S. Department of State. *Career Mobility Handbook.* Washington, D.C.: U.S. Department of State, 1983.

_____. *Diplomacy for the 70's: A Program of Management Reform for the Department of State.* Department of State Publication 8551. Washington, D.C.: U.S. Department of State, 1970.

_____ . *Foreign Service Careers*. Department of State Publication 9202. Washington, D.C.: U.S. Department of State, 1984.

U.S. Department of State. Office for Combatting Terrorism. *Terrorist Incidents Involving Diplomats*. Washington, D.C.: U.S. Department of State, August 1983.

Weil, Martin. *A Pretty Good Club: The Founding Fathers of the U.S. Foreign Service*. New York: W. W. Norton, 1978.

Wriston, Henry. *Diplomacy in a Democracy*. New York: Harper and Brothers, 1956.

INDEX